A ROAD WE ALL TRAVEL

To One of Two Destinations

Lloyd Dean McJunkin

ISBN 978-1-63630-350-5 (Paperback)
ISBN 978-1-63630-351-2 (Digital)

First Edition

Covenant Books, Inc.
11661 Hwy 707
Murrells Inlet, SC 29576
www.covenantbooks.com

Contents

List of Appendices

I would encourage you to read all the appendices before you start chapter 1 because you may feel that some apply to additional chapters that I have shown. Also, you may view your life having different "age group stages" than I've identified, but I'm sure that our first and last stages in life will be the same—that is, we each were born and we each will die. What we do between these two events will determine the choice we will make when we reach the "fork" in the road that will take us to the place we will spend our eternal life!

Preface

As you read the following pages, I pray you will see I often use the word *GOD*. That is *not* by accident but by intent. I have used the spelling of His name as GOD (all caps) to emphasize that there is no name in heaven or on earth that is greater or more important than our GOD, the Creator of all creations.

In reading, you will see there have been events happening in my life, from the day I was born to the time of this writing, that can only be explained by accepting that it was the will of GOD. It was to show my parents first, and later me (as I grew older), that GOD knew me and He had a plan for me, even before I was born and accepted His Son, Jesus Christ, as my Lord and Savior. I believe this is true for every believer. The various stages of life, as outlined on the Contents page, and some of the happenings I experienced may be somewhat like those of the readers of this book.

Throughout my life, GOD's WORD has never changed. I feel the words in Isaiah 46:4–5 have led me to this belief.

> Even to your old age and gray hairs I am he, I am he who will sustain you. I have made you, and I will carry you; I will sustain you, and I will rescue you. To whom will you compare me or count me equal?

I have come to believe there are none. Jesus tells us,

> With man, this is impossible, but with GOD all things are possible. (Matthew 19:26)

Man cannot save himself or others, just as he cannot do many things. Only GOD can do all things.

As believers by faith, we see GOD, and no one else deserves the honor and the glory for the good He does for and through His servants. Christians should not minimize the names GOD, His Son, Jesus Christ, and His Holy Spirit in our daily talk or writing. We must acknowledge the power, need, and love this Trinity adds to each believer's life. Throughout each day, we need to minimize the words *I* and *me* and emphasize *GOD* and *He.*

I have used Matthew 19:26 as a guide for writing about the events that occurred in my life. It involved much pain, and I was too young to understand *why*. You will see it was GOD who brought me through the valleys of despair, doubt, and even death. It was Jesus who led me to the mountain tops on the other side of the river of failure. I hope you will note one significant truth before starting chapter 1—and that is, there is no doubt in my mind that throughout all my life, GOD has been with me, even before I knew Him. He was *waiting* for me to come to Him. I would hope you believe the same in your relationship with GOD. Before and after I invited Jesus Christ to be my Lord and Savior; I realize I never accomplished one thing of value on my own. I didn't know that truth when I was younger than ten years old, but today I do.

Every activity that I had done that some may have viewed as kind, thoughtful, or helpful to others was done by GOD, through me. After I accepted Jesus Christ as my Lord and Savior, there were times I didn't even thank Him for using me to do His bidding.

I have tried to use the words *I* and *me* when addressing "things" I was involved with that were *not* always what GOD wanted me to do. I have tried to use *GOD* and *He* for those things I was involved with that He did through me. If I failed to do this, it was not my intention, and I ask your understanding and GOD's forgiveness. I intend to show that I believe, "To GOD goes the glory for everything He has enabled me to do, for His name's sake!"

Acknowledgments

I cannot thank GOD enough for my lovely wife, Sondra. She has stood with me in troubled times; she has been my motivation in times of disappointment; she has been my strength in times of failure; she has been my nurse in times of sickness; she has been the mother of my children. For each sacrifice I have made, she has made two or more. She has been my "sounding board" to test my ideas, views, actions, and reactions in life. She has been my general manager and secretary in keeping our daily lives organized.

Sondra has been my encourager to always look to GOD as our only hope and salvation.

She never objected to the hours I spent in writing the following pages and would often slip into my "study" and kiss the back of my neck to let me know she is my biggest supporter and helper.

To put it in seven simple emphasized words… *"Sondra, my wife, has been my everything!"*

INTRODUCTION

"For I know the plans I have for you," declares the Lord, "plans to prosper you and not to harm you, plans to give you hope and a future."
—Jeremiah 29:11

Scholars believe GOD gave Jeremiah those words sometime during the seventh-century BC. Many Christian scholars in the AD twenty-first-century felt our Lord intends for us to understand that those words apply to believers today as they did to the people in Jeremiah's day.

I have accepted the fact that I am now living in the last one or two decades of my life on earth. The thought of dying and leaving a world that seems to be turning away from the teachings of GOD's Word makes it much easier to rejoice in the promise of Salvation He has given to all who have accepted His Son, Jesus Christ, as their Lord and Savior. I found that in going to heaven, I will be able to worship Him and have fellowship with His Son, Jesus Christ, and all the saints that preceded me. And I'll be ready to welcome family members and friends who will come after me.

His Word tells us, before the mountains were formed, He knew us. That is hard to understand, and that is why we Christians believe by faith, not by sight. It is only by *faith* that man can accept all the Bible says. I feel that GOD may have created man with a limited understanding of GOD's ability. The highest level of knowledge that man seems to possess is at the level "where man is aware"—he doesn't know everything, and he can't do everything. And because Jesus said, "Only GOD can know and do all things," Christians accept it as a fact of life and believe it's true.

If GOD's Word says it is so, then I accept it by faith and don't try to understand how or why he did all the things recorded between Genesis and Revelation. Many things recorded in the Bible, I don't know how they came about, and therefore, I do not desire to debate their truth with someone who may understand them even less than I do. I believe we should never feel we have to prove GOD and His Word are right to someone who doesn't believe in Him. Many feel they are wasting their time trying to prove the truth in GOD's Word—knowing it is impossible to a nonbeliever. That is not to say we should not witness to the nonbeliever and share what He has done for us and will do for them *if* they believe in GOD's existence. I can take comfort in thinking *no one* has or will be able to prove GOD does *not* exist as the Bible has recorded throughout the centuries. He has neither a beginning nor an ending, but He does live. I believe GOD Himself is the only one that can "prove" His existence, and He will prove it in His way and in His time.

PART 1

Chapter 1

My Trip through Life (A Sinner among Sinners!)

I consider my life worth nothing to me, if only I may finish the race and complete the task that my Lord Jesus has given me—the task of testifying to the gospel of GOD's grace.

—Acts 20–24

There have been a few times GOD did things through me that helped others, but that was to show others His power. In those situations, GOD showed the world He can do "all things," even using someone that may not know His Son, Jesus Christ, as their Lord and Savior. That is how my life's story began, and I'll explain this later when GOD did something in my life when I was about three months old. But I want to first focus on the younger members of my family and all young children who are still living at home and finding it hard to understand the demands of life when they leave home.

I remember not understanding why things in my early life were sometimes very hurtful, even before I had my sixth birthday. I didn't understand why, and I didn't know how I could find the answers. It was not until I was older that GOD showed me His answers, and they changed my view, desire, and determination of how I was going to live my life. Today many young children have a feeling the world is against them and no one understands their needs. Others believe the world owes them everything they want or need. They will soon realize their future will be determined by what *they* are willing to do to have a fruitful life. Many will follow what their "pseudo friends" believe, who've chosen to take the easy way out and hope the world will take care of them. They will soon find "the world" is less forgiving when we reach our midteens. It was after I accepted Jesus Christ as my Lord and Savior at eleven years old that I realized He was the one I needed to follow, but even then, I was still encountering times of hurt, and I didn't understand *why*!

In reading about my experiences, others may be reminded of similar events in their lives. If so, I pray they have found Jesus is the only true source of strength. He is the only one deserving of our praise as He will lead us from a valley of despair to that mountaintop of freedom on the other side. If you have experienced this, then I think you will find you are on the right road to a meaningful life.

The following chapters will identify and explain how my strength in knowing GOD and how His love has brought me to the mountaintops of freedom and peace, many times. He has impacted my life in both good times and in bad times. If someone asked, "If you had it to do over again and knew what you know today, would you do anything differently?" Without any hesitation, I would answer, "I sure would!" But going back is not an option for any of us. Because of this fact of life, I have tried to follow the words of a much wiser man than I am. The following words are attributed to William Penn, who is quoted to have said, "I expect to pass through this world but once. Any good, therefore that I can do, or any kindness I can show to any fellow creature, let me do it now. Let me not defer or neglect it, for I shall not pass this way again."

If we acknowledge GOD has helped, encouraged, enabled, blessed us and allowed His Son to die on the cross for all our sins;' then shouldn't we strive to live a sinless life, knowing we will fail many times. Even when I repented of my sins and invited Jesus into my life as my Lord and Savior; I often saw how weak and helpless I was. I frequently asked myself, "Why, after accepting Jesus as my Lord and Savior, do I continue to sin?"

I recall reading the following article years ago when flying between New Jersey and Colorado on a business trip. It was titled, "Words of Wisdom," and read as follows, "Two men were debating if the Bible was true. One said, 'There is no real proof what the Bible says is true. Therefore, I don't believe it.' To this the other man replied, 'I believe the Bible on faith that it is true, however, if you are right, when I die and find there is no GOD and no heaven, then you may say, I wasted the years I lived on earth by not enjoying the 'sinful things I could have experienced,' but if I am right, and I am confident I am when *you* die, you will find that you have wasted an eternity."

(See Appendix A and E.)

As I reflect on my life, I agree with the French philosopher Montaigne when he penned the following:

> My life has been filled with many Terrible Misfortunes—most of which never happened!

I don't know how Montaigne's life ended, but I praise GOD for the words He caused that little Shepherd boy, named David, to write in his adult years in Psalms 27:14,

> Wait on the Lord; Be strong and take heart and wait for the Lord!

Paul addresses this same point in Ephesians 6:10, 11.

> Finally, be strong in the Lord and in His mighty power Put on the full armor of GOD so that you can take your stand against the devil's schemes.

When I realized the truth in those words, I came to believe, when we follow GOD's Word (Bible) and have faith in His Son, Jesus Christ, He will take care of all our needs and do it at the right time and in the right way. We may find GOD's way of taking care of our needs are not always what we expected, but later, we see they were right for us.

If you find this has been true in your life, I hope you have also come to the same belief that I have—that is, "You've come 'through it all' because of GOD's "grace," "mercy," and "love" and the resurrection of His Son, Jesus Christ. These are the reasons we can endure all things. It is because of our faith and hope in Jesus, it's not our intellect, power, wealth, or deeds, that caused it; it is because of GOD's love for us.

The following chapters are a collection of memories of my past and could be titled, "Lloyd Dean McJunkin—A Sinner among Sinners." Some of the significant dates go back to July 7, 1946, when I stood before the congregation in the Christian church in Toronto, Kansas, and confessed I was a sinner and asked Jesus Christ to forgive me of my sins and be my Lord and Savior from that moment forward. The following week I was baptized. I recall feeling so proud of taking that step of faith, knowing it was one of the most important decisions I ever made without getting permission from my parents.

I know GOD has forgiven all my sins in the past, and those I've committed in the present as well as those I will incur in the future. I'm not proud of those many times I drifted away and knowingly sinned, not once but many times during my teenage years and early twenties. I have no excuse. I have asked forgiveness, and I believe GOD has forgiven me of all my sins, yesterday, today and those I will commit in the future.

Saying this, I feel GOD has made me aware that my life on earth is coming to an end. If I can do anything to help my grandchildren to live a better teenage life than I did, I need to share with them that time in my life when I put aside the Bible and even going to church every Sunday. I felt there were so many things I could do as a teenager that would not be as available when I entered my twenties. If I can leave behind the long term feeling of shame and sorrow of those many times I sinned, thinking the world was mine and then finding it was only Satan applauding with his followers that I had followed. I had let GOD down. I had let myself down, and I felt my insides were tearing apart.

But I knew GOD would never turn His servants down. He will forgive when asked and that is what I did. So I don't mislead any of the younger readers that are thinking, "Oh, I can sin, then ask for forgiveness, and I'm home free." Wrong, I believe GOD has forgiven my sins, but until I forgive myself, I am not acknowledging that GOD has forgiven me; my recollection of those sins will linger for years because I have not forgiven myself. I also know that during the time I had drifted away from GOD's Word, I had not received any blessings from Him. And I know none of those blessings will be given to me now or later.

Many young people today are blessed by their looks, their love for their family, their academic abilities as well as their athletic talents. But since they didn't use these blessings as GOD intended, they can't find a good job and are not taking steps to be able to support themselves, let alone a family. Then they meet that one person who seems to be "the one" who would make them a perfect mate, only to find that a person does not feel the same about them. Until they decide to take advantage of GOD's blessings and use them as He intended, they will never find the mate GOD has for them. If they find someone that wants to get married, they may end up with even more disappointments in life and still not have a successful and satisfying marriage.

About this time, old Satan dumps them because he has obtained his objective of bringing the young man or woman to turn from GOD. The beautiful future He had equipped them with, is gone and Satan will leave them to suffer for their poor decisions they made. I knew this young person would never have that splendid family and career that GOD equipped them to have. I say this not in a judgmental way. I mean it because I found I was starting down that pathway when I was in the Navy. And I can't blame it on the military, I knew what I was doing, but I thought I was far away from my parents and those that knew me back "home." I felt I could do anything I wanted to do. By the grace of GOD, He opened my eyes and set me free. Looking back, I still couldn't understand why GOD would forgive me for the life I had led, and I asked myself, why would anyone do that?

Then one day, quite sometime later, while I was in a prison facility as a member of the Bill Glass Prison Ministry, I was witnessing to a young inmate around nineteen years old. As he was sharing his story with me and I was sharing the Four Spiritual Laws with him, he said, "I can't believe GOD will ever forgive me for what I have done, why would He?" Without thinking, I said, "GOD did it because He loves you, and He has a plan for you."

"I know that is true because I asked that same question when I was a couple years older than you, and GOD's Holy Spirit seemed to say those words to me. How could I not seek forgiveness and try my best to put that former lifestyle behind me?"

"You have that opportunity today, are you ready to get your life together and start serving the Lord and using the talent GOD has given you to honor Him?"

His answer was, "Yes, I am."

We prayed the sinner's prayer and for his forgiveness and when we finished, I noticed tears were running down his cheeks, and for the first time he had a smile on his face.

I hope my grandchildren might read this and think twice before making the mistakes I made. I knew I needed to confess the truth in my past, and I know GOD forgave me when I accepted His Son, Jesus Christ, as my Lord and Savior. He has given me a life and lifestyle that I never thought possible. If we have Jesus Christ as our Lord and Savior, our sins will be forgiven, if we ask, because GOD is the forgiving GOD! Hopefully, our grandchildren will not make the same mistakes as did a young man I witnessed in prison several years ago. I will share his words with you a little later. Our sins will be forgiven if we repent and ask forgiveness; however, the blessings we would have received during the time we turned from GOD, are lost forever. But now is the time to come back to GOD, His Son, Jesus Christ, and the Holy Spirit. Remember, GOD is waiting and the clock of time is running. When that day comes, it will be impossible to change your mind.

If my memory serves me right, I have never discussed the first eighteen items (following) with any of our children or grandchildren. I felt they would not be interested in some of the events I encountered after my birth or my early relationship with my earthly father. Now that my time on earth is coming close to an end, I feel they should hear these events and see how Jesus Christ made all the difference in revealing the cause of why my dad did what he did. My prayers have always been that our children will not have to experience like type happenings, especially those in our family who do not have Jesus Christ as their Lord and Savior. I also pray for those who will be reading the following chapters to understand the danger in "judging" others based on what they see rather than "knowing" the cause of another person's actions. GOD showed me, in His time, the cause of my dad's actions. Even during those hurtful times, at a very young age, the Lord assured me my parents loved me. It was after I was in high school that I found what the cause was for my dad's actions, and only then did I understand why they happened. It was then, my dad and I came together as all fathers and sons should. It was with faith in GOD, and belief in His Word, and trying to follow His Commands. Today I believe my dad, and I will have an eternal future, together in GOD's heavenly home. I also pray all the members of our family will be with Sondra and me when their days on earth come to an end.

You will see, in the following list, areas that GOD showed me the power He has in my life. Within the first few months after my birth, he gave me life a second time. All the events following my rebirth paled in importance as to what He can do when we see and believe what He has done for us, and why we must follow His commands until He brings us *home*!

Significant *events* from my birth to the time of this writing. I will explain in more detail in later chapters.

1. I was born in a church and *died* about three months later! I'll explain the truth of this in chapter 3.
2. My McJunkin Grandparents had four boys and two girls that lived to maturity. They had a total of eleven children; but five died at birth or before their first birthday. Today this would make the front page of our morning newspaper, but in those days, doctors and hospitals were not as plen-

tiful as they are today. As bad as that was, it was not that uncommon at that time.

3. My father started working in the oil field in his early teens. He lived the life of a "roughneck"—that is, he drank, smoked and fought, but I never saw him in a fight, and I never heard him use the Lord's name in vain.
4. My mother never took me to church because of my dad's reputation, but she always saw that I attended.
5. I accepted Jesus as my Lord and Savior when I was eleven years old, almost twelve. (See Appendix C.)
6. Boy Scouts impressed me even before I was old enough to join. As far as I know, in 1950 my friend, Hoyt Black and I were the first Boy Scouts in Toronto, Kansas, to receive the Boy Scouts Eagle award. I explain this in more detail in chapter 4.
7. I was active in sports, especially basketball and baseball. I tried to be a "team player," but I also developed a competitive attitude with myself. Sports was another part of my life, in a somewhat unorthodox way. I will explain this in chapter 4.
8. By riding my bicycle seven miles each day, on my paper route, during my junior high and freshman years, I developed rather strong leg muscles and could out jump the varsity players on our basketball team my junior year. I explain in chapter 4.
9. About this time in my life, I started noticing that you don't have to be the smartest, the biggest or even the most talented at accomplishing good things in life. But you do need to have a desire and be willing to work for what you want and ask GOD to guide you.
10. In 1952 after graduating from high school, I joined the US Navy during the Korean War. In boot camp I was assigned to company number 422, in Squad Three. In less than four weeks, I became the leader of squad 3 and retained that position throughout the remainder of boot camp. I explain how this happened in chapter 5 and 6. GOD showed me

when you are in the military, "You abide by the rules, or you are not going to enjoy the game of life in our Armed Forces." I later found this rule also applies to civilian life outside the military.

11. I started college after my tour in the Navy in 1955, utilizing the GI bill. I soon realized I did not have the patience to tolerate all the young "kids," right out of high school, acting like a bunch of children in many of my freshman classes. I guess that is what happens to you if you go into the Armed Forces right out of high school. Whatever the real reason was, I ended up dropping out at the end of my first semester. You will see this proved to be a blessing in the following years. As bad as I felt in leaving college, I found my faith in GOD would take care of my needs in the future if I would follow and not try to get ahead of His plan for me.

    It was then He showed me He alone could do all things, and realize we must have faith and follow Him.

    > With man, this is impossible, but with GOD, all things are possible. (Mt. 19:26)

12. I explain at length in chapter 7 how GOD arranged for me to have an interview for a job with the Santa Fe RR in their Fort Madison, Iowa relay office. Later I found this had *no* connection with the real job GOD had for me. I've since realized He sent me there to find what I needed to help me throughout the rest of my life to complete the plan He had for me!
13. Mrs. Jones, my landlady in Fort Madison told me something that started a series of events that turned out to be the second-best thing in my life and it took place on November 24, 1956.
14. My job with Santa Fe was not what I was led to believe. I soon found that GOD was arranging not only my real job, but so much more. When He started revealing how great

His overall plan was for my future, I realized you can never outdo what GOD wants to do for you; in His way and in His time frame, In the following six months He showed me His view of my future was much better than anything I had imagined, and it turned out much better than any of my ideas. I reveal this part of GOD's proposal for my future in chapter 8.

15. GOD next led me to a new career that included different job responsibilities, including living in different parts of America. I addressed this in chapter 9.
16. GOD continued to amaze me in how He does things that cause us to say, "Wow, I never would have realized that if I hadn't experienced it, firsthand." During that time GOD provided me opportunities that resulted in positive experiences I never thought would happen. And all GOD asked of me was to put forth the effort that showed I was *willing to do my part*, which is so essential if we want to serve GOD, His way.
17. Looking back, I feel GOD has always been the controlling factor in my life. Even in my early days of life, I, couldn't understand why I was experiencing hurt, and why things in my life could be so painful, I feel now GOD had His protective hand on me and leading me each day. I praise Him for the love and care He gave me.

    I know He will do the same for you. He only wants us to ask Him to help us in our time of need. I didn't know how great GOD was when I was in my preschool years. Later I realized many of those experiences GOD brought me through were during my early years of life. As I grew older I saw some of the people He was bringing me in contact with had experienced more pain and hurt than I had. It was then I understood the importance of having love and understanding for those who had a greater need than I did. I could share with them and let them know I understood, to a lesser degree how they were suffering. This often opened the door to tell them about GOD, "the

Great Physician," and how He could help us through some of the pain and suffering we encounter during our journey through life. All this has helped me to witness to young people in the prisons (sometimes my wife went with me when we were in a juvenile unit), the gyms, and in recent years GOD has led us to witness to waiters in restaurants.

In doing the above, I am not talking to these young men as a "counselor" would speak to them. But it has enabled me to talk and speak with these young people as a "friend" and let them know I am not in any way judging them. Once they feel I am there to talk about someone that can help them today. Someone that can guide them in the future as they start their journey through life. I am there to witness to these people about, Jesus Christ and what He has done for all mankind.

18. Before I realized how GOD was guiding me, there were times I asked, "*Why* me, Lord?" Then I started to see things were happening to me, and I didn't understand why. I will cover In chapter 9, how this portion of my career was not always a smooth and joyful experience. (Appendix F number 2.)
19. It was sometime before I retired that GOD led me to teach adult Sunday school (SS) classes. I gave GOD many reasons why I couldn't teach—that is, I didn't have the talent, I didn't have the time, and there were people in our SS class more qualified than me. He agreed with my last reason, but He seemed to say He wanted me to teach, and He would take care of the other excuses I had given Him. He won out, and that started a period In my life, when I taught adult SS classes for some twenty-five-plus years, teaching full-time or part-time. One small church in New Jersey we attended, grew into a much larger group, and' we built a new church building and became a close-knit Christian family. (See Appendix A and F number 10.)
20. Over the years and many locations that GOD moved our family; we always attended church. Usually, we joined the

church within the first year at our new location. Throughout my adult life, He enabled me to serve as a deacon, elder, and chairman of the elder board in churches in the Midwest and Eastern States. This experience revealed some biased views I had toward different denominations and social norms; things that did not conflict with the Bible but differed in "how or when" they were utilized. I doubt if this would have been noticeable to me if I had lived all my life just in the Midwestern States. GOD showed me Christians shouldn't view other Christians by their denominations as being wrong (maybe even sinful) because they do things differently from the way, "We did in the denomination and church I attended back in Kansas." Isn't that what GOD's Word tells us is "judging others"? In discussing this point with my wife, Sondra, said she had experienced the same feeling throughout our moves and, like me, had to focus on "stopping it" when others did things like passing the "offering plate" at a different time during the service than the way we did back home in Missouri."

But back to my point of being initially hesitant to accept things I was asked to do in the churches we attended. It was not because I didn't want to serve when needed; it was that I felt I wasn't the most qualified.

Then GOD informed me He would never give me, or anyone, the opportunity to serve Him if He hadn't already equipped me to do the job. I then realized I could not serve GOD the way He wanted me to if I didn't accept the opportunities He was giving me. So I accepted on *faith* that He would guide me along the way, and He did.

21. After giving me life at birth, three months later, He gave me life a second time after the doctor pronounced me dead.

    Then on January 9, 2001, at sixty-seven years old, GOD gave me a third chance to live. I had what my doctor called, a "sudden death syndrome" attack. I believed GOD is all-powerful and that experience proved to me He is. He brought me through that serious attack, including a triple by-pass surgery four months later. GOD showed me how great His love is. He showed me how powerful He is in guiding, forgiving and giving life; if we are obedient and follow Him. GOD has shown me many times, He wants to help us, but we must show Him our faith, hope, and trust by asking for His help and then be obedient. (See Appendix C.)

22. On the twenty-fourth of November 2019, I celebrated our sixty-third wedding anniversary with my wonderful and beautiful wife, Sondra. At that time, GOD had given us three wonderful children, nine grandchildren, and eleven great-grandchildren and, at this writing, one great-great-grandchild and probably more will come.
23. The above experiences were the motivation for me to write the following chapters. Once I started, GOD showed me that it is not just My family that has these multiple age group challenges. Some of the same concerns exist in families throughout America and the world. I encourage the readers to think of this truth as they read the following chapters. They may ask, "Is this a book I can relate to and act on versus just a story about the life of a "small-town boy from Kansas?"

    Remember, if we feel we serve the GOD of the Bible, then we all serve the same living, loving, and forgiving GOD.
24. I hope as the readers continue they will ask not only, "Does this relate to my family and me, to my children and maybe my grandchildren and beyond?" But also, "How am I addressing my children's needs today?" If you say, "My children are still living at home." Then ask yourself, "Am I guiding my children to make GOD, Jesus Christ and the Holy Spirit a significant part of their lives?"

    "Am I taking them to church, are they involved in Christian youth groups in our church, are they attending Sunday school teach Sunday?"

If you have a close-knit family, praise GOD, but what is more important is being a family that is saved. The two are not synonymous, and when your family's life is over, they may still be a close-knit family, but if they do not have

Jesus Christ as their Savior; they will not be in heaven. Jesus Himself said,

> I am the way, the truth and the life. No one comes to the Father except through me. (John 14:6)

As parents, we need to ask ourselves, "Am I satisfied my children know Jesus Christ as their Lord and Savior?"

"Have I done all I can for my children's salvation? "Have I given them the guidance they need to know and follow Jesus Christ as their Lord and Savior?"

"Will I be accountable when I stand before the judgment seat of Jesus, knowing some in my family may never go to heaven?" Do I ever ask GOD, "Please help me to understand, as a parent, that, I *cannot* save my children, and help me to *not* to be a reason my children may never know Jesus Christ as their Savior when they die?"

As a mother or father, have you told GOD, "I love my children so much and want to help them to understand the meaning of Jesus's words to people over two thousand years ago when He told them, He is the only way to Heaven. Not a way, but the *only* way. As parents, we must ask GOD, to guide us, and our children, and help us study and understand His Word (Bible).

One thing we must be sure we are *not* guilty of, is doubting the truth in what GOD's Word is saying and do this because of the bad experience we had in a church we once attended. It may have been a comment a church leader made about something we did in our youth that was wrong or something we felt members of our own family have said that we felt they were "judging" versus "their words of witnessing that is supported by GOD's Word" (e.g., Matthew 12:30, John 14:6, Romans 14:12, and 1 Corinthians 3:16).

Sondra and I pray for all our family each evening, and especially for the younger members that are still living with their parents. We pray they will be taken to church and attend Sunday school with their friends and sit with their parents during church services.

Time spent together as a family today will often help Mom and Dad praise GOD in how their children grow up knowing Jesus as their Lord and Savior. Hopefully the day will come when their children are saved, baptized; and attending SS and church on Sunday.

If this becomes the norm on Sunday morning; the day will come when Mom and Dad will see their children and their grandchildren following the same practice. And they will look at each other, with a smile and a kiss and say, "Thank You, Father,"

"It was worth it all," and "GOD is good—all the time."

Chapter 2

Grandpa Lloyd D. McJunkin's Memories

But in your hearts set apart Christ as Lord. Always be prepared to answer everyone who asks you to give the reason for the hope that you have. But do this with gentleness and respect.

—1 Peter 3:15

At the age of six, I assumed my life was normal for all children my age. I often felt hurt and didn't understand *why*. I thought other kids my age were experiencing the same feelings. I realize today these were events in my early life when I was too young to understand *why* they were happening, and "Why to me?"

I now understand that at the young age of six going on seven, there are many things in the world children that young don't understand. Let me share a few events that took place in my life at that young age and even extended into my teenage years that caused me to react the way I did. I was much older when I found out the (causes) behind the actions of my Father. In my preschool years, I only knew they affected me in a "hurtful" way! But saying that, you will see, I always felt my dad and mom loved me.

GOD showed me, as we mature into our teens, we should never judge another person, and we should always seek to understand what *causes* a person to take the actions they take. We should learn how to forgive those who have wronged or hurt us. The Apostle Paul tells us this in (1 Corinthians 4:3–4), when he stated,

> I care very little if I am judged by you or by any human court; indeed I do not even judge myself. My conscience is clear, but that does not make me innocent. It is the Lord who judges me.

An example of this came about in my early years of life. It centered around the relationship I had with my father. I will address this in more detail in chapter 3. But first, I want to share some of the memories I have that shows how important GOD has been in my life and why I want to give Him all the praise and glory for bringing me to the end of my journey on earth with far more blessings than I deserve. In the following chapters, I will share some experiences with my own younger families (preteen and teenagers) that still live with their parents. I can recall when I was their age and, being an only child, I would sometimes ask my Grandpa McJunkin questions that I felt I needed to know the answers. As a reader, you will see I listed some of the issues that might be of interest to my grandchildren. These events in my life took place when I was close to their age and how I coped with certain "unknowns" that was very difficult and hurtful by not having any siblings.

My children and their children will be reading the following, for the first time, some of the things in my early preteen years that were impacting experiences and some that were hurtful, because I was too young to understand why they were happening. I hope they and all who read the following will see how Jesus Christ made all the difference in my life in bringing me through those years. Some of my grandchildren may experience like type experiences in their younger years. If they do, I pray they will see that even before we accept Jesus Christ as our Lord and Savior, He is watching over us and He is waiting for us to invite Him into our life as our Lord and Savior. Until we do that, we will never realize what "being saved" really means. This is true for all families of all generations.

From chapter 3 forward, I discuss, in more detail, my walk "through life" once I knew Jesus was always holding my hand. I became aware of the need and the value of having HIM as my Lord and Savior in the passing of each day. But Did I stop sinning? No, and neither will you, and that is why Jesus Christ makes all the difference; He died for all our sins, past, present and future. GOD has shown me many times, and He will do the same for all who follow His commands, what He has done in my life, He will do the same for you. Jesus makes this point in (John 14:6), if we ask Him and obey His Word, Jesus tells us, "I am the way, the truth, and the life. No one comes to the Father except through me." It's as simple as that.

The following are preteen "Questions for Grandpa" that reflected my concerns during my six to twelve years of age. The remaining questions and chapters are written with older readers in mind, including my older Grandchildren. It would be those who have moved away from Mom and Dad and are on their own. Hopefully, they will be reassured, by the love of GOD, they can get through their valleys of hurt and pain IF they have Jesus Christ as their Lord and Savior. I hope they will see He will do the same for everyone if they ask and obey His Word! Going to church and Sunday school class is the best way to understand *why*.

The following scenario was initially started several years ago when I recalled how I had talked with my Grandpa David Grant McJunkin, during my preteen years. He and I became the best of friends, and in many ways, he was MY Hero. Some of the following are like-type questions I recall asking Grandpa. Other questions that I've listed are what I felt I would have asked him as I grew a little older, but he and Grandma McJunkin had both gone to their eternal home in heaven by the time I reached my teens.

The next questions I've listed are questions I think some of my older grandchildren might ask today. So read chapter 4 in that context. Should a question or an answer remind you of an event in your life, maybe the way GOD handled my experience will cause you to look at how He is involved in your life today?

If one of my grandchildren, great-grandchildren, or beyond were to ask me, "Grandpa, can you tell me about our McJunkin family?" I think my reply would be. "Yes, what do you want to know?" I would reply that way because that was how I recall Grandpa McJunkin responded to me many years ago.

*****

Grandpa, can you tell me about our McJunkin family tree?

I have a couple of documents, and one goes back in time before our forefathers came to America. I can't guarantee their accuracy, but they are quite interesting. However, I think they may contain some information that would be hard to understand until you get to be a little older. Depending on your questions, I will share some of the contents from those documents when they relate to what you are asking. But for now, ask me any question about our family, and I'll do my best to tell you what I know.

Grandpa, can you tell me your full name as well as Grandma's?

Lloyd Dean McJunkin (October 13, 1934) and Sondra Lee (Klein) McJunkin (August 29, 1938)

Grandpa, can you tell me what the full names of your and Grandma's mother and father?

My dad's name was Lloyd Earl "Mac" McJunkin (March 5, 1910 to March 12, 1972).

My mom's name was Gladys (no middle name) Garrett-McJunkin (January 28, 1915 to September 17, 1971).

Grandma's dad's name was Horace Adelbert Klein (March 13, 1908 to June 1, 1975).

Her mom's name Mildred Pauline Lamb-Klein (November 3, 1914 to March 10, 1964).

What were the names of your grandpas and grandmas?

Dad's parents were Grandpa David Grant (August 16, 1868 to March 24, 1944) and Grandma Nancy Umbel-McJunkin (March 31, 1874 to October 28, 1942)

Mom's parents were Grandpa Norman (Nance) (January 24, 1879 to March 28, 1951) and Grandma May Alberta (Lewis) Garrett (May 2, 1875 to July 23, 1955).

Sondra's dad's parents were Grandpa Martin Frank Klein (?) and Grandma Mary Lucinda (1866 to 1886).

Sondra's mom's parents were Grandpa Thomas Arnold (1826) and Grandma Mary Lucinda Gammons (1836).

My dad's grandparents (my great-grandparents) were William and Hannah McJunkin and married in Ohio, where my Grandpa David Grant was born. From their home in Ohio they moved to Kentucky where my Grandpa, David Grant, spent his boyhood days. From Kentucky, the family moved into the Indian territory and the small town of Alluwe, in the northeast part of the State of Oklahoma.

In the fall of 1890, Grandpa David Grant was united in marriage to Nancy Umbel, in Independence, Kansas. They returned to Alluwe, Oklahoma, to make their home, where he was engaged in oilfield work. To this union were born eleven children, five of whom passed away before their first birthday. It was while they were in Oklahoma that most of their children were born, among them was my father, Lloyd Earl McJunkin born on March 5, 1910. He was next to the youngest of the surviving children. In the spring of 1916, the family moved from Oklahoma to Toronto, Kansas.

How many brothers and sisters do you have?

I was an only child.

Where did our family come from initially?

One story says we started in Denmark with the name of Junkovic. They later moved to Scotland and changed their name to MacJunkin. A few years after moving to Scotland they moved to Ireland where the spelling of their name became McJunkin. I don't know if there is any connection, but the many moves by our forefathers in Europe seemed to continue when they came to America. Moving seems to have continued being a part of the David Grant McJunkin's branch of our family tree. You will see later, I have done my part in keeping the "Moving Trend" going.

A family story that was shared with me by a man with the last name of McJunkin: I received most of the following, not from my family but from a family named McJunkin living in New Jersey in 1972. It listed several of the McJunkin names that I knew were names in our family. It also included information I already had that matched with what my Grandpa McJunkin had recorded in his file.

It goes something like this...

While our ancestors were still living in Ireland, a somewhat strange event took place. One of the McJunkin men was digging potatoes in his garden when he unearthed a leather pouch that contained gold coins. These coins were enough to finance passage for his family to sail to the new country known as the United States of America. Several years later, some of his brothers and cousins came with their families to America. In a short time, they all settled in the same area in Pennsylvania and became farmers.

One day while the men and older boys had gone to town for supplies, a band of outlaws (not Indians), attacked the women and children. They killed some of the older children and molested several of the women. As they left, they set fire to the barn and other outbuildings and took some of the livestock with them.

When the men returned and found what happened, they went in search of the outlaws. They found them camping several miles from the McJunkin farms. Most of the outlaws were killed, and only a few were able to escape. Feeling their story would not be believed by the law, the men went back home, loaded their wagons with food and anything that was still usable or had value, and with their remaining family members, headed out of Pennsylvania in several directions. Some went south into Virginia; others went farther West into Kentucky, Ohio, Iowa, and later into Louisiana, Oklahoma, Kansas, and Texas.

The interesting part of this story is that in 1974, I located another family named McJunkin living in Pennsylvania. In 1984, I became aware of McJunkin families in New Jersey, Virginia, and Louisiana. Several had large businesses in their family name, e.g., "McJunkin Iron and Steel." Shortly after retiring to Texas, I came across a family in the De Soto, Texas area by the name of McJunkin, also with a good-sized business in the name of McJunkin. I laugh when someone asks me if I checked to see if we were related to any of these other McJunkin families. I would reply, "No," because in finding out more about them, I determined they seemed to all be quite wealthy. Since many seemed to have companies in their family name, I knew they probably were not related to our branch of the "McJunkin family tree." (Just kidding.)

Since our name is not a common name, at least with the same spelling of McJunkin, it seems the story of how we were motivated to leave Pennsylvania, at least until things cooled down, may have some truth to it. My Grandpa, David McJunkin told me when I was still in grade school that he had come to Oklahoma from Kentucky. He said he knew of one brother (Fred) who had moved on to one of the northwestern states, but he had lost track of him and was not sure where he lived at that time. Years later Grandpa was contacted by this brother who, as I recall, had settled in Oregon and some of his children were living in the State of Washington.

Grandpa, can you tell me about your very early days?

When were you born?
October 13, 1934.

Where were you born?
Toronto, Kansas, in Woodson County.

How did your mom and dad pick your name?

My first name is the same as my dad's. My middle name, Dean, was taken from the last name of a famous major league baseball player at that time—that is, "Dizzy" Dean. I've always been thankful my parents didn't select his nickname for my middle name! Some may feel that the nickname, "Dizzy" would have been more appropriate.

What was your childhood like?

Since Dad had to travel often to find work in the oil field business, I went to several different schools during my first three years of school. We always rented apartments, knowing we would only be there for a short time. When I was in the fourth grade, we had moved back to Toronto (for good), and that is where I graduated from high school. The first house we owned was a small wood-frame house in Toronto, Kansas, only one block from Main Street and one block from the school. When our children were in junior high and high school, and we were living back in New Jersey, they would sometimes talk about how cold it was on the bus going to school in the morning on a cold winter day. I would kid them by saying, "Spring, fall, or winter, you don't know what bad weather is. In all my school days, I had to walk to and from school each day, in the rain, snow, or hot sun." Then I would remind them, "At least you get to ride in a bus." They would be quick to remind me of another difference by saying, "Yes, but you only had a block to walk, and we had several miles to ride in the bad weather!"

I have a lot of fond memories of the house I grew up in during my junior high and high school days. (During my preschool days, before my parents bought our first house, we rented, and my memories of things in my life are not as pleasant during that period. I will talk about that in chapter 3.)

Grandpa, can you tell me about your life as a child? What did you like most about your childhood?

Once we had settled in Toronto, I developed some close friendships. I liked the freedom to run and play in the safety of our small town. We boys made many of our toys out of sticks, scrap wood, or whatever we could find and pretend it was something that we couldn't afford to buy. We made up new games and modified old ones that we and many of the kids our age played. I remember kick-the-can was the most popular game.

What is one of your favorite memories of your mom and dad?

Mom always had a large garden. She would "can" all kinds of food for the winter months. While she was canning, she would let me eat some of the fresh food before she filled the jars and sealed them so the food would keep until the winter months. I recall telling her how good it was, and she would reply by saying, "It will taste even better this winter when we have it to eat." Dad carried a lunch box to work. Often, he would leave some of the food, like an apple, and bring it home, knowing I liked to check his lunch box each day to see if he brought anything home for me. I know he could have eaten everything Mom had prepared since working in the oil field was hard work, and Dad had a big appetite.

Did you have chores to do each day?

Not many while I was a preschooler or young teenager, however when I started junior high, I began to mow yards with a "manual" powered (meaning *me*) "push lawn mower." If you find one today, take a good look at it and imagine mowing your yard next summer with it each week. At the year I went from twelve to thirteen years old, I started mowing one to two yards each day for an average of six days each week. I would get $0.25 for each small yard and as much as $1.50 for a yard that took me all day to mow. I only had one large yard that included a vacant lot plus the normal yard of the home owner.

What were your favorite and least favorite foods?

My favorite food was homemade chocolate or pumpkin pies. My least favorite food was spinach (and still is).

Did you have a favorite movie or TV program?

Cowboy western movies were my favorite. I also liked going to the movies once a week. (It cost ten cents.) Before the film, we would see World War II previews since we were still fighting World War II at that time. Television was not available in towns outside large cities. Before the movies would start, they would show a news film of the events going on in the war. I think it was called "Movie Tone News." I had two uncles and several older cousins in the military during World War II, and I would always look for one of them in the "News" shown before the movie started.

How did you pass the time during a free afternoon?

In my preteen years, TV was not available, but I would listen to some of the afternoon serials on the radio, like, *Jack Armstrong the All-American Boy*, *Captain Marvel*, *Superman*, and others. If the weather was nice, I would be out playing with some of my friends.

Where was the best place for you to play as a kid?

Anywhere in town. We never had any fear of being hurt by strangers, and everyone in town knew everyone else, and some of them became "lookouts" for our parents.

A few of the elderly ladies kept an eye on all of us kids and would call our parents if they felt we were getting "out of line."

Grandpa, can you tell me about your school days? Anything special? Do you remember when you were a schoolboy?

I remember much of my boyhood school days better than I remember some of the things I did last week!

Where was your first school?

I started the first grade in Toronto, Kansas, and ended in Elizabethton, Tennessee. There was no kindergarten at that time in Toronto. I started my second grade in Toronto and ended up in Mound City, Missouri. I went to the third grade in Oskaloosa, Kansas. Then we returned to Toronto for the rest of my schooling through high school.

Who was your best teacher?

Mrs. Ireland (fifth and sixth grades) in the Toronto school. She was a great teacher.

What were your favorite and least favorite subjects?

I liked math and disliked history.

Did you go to college?

Yes, but I didn't go to college right out of high school. At the time I graduated from high school, we were fighting North Korea, and I joined the Navy a week after I graduated.

In chapter 9 you will see what GOD enabled me to do in going back to college at a time some would have told me, "There is no way you can do that and hold down a job in New York City." Remember, "With GOD, all things are possible." Sometimes GOD will test our faith, and when He does, we are much better off in following His lead.

What kind of activities were you involved in throughout your high school years?

I liked sports in high school and played baseball, basketball, and one or two years we had track and field. I was in the high school annual plays my junior and senior years and played the bass drum in the marching band (briefly) one year (that was a joke as you will see later). I was senior class president and captain of the high school baseball and basketball teams my junior and senior years. Before you think I was quite smart or talented, and better than I was, keep reading. You will see that GOD does miracles in ways you would never believe He would.

Grandpa, did you have a pet animal when you were growing up?

Yes, a dog named Spike.

If you could've had any pet as a kid, what would you have chosen?

My dog Spike. He was a very loyal pet and always wanted to go with me when I went to a friend's house.

Did you let your children have pets?

Yes, they had two cats, two dogs, two horses, but not all at the same time.

Grandpa, can you tell me…more about other things when you were young?

What was your favorite season of the year, Grandpa?
Spring.

Have you visited your hometown lately?
The last time was in 2008. How had it changed? It was almost a "ghost town"! In 2019 I received an e-mail from my friend Hoyt Black, saying they had demolished the schoolhouse!

Did it bring any memories back to the time you lived there?
Yes, and I still have many fond memories that only other kids my age, and I could understand and know why they were so special.

Which years of your childhood are most dear to you?
They each have a special meaning for me when I think of the fun and pleasure I had as I passed through the different stages of my childhood. There were a few exceptions that were difficult to understand, and I'll touch on them later.

When did you first think about your future?
When I was twelve or thirteen years old and started mowing yards, I saw if you earned money you could buy things you wanted and not have to depend on someone like your parents to buy them for you. It was a great feeling of maturity. As to what I wanted to be when I grew up, I don't think that happened (seriously) until I was a junior or senior in high school.

When you played as a child, what was your favorite outdoor activities?
Since World War II was still going when I was a child and most of our playtime centered on being soldiers fighting to defend our country. Contrary to many beliefs today, I don't know of any of my friends that ended up a gangster or killed anyone because of them playing war games as a child. I think quite the opposite. It instilled in

us the need to fight for the freedoms of the people in our country—that is, the good old USA!

What do you think is the key to happiness?

I have found real happiness comes only through having faith in GOD through His Son, Jesus Christ. But to have that level of joy, you first must know and accept Jesus as your Lord and Savior. (See Appendix F numbers 12, 13, 14, 15.)

Did you have a favorite toy?

I had a toy tractor that would be a collector's item today, but I no longer have it.

As your children grew up, what games did you play with them?

Mostly card and board games.

Do you have a fond memory of attending or participating in a sports event?

Many. I played baseball and basketball, on our high school teams, I think we went to two district tournaments in basketball and, as I recall, we took second place in one, but we didn't win either of the tournament finals.

When were your children born?

Vicki Lynn was born on July 13, 1957 (in Wichita, Kansas).

Stephanie Luann was born on February 27, 1959 (in Wichita, Kansas).

Grant Wade was born on December 29, 1964 (in Pueblo, Colorado).

Did any of your children participate in sports?

Yes, and my most fond memories in sporting events were not of those I participated in, but they were those their Mother and I attended that involved our children.

These involved our daughter, Stephanie, whom on weekends we took and her horse, Kerri, to horse shows in New Jersey. She became a very accomplished rider. We enjoyed seeing her win many ribbons on her horse Kerri.

When our son, Grant, was in high school, I believe we attended every one of his wrestling matches and football games. He was a good wrestler and made the second team all-state football team in New Jersey his junior year. His team won the state championship his junior year in their division. He and one other junior were the only nonseniors on the starting varsity team that year. As I recall, our son's high school division was next to the largest high school Division in New Jersey.

I enjoyed seeing our children excel in sports, much more than I did in any of my (few) sporting accomplishments.

Our oldest daughter, Vicki, did not go out for sports. However, we were equally proud of her accomplishments in the academic area. She improved her skill after finishing high school and schooling in the medical field. She also raised her oldest daughter under some very challenging circumstances, after becoming a single parent. Later, she and her second husband raised a second daughter while they were both working full time. She continued her work in the medical field and retired after having a successful career in that area.

Can you recall the landscape that surrounded your town as a child?

Toronto was a small farm community in the Southeastern part of Kansas. During my high school years, we had seven churches—all Protestant; none were Baptist, Catholic, or Jewish. At that time, the population of Toronto was under a thousand. However, we often had about as many farm children in our school as those living in town. By living outside the city limits they and their parents were not counted in our city population. This made the size of our school much larger than the city population numbers would indicate. Since the farm families lived outside the city limits, they were not counted in our city's population. We had a bigger high school than our city population might indicate. Toronto was surrounded by hills (not mountains), two rivers and all kinds of wonderful places to play, swim, hunt and be safe.

Did you ever make a fort in the woods? A trail in the meadow? Or tree houses?

Yes to all three, and I made them more than once in different places.

If you could show me one special place in nature close to Toronto, where would it be?

It would be a place close to Toronto but outside the city limits about a mile. It was called "The Bluffs." It was a high cliff overlooking a widening in one of the rivers. At that spot, the water was about ten feet deep and was a great place to swim. As I recall, the cliff was at least thirty feet high, and about six feet below its top was a "natural" cave that was about four feet deep.

It was somewhat hard to climb down to the cave, and as a young boy, you were considered by the older boys as being "one of them" when you were brave enough and succeeded in climbing down to the cave and back up, without any help. I don't recall any boys falling into the river below, but some were older than others when they made it to the cave and back, without help! I don't recall how old I was, but I made it without falling, and I felt like I had done something "really great." The story surrounding the Bluffs was that it had been part of an Indian camp many years ago.

Grandpa, can you tell me about your beliefs during your youth?

I assume you mean my belief in GOD and Jesus Christ, right? My mom and dad did not go to church. However, they both grew up in the church. Mom would always make sure that I went with one or both of my older cousins, Beverly and Rheta.

What was your favorite prayer for bedtime and mealtime?

At bedtime, I sometimes asked GOD to make my mom and Dad go to church with me. Since I didn't have any brothers or sisters,

I would often talk to Jesus and ask Him why certain things happened or didn't happen in my life. I even asked for an older brother, not realizing that was impossible in the laws of human nature, but I was around eight or nine at that time, and desperate!

As I look back to my younger years, I realize I had a very close relationship with GOD via Jesus since He was the only one I knew that I could share my true feelings. At mealtime, we didn't ask a blessing, but Grandma and I do today, even when we eat at a restaurant. When we eat out, we ask the waiter who serves us if they have anything they would like for us to ask GOD to take care. We started asking that question back on January 12, 2015, and it has led us to what has become our "R" (restaurant) ministry. (See Appendix D for details.) It has blessed us in witnessing the willingness people have to share their needs with strangers, and it has shown us the power of prayer and the opportunity to pray for strangers in need. At first, it was a surprise to see how the waiters seem to welcome our asking them if they needed what only GOD could provide. At the end of 2019, we had only three people who refused to give us a prayer request. Some of the waiters' comments have led us to believe they gave us their need because they felt we genuinely believe in the power of prayer. More than one told us they thought GOD sent us to support them in their need for prayer. One told us they needed prayer that day and praised GOD for sending us. Those kind words from many of the waiters we prayed for have been such a blessing. It was not too long after we started praying for waiters, that we felt GOD had confirmed this as a ministry for Him. That feeling has increased in the years following our start on January 12, 2015.

GOD has blessed our prayer ministry in so many ways, and we give Him all the praise and glory. One example of this was when a waiter told us, "You will not believe this, but prayer is what I needed, and my prayer request was for someone to join me in asking GOD to help me with a problem I have. I didn't expect He would send someone so fast." The waiters always thank us for being a reminder to them, that He is the only one that could take care of their need, and today, you folks have reminded me of GOD's power. He knew, but He wanted to hear me ask for His help, and He did it through my asking "if I had a need." Thank You so much!

What is your favorite memory verse?

John 3:16 was the first verse I memorized. This one verse shows how GOD continues to love us. Just before I accepted Jesus Christ as my Lord and Savior, His words moved me when He said in (John 14:6) "I am the way and the truth and the life. No one comes to the Father except through me." I was about eleven years old at that time. (See Appendix B.) Before I accepted Jesus as my Lord and Savior, I looked at Peter as my Bible hero. However, it was not so much for his works with and for Jesus, but more for being a man who let you know his true feelings, even if you didn't agree with him. After I accepted Jesus Christ as my Lord and Savior, I changed my role model when we were studying about a man the apostles called Barnabas, meaning "Son of encouragement." When we studied in (Acts 9:27), how Barnabas brought Saul (Paul) to the other apostles (who were afraid of Saul) and told them of Saul's encounter on the way to Damascus and how he later preached fearlessly in the name of Jesus to the people in Damascus. I realized Barnabas was a man that seemed to put others first and did his best to "encourage" them to do the work of the Lord. That's when I chose Barnabas to be my real hero, and I've tried to follow his way of serving the Lord as I have grown in GOD's Word. Like Paul, I have also met with disagreement from more than one person, often in their denominational belief versus GOD's Word.

What is your prayer for me, Grandpa?

My prayer for you and each of my grandchildren (and great-grandchildren and beyond) is that you will come to know and accept Jesus Christ as your Lord and Savior before it is too late. I pray that none of you judge your parents or others for the mistakes they have made but, strive not to repeat their faults in your lives. I pray you each keep your focus on Jesus Christ, acknowledging that He died on the cross for your sins and only He can forgive us and take care of our needs. Jesus tells us in John 15:5,

> He who abides in Me, and I, in him, will bear much fruit; Apart from Me, you can do nothing [of lasting value].

When you were young, what were some of your good times that made you happy?

Not to be redundant with my previous comments, but I accepted Jesus Christ as my Lord and Savior when I was eleven years old and made my profession of faith before our church congregation on the week of July 7, 1946, and I was baptized the week of July 14, 1946. Although I didn't fully understand everything I had done at that time, I knew I had received GOD's Holy Spirit to guide me. (See Appendix F number 6.) At that time in my life, I was happier than I had ever been. Before having Jesus as my Savior and a *real friend*, I had no one to talk with about things that every young person needs to discuss with someone. As a preteen, I knew kids at my age needed someone that would not "blab" to others or make fun of us. When I talked with Jesus, I felt so many things that were "important" to me were things Jesus wanted to hear, and I needed an answer to my questions. It seemed many of my fears would go away, and sometimes I felt so happy that I forgot to thank Him for taking care of me. I know now that Jesus reads our heart even when we fail to tell Him with our mouth how we are thankful for His love and blessings. As I have grown older, that same feeling has kept me going, time after time. Jesus truly means "all the world to me."

What hobbies or activities have brought you joy over the years? (*Note*: The following answer would be what I would give to one of my older teenage grandchildren to this question.)

My answer to the above question would be the following:

Being willing to work and prepare myself for things I felt important. For example, I worked hard in the Boy Scouts and earned the much-coveted Eagle Scout badge. (Covered in chapter 4.) I was appointed one of four squad leaders while going through Navy boot camp, and I made E-5 (second class petty officer) in the Navy in less than three years. (Covered in chapter 5.) After returning to civilian life, I spent thirty-plus years with AT&T, ending my career in their headquarters office on March 3, 1987, as a district manager. (Covered in chapter 9.)

It was during those times, the trend within headquarters seemed to be "next to impossible" to make district level without having a college degree. The reason for this trend was because we were in a "buyer's market," and AT&T was receiving applications from graduates coming from some of the highest accredited colleges in the United States.

After interviewing some of these candidates, I was so impressed that I wondered if I might be reduced in level to open a slot for a younger person with one or two PhDs, and I knew these people existed at that time because I had interviewed several of them.

More than once, I prayed to GOD that I would not be transferred to a lower-level job and have my pay reduced. I had more than one conversation with GOD on those long train rides home from my office in NYC. He heard me, and to this day, I don't know why He answered my prayers the way He did. I've always felt it was a little too much to be "coincidental" with all the trends going on in headquarters. Think about this: I did not have a college degree; my job was requiring me often to travel to locations throughout the United States, and AT&T was receiving applications from graduates of major colleges. Some of these were students who graduated in the top percentile of their class, and at a minimum, they had a master's degree and more often a PhD in an engineering field. How could I hope to get a college degree, continue to work, and maintain a high enough rating within the company to keep the level of job I had? My job at that time was, codirecting and supervising the development of a Bell System-wide project called "common language." It was about to be completed, and my future did not look too secure. I felt pressure in several of my earlier assignments, but at this point, I was feeling a lot of pressure and stress, and I tried to hide it from my family. There were times I found this was next to impossible, and that increased the pressure even more.

Although I was not aware of it at that time, but GOD was preparing me for the future He had for me. I'll explain this in detail in chapter 9. Not only was my life about to change, but it would be in ways I would never believe. Once again, I recall what Jesus told His disciples when He told them, "With GOD, ALL things are possible."

Grandpa, what do you think is the key to happiness?

I touched on this earlier, but real happiness comes only through having faith in Jesus Christ. But to have that level of faith, we first must know and accept Him as our Lord and Savior and follow His commands according to His will.

What sporting event do you hope I will play?

As a child, I would hope you would learn and play all the sports that you enjoy. If you decide you enjoy one or two sporting events more than others, then you should focus on them and try to narrow them down to the one or two you like and seem to excel in. Even if you feel you will not make All American, enjoy the sport while you can. But never lose sight of one thing; playing a competitive sports game is not the important thing you need to keep in mind. For maximum satisfaction and recognition, you need to focus on being viewed as a "team player." The team that wins the championship is most often known as a team whose players are, "team players." Years in the future people will remember the name of the team that won the championship; few will remember the player that scored the winning point(s). If you are viewed as a "team player" while in school, chances are you will be known as a "team player" when you become employed in the job market.

I found during my career, more good jobs were offered to "team players" than to those whose philosophy was "I'll do it *my* way." The earlier you show you are a "team player," the earlier you will enjoy its rewards; in sports and the work-a-day world. It is true in civilian (private and corporate sectors) as well as choosing a military career. This fact of life should not surprise anyone. Think about it; wouldn't you want someone working with you or for you that you knew you could rely on and know they would be working for the good of the group, company, as well as themselves?

Remember this: If you are good at what you do, you do not have to tell others. If it is true, others will tell you. Never forget, what we have achieved that is good, is only possible because GOD has made it possible, not we by ourselves. We are GOD's instruments, and we are where we are, to glorify His name. If we are faithful to Him, He will do all things for us.

Grandpa, can you tell me about some of your friendships?

Did you have a best friend growing up? I had many friends, but I think the ones I considered my best friends in high school are the following:

"Hoyt" (Bill) Black—now a retired officer after a career in the USAF. He and his wife Joanne live in Kansas. Meredith McCurdy retired as an architect with a firm in Texas. He passed away on March 11, 2017. His wife, Molly, continues to live in Texas where their children live.

"Hody" (Charles) Moon retired from AT&T. As I recall, Hody died in late 2003 or early 2004. His wife, Joyce, the last I heard, lives in the Chicago area, close to their children. I also retired from AT&T and along with Grandma (Sondra) moved to Texas to be closer to our children. Today all three of our children are married and have children.

Our oldest (daughter), Vicki, and her husband (John) are retired and moved back to Oregon from Washington State. They have two of our grandchildren, both girls and five of our great-grandchildren. We also have a great-great-grandchild. Their children are all living in the State of Washington.

Our middle child (daughter), Stephanie, and her husband (Jay) are semiretired and lives in Texas only ten miles from us. She and her husband, who is still working, live on a farm on the West side of Waxahachie, Texas. Our three grandchildren in Stephanie's family all live in or within a short distance of Waxahachie. They are all married, and at this writing, collectively they have four of our great-grandchildren. Each of the girls has two boys. Our grandson and his wife are expecting their first child near the end of 2019, a girl.

Our youngest child (son), Grant, and his wife (Jennifer) and family live in Florida. Their two sons are out of high school, and the oldest has completed college on an athletic/academic scholarship. Their two daughters are still in high school. Grant has an older daughter who is married and lives with her husband and their son and daughter in South Texas.

Now, back to my three best friends.

During my high school days, some people in Toronto referred to the four of us boys when we were in high school as "the big four." When they saw one of us, usually there were at least one or all three of the others nearby. I was the youngest of the four and was one year behind the older three in school, due to my birthday being after the school year started. After we graduated from high school, married, and started our families, we drifted away from each other because we had our careers, family, and lived in different parts of the USA. We became involved in many different occupations, interests, and activities involving our families, but we still recalled our days when we were all part of the Trojans of Toronto High.

Were you shy or outgoing?

In high school, I felt I was rather shy, but my friends may have seen me as being more sociable.

Serious or funny?

I never saw myself as "funny," but I didn't think I was overly serious either.

What quality do you think is most important in a good friend?

By being there when your friends need you.

Do you recall a story about having a good time with your friends?

One summer, as I remember, we camped out all summer in a large tent in the backyard of my friend Meredith. As I recall, at least three of us spent a week camped on the riverbank outside the city limits and prepared our evening meal each day. That was because it was a requirement for earning our "camping merit badge" in the Boy Scouts. We had a blast, and as I think back, remembering how little sleep we had at night, I don't know how we made it, but it was a lot of fun. I address this in more detail in chapter 4.

Do you remember when there weren't computers or cell phones?

I can even remember when there were no home television sets. I remember when the transistor made the vacuum tube a thing of the past, almost overnight. The transistor made it possible to construct a piece of equipment that formally had been too big to carry in a suitcase but, in utilizing transistors, that same piece of equipment was made small enough to be carried around in your shirt pocket.

Grandpa, can you tell me about major changes in your lifetime? (This type of question would probably come from some of my older grandchildren because I think they would be questions I would have asked my grandpa McJunkin if he had still been alive in my teen years.)

What do you think were some of the best changes that came about in your lifetime?

Knowledge and the advancements in all fields that have helped the human race be what our creator wanted to see in us. However, I feel there has also been a downside to what we have done with our newfound knowledge. We have used it in all areas. Some knowledge has been used in hardware that is used daily by many people, young and old, in ways that tend to isolate them from society. If you doubt this, try saying, "Hello" to the next person you pass that has a set of "headphones" plugged in both ears and see what response they give to your friendly greeting. Today the reason they may not reply to your greeting is that they have the outside world "blocked out" and only what they want to hear is permitted to come into their ears.

Right or wrong, it has resulted in a habit that is creating people with hearing problems and possibly, people who will not be able to take over the controls of running our nation in the future.

GOD has given man two very important freedoms: We have the freedom of choosing to *do* things, *and* also the freedom of choosing *not* to do things. These are better known as "the freedoms of choice."

When we think about the society our children and grandchildren will be responsible for, will it be one they are prepared to receive? "How are they using the two freedoms of choice today, that GOD has given them?

If the future leaders are not prepared to take over the leadership of America, they may blame their parents but, in the end, they will realize that they were the ones that chose to isolate themselves from what was going on in the world that their generation would now become its leaders.

Okay, enough of Grandpa's thoughts on what is causing many problems today. I do pray our younger generation will not be influenced, in a negative way, when they encounter poor decisions taken by earlier generations. Actions that did not improve the future that made America the great country GOD once enabled them to have by believing in Him!

Grandpa, what did your father teach you as a special craft?

Nothing as a craft or trade because the only thing he worked on from an early age around fourteen or fifteen was working in the oil field. He made it clear to me when I was in high school that he never wanted to hear of me working in the oil field. In his way, I think my dad felt he did not have a good education, and he wanted me to do better in life than he had done. However, Dad did have some qualities that many people with college degrees do not have. Some of Dad's most notable qualities were his honesty, integrity, and hard work ethics. More than once, after Dad died and even a few times while he was alive, his friends told me how they respected Dad for how his life reflected those qualities I just mentioned.

I know he wanted me to have a better education and job than he had. My father did teach me many things. One of the most important was the value of having integrity. He taught me, "Never tell someone you will do something and then not do it. Even worse, is to do something that you said you wouldn't do." He, like me, had faults, but lack of integrity was not among them, for my dad. He was a very caring and emotional person, but being raised in the oil field, he tried not to show his emotions. I guess you might say, "He felt tough men don't cry," but today, I know he loved his family, and it hurt Dad when he was not able to provide for us the way he wanted.

Grandpa, what are some of the memories you have that you would like for me to know?

There have been so many things in my life that I would love for you to experience. However, there are probably an equal amount I hope you will never encounter. I remember the events that existed the day each of our children was born and where they were born. I also remember those days we made phone calls to our relatives and friends to tell them we were parents, then years later, with the same pride, we announced we were grandparents and still later, but with the same pride, we announced we were now great-grandparents. As the years seem to pass by faster now, we find Grandma and I will sometimes talk about those wonderful events in years gone by. When we recall a past family event, for a moment, I am back in that time period twenty, forty, sixty years ago, living those beautiful moments over again. And I see how wonderful GOD has been to Grandma and me by giving us such a beautiful family. The sad part is our oldest daughter lives in Oregon and we can only talk with them by phone. We don't see them very often. Our son and his family live in Florida and we don't have much contact with them, other than what one of their children's cousins tell us, and that doesn't happen too often. But the sun still comes up in the East and life goes on. The one thing GOD continues to remind us are the wonderful memories of yesteryear.

Did you have any family traditions?

When I was still living at home we didn't have a lot of family "traditions." Remember during most of that period; our nation was still recovering from World War II. Families were still searching for ways to survive and rebuild their lives. We would go to Grandma Garrett's (Mom's parents) house on holidays. She and Grandpa Garrett were farmers, and they always had homemade or home-grown food. In the summer, we would often go to their farm on the weekend and make homemade ice cream, and sometimes I would get to crank the ice cream maker. Once each year, the McJunkin "kinfolk" would have a big picnic at a place called Rocky Ford. It was at a river crossing that, when the water level was low, it had a sandstone crossing at one place. It was great for a picnic, and there was plenty of water for everyone that wanted, could swim. I recall when the water level was low you could still see where the wheels of the covered wagons from years gone by had cut into the sandstone time after time when the Pioneers had crossed in their following Horace Greeley's advice—that is, "Go west, young man, go west!"

Grandpa, can you tell me...more about your hopes and prayers for my future?

I touched on this earlier, but to add to the above, I pray all three of our children will have shown their children, while they were still living with them, that they are experiencing one of the ideal places and times to prepare for their eternal future. Some jokingly call it the "Stage before being kicked out of the nest." It is that time in our children's lives that we begin to realize everything good in life comes from the need (sometimes even sacrifice) on their part, to perfect and use the talent GOD has given them to glorify His name. It is a time they each will exercise their freedom to do something or not do something that will open the door of their future for each of them. If they don't have Jesus as their Lord and Savior, their chances of doing GOD's will be reduced.

The following applies to both parents and children and realize it applies to all humanity in different ways at different times in our lives.

It is the responsibility of each person to decide who they will look to for guidance to be a better person and to improve their ability to be successful in life. As a freshman in high school, we can easily find an upperclassman more than willing to advise us about anything and everything. He or she is that "braggart" that all high schools seem to have, who brags about how great they are. Or we can listen to our parents who tell us how good we can be if we study and develop the talents GOD has given us. The child, based on what their parents have taught them, will decide who to follow. Some might feel they don't agree with their parents because "None of the kids at school believe their parents" (a typical young person's exaggerated view, at least it was when I was a teenager). Parents teachings should be for the good of their children's future. When a child follows someone that could turn them into a "braggart," and the child tends to believe what they hear at school versus at home, the child's future is in jeopardy. That does not help the child, and it can impact their future development.

If parents and their children follows the teachings of our Lord's Word, as taught in Sunday school and church, they will experience much more, the thrill of competing, in a friendly way; with their classmates in the classrooms and with students from another school in sports. They will have a feeling of fulfillment they never experienced before. Hopefully, they no longer believe the anti-Christian comments other students talk about in school. Will your children recall those times Mom insisted their homework had to come before going out with friends or talking to them on the phone. Will they remember, it was Dad who pointed out things they could do that they weren't sure they could, but knowing Dad felt they could; they tried and succeeded, especially in sports. Then they found others also encouraged them to do their best in the events in which they participated. When we think of these things as we get older, we should also thank GOD, who made it all possible. When we children show Him, we are willing to do our part in learning, and following His commands, we will find He is ready to lead us to do His will in our lives. Mothers and Fathers, compared to GOD, are limited as to what they can do, and so are their children. GOD has no limits, He can do all things, and He will IF we believe in His Son, Jesus Christ, and show Him we are willing to do our part and work for our dreams to come true.

Remember, the world does not owe us anything. I've found the following rule is so essential for real success, "Ask GOD for what you need for future success, *not*, just your desires for tomorrow." Then strive to do your part in following His guidance. This fact of life is true in education, sports, and life in general. By your parents instilling this in you while you are with them, by words and by deeds, it is then up to you and your siblings to decide what kind of a future each of you are willing to work for and obtain. If your parents didn't or couldn't encourage you for some reason, *you* still have the responsibility and capability to serve GOD and receive the fulfillment of your dreams and the plans He has given you! One of the best ways for parents to guide their children is taking them to church and Sunday school on Sunday. Did your parents do this with you?

Parents, what are you doing to help your children? Often, young children place more truth in what they hear from those who are only a year or two older than they are. GOD expects us to follow His Word and hear the truth from their parents and their church. He has given all parents specific guidelines to follow in what they tell their children, to prepare them for their adult life. We should always pay attention to our parent's instructions because they will be accountable for parenting their children.

We must remember humans are not perfect, GOD is, and we must always strive to follow His commands if we want real satisfaction and fulfillment. We should be careful not to judge what seems to be a weakness in our mother and father while we are still living with them. Later we may find they were only trying to keep us on the road to salvation.

If you refuse to accept the truth in GOD's Word (Bible) as to how He wants you to live; there will be consequences. You will find you cannot blame your parents or friends; it will be your decision in not accepting GOD's Word. The bottom line is, if you don't have Jesus Christ as your Lord and Savior, you will never realize your full potential. You will never understand it is GOD that gives you the abilities you have. When you refuse to accept His truth, the day will come when it will be too late to change your mind. (See Appendix F numbers 7, 11, 12, 13, 14, 15). If you live your life not accepting or acknowledging what GOD has done for you, through His Son, Jesus Christ, the Bible tells us, *you* will have chosen the road to follow that will take you to your eternal home. Unfortunately, it is not the road to heaven! Are you willing to gamble that the Bible is wrong? If you find *you* are the one that is wrong in your belief, do you understand what you will lose, for eternity?

Grandma and I both have fond memories of seeing our three children grow up in the church and accept Jesus Christ as their Lord and Savior. We enjoy the memories of their accomplishments after they left home to follow their dreams. It has, however, been very hurtful at times, seeing and feeling some may feel we were not proud of them. Some have drifted away from the church and its teachings and may not have exposed their children to the truth in GOD, the meaning of His Word (Bible) and why everyone needs to have Jesus Christ as their Lord and Savior. I pray that my grandchildren who do not have Jesus as their Lord and Savior will understand they will not be able to blame their parents, once they are at the age of accountability.

Now that *we* are grown and accountable for what we do, say and believe in the eyes of GOD, not man or ourselves, but GOD; the decision we make when we become accountable will be the one that GOD looks at in deciding where each of us will spend our eternal life—that is, in heaven or hell. I pray we all have or will make the right decision—that is, knowing none of us knows if we will see the SON or the sun in the future.

It is easy for young people to overlook the fact that often parents must sacrifice time with their children and spend more time on their job so they can provide their children with a lovely home, adequate food, opportunities for them to go to summer camps and events that are so important to them during their younger years. Hopefully, these children will have forgiveness in their heart if they feel their parents have failed them. I pray if you are a parent, you have forgiven your children for misreading your intentions and forgiven yourself when you did fail them, because you know God has forgiven you. It is not too late for your family to come to the Lord and Savior, asking forgiveness for the times they have failed Him, you and your family. It's not too late as an individual or as a family to get on your knees and lift your eyes to the one true GOD and ask His forgiveness.

Each of us will be responsible for our decisions as to how GOD, Jesus Christ and the Holy Spirit are a part of our earthly lives. We each will choose to live the life we desire. In doing this, we should understand there will come a time when we will not be able to change our decision. We will all be "judged" by the only one who has that authority—that is, GOD the Father. At that time, our earthly life will be over, and our "eternal" life (outside our earthly body) will begin, and there will be no going back. My prayer is that everyone who is reading this has or will make the right decision before they arrive at that point of no return! The sooner we decide to make Jesus Christ our Lord and Savior, the earlier we will experience a more fulfilling life in our remaining time on earth—learning, understanding, and experiencing an earthly life as GOD's servant. The decision we make will be the most critical decision we will ever make here on earth. We will be determining where our eternal destination will be. YOU and I both will decide if our eternal home will be in heaven or hell, determined by what GOD sees, what and how we believe versus what *we* feel, *what* and *how* we believe. These are not my views; they are GOD's words that are pointed out many times in the Bible.

GOD's rules and requirements for humanity to enter heaven for their eternal destination are clear, and we must adhere to them. We must also remember, Satan will tempt us in a way that sounds like he can give us all kinds of fun and enjoyment if we follow him to his eternal destination. *We* will choose the "road" we will follow!

Grandpa, is there a tradition you would hope I will share with my children someday?

So many things we did when I was living with my parents are very hard to do in the world we live in today. Our society seems to offer so many "things" for young people today that don't include "Mom and Dad." However, when you can, be involved in your children's activities even if it is only as a "spectator." You will recall those times, years later, and if you are lucky, your children will also.

Grandpa, can you tell me…about your meeting, Grandma?

Yes, any specific questions?

Do you remember where you first met Grandma?

Yes, in Fort Madison, Iowa. Mamie Jones, the lady I was renting an apartment from, introduced us. Mamie was a friend of your grandma's aunt, and she told me she knew a nice young girl that she felt I would like, and the rest is history! (I explain this in more detail in chapter 7.)

What did you do on your first date?

I think I took her to a movie, but soon after we started dating, we went roller-skating on most of our dates. Not to boast or brag, but we both were pretty good skaters, back then!

How did you propose?

I would not have won an academy award for my performance because I was very nervous. I proposed on the front porch of her house as I was bringing her home one evening.

Where did you get married?

In Burlington, Iowa, on November 24, 1956, in the First Christian Church. This was the church Grandma attended years earlier when her parents were living in Burlington.

What did you like most about your wedding day?

That's a rather personal question. (LOL.)

You'll understand the thought behind that answer when you get a little older. But I think the realization that I was now a married man, really made me feel good. Like most men getting married, I thought of all the wonderful things that were to be in our future. Looking back, many of the things I thought would be tremendous and essential did not come about, and some would not have been that great. Other events that did come about have proven, to be very important and have provided me with beautiful memories, especially the older I get.

What have you liked most about your shared life?

Being with Grandma! I cannot think of anyone I have ever known that I could have enjoyed more than I've enjoyed over these sixty-plus years I've spent with "Grandma." She put up with my crazy antics, nursed me when I was ill, did not complain when she had good reason to do so, and has been the best soul mate I could ever want. There is no doubt in my mind, she was sent by GOD to support me in doing many of the things He had for me, and no one else, to do. (See Appendix F, number 17). Grandma has been a wonderful wife and a super mother and never put herself before her family. I pray before she goes to her home in heaven, that all our children will recognize how much she did for them in those years they were growing up. If they haven't done so already, I pray they will let her know how much they appreciate all she sacrificed for them.

Did you ever give Grandma a special gift?

Yes and no. The first year we were married, I bought Grandma a dress I thought was gorgeous. Grandma took one look at the dress, and one look at me, and I knew I would never see her in that dress! I think she took it back and exchanged it for something she liked and would wear. I never bought her another piece of clothing in all the years we were married. I would often tell her, "If you like that dress, get it and think of it as my gift to you." I think she was grateful for that decision, especially in matters that involved her wardrobe.

Grandpa, can you tell me some special memories you have about your life with Grandma?

Your grandma always amazed me with some of her characteristics. For example, when our children were very young, and a storm was raging outside at night, she would never wake up. However, if one of the kids whimpered a little, even during the storms, she would be wide awake and jump out of bed to see if they were okay. I can never remember a time when any of our children wanted her to help them do something that had to be done dealing with school or other things, that she ever said *no*.

After all these years, Grandma still asks me what I want for dinner. She will often make a dish and not tell me what is in it when I ask. She will laugh and say, "Just eat it." She will sometimes fix a dish and watch me pick at my food trying to figure out if it is something

I don't like. When I look at her, she will be laughing so much she can't talk. But she knows what I don't want to eat, and she never fixes a dish that has any of those foods in it. I like to think, "Grandma's actions are typical for a mother, grandma and a wife to do, but to me, she is something much more than typical, she is special in all of those categories."

Life with Grandma is a life of many surprises and so many pleasant moments when compared with what some would consider a healthy marriage. Life without Grandma would be unbearable, and I don't like to think about that. In our evening devotions, we pray together and often ask GOD, "When it is time for one of us to come home, please bring both of us at the same time to our heavenly home You have promised us." That would be a wonderful blessing for me because I can't imagine life on earth without Grandma. We both agree that as long as GOD leaves us here, we know we still have not completed the plan He has given us to fulfill. We know when it is GOD's time to bring us home, He will.

We know He never makes a mistake and we thank Him each night for all He has done for us that day. We thank Him for walking with us throughout the day, helping us to be obedient and always guiding us back whenever we go astray.

I hope you see that Grandma and I have had a beautiful life together. When you find that "special one" you feel you want to spend the rest of your life with, I would ask you to read and remember the following events that I encountered, starting from the very beginning to the very end of my life. They are not to scare or discourage you but to show you that with the valleys of despair we all will pass through, from time to time; there is always a mountaintop beyond if we have Jesus as our Lord and Savior (along with the "helpmate" He has given us). I hope you will see when bad or hurtful times come your way, Jesus is the only one who can lead you to that mountaintop on the other side.

I pray you will come to know and follow the words of Jesus Christ as your Lord and Savior, in the good times and the bad. Try to develop the strength and wisdom to be a strong "helpmate" when your spouse needs your understanding, and your children need your warmth and guidance. Recognize, you will fail many times in both, but if you do the best you can, and others feel you failed, you can take comfort in the words of the Apostle Paul as he wrote in 1 Corinthians 4:3–4,

> I care very little if I am judged by you or by any human court. Indeed I do not even judge myself. My conscience is clear, but that does not make me innocent. It is the Lord who judges me.

If you have done your best, but at times you were not able to do what you wanted to do, then GOD's judgment is the only one that counts. If friends or family do not agree, that will be between them and GOD. If you do your best and you stay in daily contact with Jesus Christ; when you reach the end of your time here on earth, you will be able to look up and say, "Thank You, Jesus. Amen!"

I pray that you and all those in your family will be able to live a life that is pleasing to you and one that GOD wants you to live.

Chapter 3

It's an Unforgiving World—Without GOD

GOD has given us everything we need for a fruitful life. In 2 Peter 1:4 it says,

> Through these He has given us His very great and precious promises, so that through them you may participate in the divine nature and escape the corruption in the world caused by evil desires.

I hope you agree if the procedures, beliefs, and rules that are spelled out in GOD's Word are ignored, or discounted; having a successful and meaningful life on earth, is virtually impossible. It has nothing to do with how much money we acquire or how great the sounding of a title we possess or how much control and influence we have over others. Throughout most of my adult life, the underlining pathway to attaining a fulfilling life was when I believed GOD's Word tells us the following, "The only way we can repent is to acknowledge our sins. The only way we can move forward in having a meaningful life is to ask those whom we have hurt, to forgive us. The only way we can feel worthy of serving GOD is first to forgive those who have wronged us. And the only way we can have comfort in GOD's forgiveness is to believe He has forgiven us and *then*—forgive ourselves."

I know I was not born with a silver spoon in my mouth or a "halo" above my head. That is another way of admitting, "I have never lived a perfect life." There was a time I drifted away from the teachings of GOD's Word. I have sinned and fallen short of the will of GOD, many times. Without one bit of pride, I admit I have been "around the block," more than once, in my young adult years. I have seen and done things I am not proud of and don't care to discuss them because I believe GOD has forgiven them.

I find no comfort in saying, "Yes, but I can name many who have done much worse than I have." GOD's Word makes it very clear that He does not judge us with one another. It is Satan who tries to get us to compare our sins against those of others that our society might agree are much worse than ours. When we let Satan influence us this way, we set the stage whereby we will never feel the real love and forgiveness of GOD.

It is so important to know the facts surrounding the actions we take in responding to life's unpredictable encounters each day. Said a different way, we need to go beyond knowing what steps we are taking. We also need to know the answer to the question, "Why do we react to a given situation the way we do, time after time?" OR., better yet, "What is the cause that is bringing about the action we take?"

And knowing the cause is also essential to identify when we are the observer of the actions of others. The cause can be actions taken by our parents, our children, other close family members, and even friends and coworkers.

If we react only in seeing what people do but never try to identify the cause, then we are "judging" them. Not knowing the cause can be harmful to others, and it can bring about the loss of good friends. The action word in the above statement is *cause*. Failing to know the cause can lead us to "judging" others, and that is the work of the Lord, not yours, not mine.

In reading about the events in my life, you may recall similar occurrences in your life. They may remind you of related happenings in your past that resulted in you making wrong decisions that were hurtful to you and others? If the answer is *yes*. I would ask you to think about what GOD's Word says. His Word has shown me it is vital for us to understand there are times in our lives that we may not be old enough or wise enough to understand the cause(s) behind the actions we take, as well as the cause(s) of actions taken by others. Knowing the cause for one's daily activities—that is, for a friend or ourselves—can bring about forgiveness, stronger friendships, and even a better understanding of our own life.

Prejudging another person by what we see can cause "hurt feelings" within families and friends. It can bring separation from people that are close to us and important in our life. We need to identify the "cause" and see if we may be able to help the person overcome the "situation" that is controlling his/her life. Wouldn't it make you feel better, knowing you have helped someone overcome an "action" that has resulted in their losing friends? If you get to this point, you have "stopped judging" and started understanding and probably made a friend for life. Remember, it makes no difference which person is not following GOD's Word, it can be the other person, or it can be us. To identify the problem, without judging the other person, must be the objective.

Over the years I and maybe you have been guilty of stopping short of finding the cause behind the action of another person, or even yourself. Later, you will see, in my early teens, my prejudging almost brought about my rejection of my father, until I found out the cause for his actions. When we don't judge others, we will find it is easier to forgive them and forget the hurt they caused us and, in some cases, we may be able to help them overcome their hurtful actions.

We need GOD and His Son, Jesus Christ, with the Holy Spirit in our lives if we hope to survive and accomplish anything of value in the short time we are traveling through this place we call planet earth. I have no doubt GOD, Jesus Christ and the Holy Spirit are real, and each serves a different need in our lives!

Now may be a good time to explain in more detail, the David G. McJunkin clan, and especially how my dad fit in. Grandpa David McJunkin, being an "oil contractor," seemed to have a lot of influence on all his sons. They all worked in the oil field as drillers, tool dressers, or "Roughnecks," at least a portion of their lives. Only my dad made it his lifelong occupation until his later years. In those days, the above titles denoted men who operated "cable-tools" equipment to drill for oil. With advancements in technology, the drilling equipment was starting to be modernized to use a "rotary" technique. However, the titles of the workers, for the most part, remained the same.

Dad, in his school days, apparently was considered a good football player and played fullback in junior high and high school, but he never graduated. The rules at that time were quite different from today. If you were good enough to play on the high school team when you were still in junior high, you could, and that is what Dad did. Also, at that time, boys were going to high school and playing sports when they were twenty-one years old!

After finishing junior high, Dad continued to go to high school four years in a row (during football season), always as a freshman. As soon as the football season was over, he quit school and went to work in the oil field until school started next year. On the fourth year, Grandpa McJunkin gave Dad an option, "You finish high school and quit playing football or, you drop out of high school." Dad chose the latter and dropped out of high school and started working full time in the oil field.

During the "cable tool" days when drilling for oil was being converted to the "rotary technique," a lot of the dangers between the two techniques were removed. Some of the men from the "cable tool" era that Dad was a part of would have you believe, "You didn't have to be as tough to work on rotary drilling as you did to handle cable-tool drilling." I'm not sure that was ever proven to be true, but the reputation of cable-tool oilmen seemed to center more on their ability and desire to fight, drink and cuss rather than their skill in the oil field. My father never talked with me about that part of his life, but one of his close friends did (I'll call him Mike). Mike and my dad were close friends during their school days and beyond. Mike became a farmer, and I worked for him a couple of summers baling hay during my high school years. When we stopped for lunch, he often shared with me some of his and Dad's experiences when they were, as Mike put it, "Young and foolish."

One such event took place at a "barn dance'" Mike and Dad went to one Saturday night. As they arrived, they saw a crowd of people circling two young men, "slugging it out." One of the men knocked the other one to the ground and immediately started beating him around the head. As Mike revealed the story to me, Dad (who was smaller than either of the fighters) grabbed the one on top and pulled him off and said, "Okay, you've whipped him, let him go." The guy got up and took a swing at Dad, who dodged the blow and in turn punched him in the nose and broke it. The fight ended, and everyone went inside and danced, except the guy with the broken nose, who went home. That was one of many stories Mike shared with me about Dad's fighting reputation throughout Woodson County.

At that time, the effects of the depression were still impacting most families. Dad's two older brothers had married, and I'm not sure if they ever lived with Grandpa and Grandma McJunkin in their "church home." Both ventured into other work areas, unlike oil field work, once the family arrived in Kansas. Dad's younger brother Everett was in the military during World War II, and when it ended, he worked for a while in the oil field but later started his own business. Since Dad had no experience in any other occupation than working in the oil field, he continued in that line of work. I can't help thinking there were many times Dad regretted that decision, especially after he and Mom were married.

I never knew why Grandpa and his family settled in the small town of Toronto in southeastern Kansas. They moved from Northeastern, Oklahoma, and Dad and his two sisters came with them. Their two oldest boys were married and may have come with them at that time but it seems they never lived with Grandpa and Grandma in their 'church' home. Grandpa was an "oil contractor," which meant he would contact landowners who wanted someone to drill for oil on their land. Then he would contract with a drilling firm to drill the well. When he and Grandma moved to Kansas, he continued that occupation.

According to my aunt Lora, my grandparents had eleven children (five died in early childhood), six children survived to adulthood. Of these six children, all were still living when I was born; I was about ten when the first of the six children died. That was Uncle James or as everyone called him "Short." He died of cancer while still in the military during the latter part of World War II. They have all passed away now, and I pray they are all with the Lord. I still recall each of them as if it was yesterday at one of our annual family reunions out at Rocky Ford, about a mile outside of town.

When the family arrived in Toronto, Grandpa had to find a house large enough for his family of two girls and two (?) boys to have some privacy. I'm not sure if their son Everett had been born at that time. After much searching, the only place he could find, that had the square footage he was looking for was a church building that had been vacated a year or so earlier. I'm not sure how that fit in with Grandma's plans for a home, but that became their new "church" home, and significant remodeling started immediately in creating additional bedrooms.

Dad, along with two older sisters and one younger brother were still living with Grandpa and Grandma at the time Dad and Mom were married. They were married soon after Mom graduated from high school. She never indicated she had any regrets in being married so young. However, I expect Grandma Garrett (Mom's mother) may have had some second thoughts since Mom graduated at the top of her class in high school and was offered a full scholarship to the teachers' college at northwestern Missouri. Since they didn't have a place to live, Grandpa and Grandma McJunkin said they could move into their church home.

At that time, I'm sure Dad and Mom were thankful that Grandpa and Grandma were thoughtful enough to make their offer. Once they had their own bedroom, life was normal for the newly married couple.

About a year later, I made my entry into the world. As most fairy-tale stories start, so did my life… "Once upon a time, on a cold winter's night in the small town of Toronto, Kansas." The difference between fairy-tale stories written as being untrue events; the following is a real account of my birth and my life with Jesus Christ as my Lord and Savior.

I hope you can see why I have all the proof I need to believe everything the Bible says about GOD the Father and Jesus Christ His Son and His Holy Spirit. There is no doubt in my mind, knowing what I have experienced from my first day on earth that GOD has shown me His love, power and forgiveness are real. These experiences have now been spread over more than eighty-five years as of October 13, 2019. Sometimes I was not living by His Word. "Why?" Because I am a sinner. But through it all, I never doubted His love and forgiveness, were always present. I will admit there were times I couldn't understand *why* GOD would continue to forgive me.

My life began in what seemed to be a short, predestined, and meaningless life that would shortly end. But praise the Lord, that was not GOD's plan. He has shown me that we never want to assume GOD is not in control of *all* things! What began as a life that seemed destined to last for only a few months, GOD is still using it over eighty-five years later, at the time of this writing. My prayers today are that my life will have some value in the eyes of GOD when it comes time for Him to bring me home.

In some ways my life did start almost like a fairy tale—that is, early one cold October, on Saturday morning in the year of 1934, at 4:00 a.m., I made my entry into the world. The bedroom area Mom and Dad used was in a part of the sanctuary area of the original church. Now you know why I jokingly claim the honor of being born in a "church." I joke with some of my friends saying, "The first time anyone ever saw me, I was in the church in a crib. The last time anyone will see me, I expect to be in the church in a casket!"

Having one more adult living with Grandpa and Grandma was no big deal when it was my mother. However, when I joined them, I expect my crying at 2:00 a.m. when I was ready for breakfast and continued crying because my stomach started aching from consuming too much milk; things started changing fast. Within weeks after I was born, Dad and Mom found a rental house that was adequate for the three of us, and for the first time, my home was outside of a "church" building!

I'm sure my parents had several discussions about things, not going as they had planned. THEN, when I was about three months old, I came down with a bad cold. At that time in small towns throughout America, when a person was sick, the doctor was called, and he would tell them when he would be out to their home to check on the sick one.

Mom never told me until I was in high school, about the events that took place that day when she had called Dr. Newman. As she revealed what happened, I understood why she had not told me earlier. I realized, for the first time, more of the causes and actions that brought about some of the hurtful events, starting in my preteen years.

Mom talked to Dr. Newman; our one and only doctor in Toronto. After hearing my problem, he said he would come out within the hour. When he arrived, he immediately started examining me. He was nearing the completion of his examination when he told Mom that it looked as if my bad cold had now developed into pneumonia and things didn't look good. As he continued to check different parts of my body with his stethoscope, suddenly he murmured, "Oh no!" He then looked at Mom and said, "I'm sorry, Mrs. McJunkin, but he's gone."

Mom went into shock. Dad was at work, and there was no way to contact him, and Cell phones did not exist at that time. Dr. Newman said he would stay with Mom until one of Dad's sisters could come down to be with her. Aunt Lora came down as soon as they contacted her.

Today I can understand the shock my mother was going through at that moment when Dr. Newman informed her I had died! It may have been that Dr. Newman didn't know what to say or do that would be of comfort to Mom, but for some reason, he again moved his stethoscope on my chest, and, maybe at that point, GOD was taking over! Dr. Newman, after placing his stethoscope on my chest and again, started to move it around to different parts of my upper body. Mom said he continued this process of moving his stethoscope as he had earlier. All of a sudden, Dr. Newman stopped, adjusted the earplugs, and looked at Mom. His eyes were open wide when he said, "I think I am getting a faint heartbeat. Yes, it is! "He's *alive*!"

I joke about this today and tell people I'm living proof that GOD does give some people a second chance in life! I can't help but think, this second announcement from the doctor within seconds after he had told Mom I had died, and a short time later he was now telling her, "I was alive. What was going through her head? Was the doctor mistaken, and was he going to say in a few more seconds?"

"Oh, I'm sorry, he *is* dead."

After first being told I had died, then hearing seconds later that I was "alive!" I can't help but wonder if my mother had some doubt if I was going to stay alive. Was she praying I would remain alive, and at the same time, doubting if what she was now hearing was true? I can understand better why, in the short time I had joined the family, I was causing a lot of unexpected concerns for my newfound parents.

They probably wondered, "What is he going to do next?"

It was that event, as I grew older and realized how the unplanned illness that I brought into our family shattered many of my parents plans to enjoy a pleasant and enjoyable married life. I didn't understand how my becoming a part of my parents' family was not something that made their lives fulfilled and more pleasant. However, my view of my dad changed when Mom revealed the above experience I encountered. I especially started changing my feelings about my dad and started to feel, even more, his love for me.

Dr. Newman told Mom I would probably develop a cold each winter, and they would have to pay close attention to me because a cold could develop into pneumonia again. His prediction proved to be correct. Until I was in the first grade, I would catch a cold early in the fall, during the first days of severe weather, and it would last until spring.

After starting school, I would often miss several days at a time. As time passed and I became more active and gained some weight, my severe colds became fewer and less severe each year. However, in those first five years, I did not make a life for my parents more pleasant.

Not finding out about all of this until I was in high school, I could see *why* it caused my parents even more problems in trying to keep me healthy and at the same time, cope with the Great Depression problems that still existed. For about four years, they had to deal with a sickly son. These two factors caused certain "challenges" in their early married life that many other families did not have to experience. Even today, I thank GOD for enabling my parents to do the best they could to give me a chance to live.

I expect it was when these events were taking place; my parents decided there would only be *one* child in their family. The care and attention I required did not make their first few years of married life anything as they had planned.

As my health began to improve each winter, I started making more friends, especially after I started school. It was then that I noticed most of my friends had a brother or sister. Quite often, they would tell me things they had asked their older siblings. These were things they were afraid or too shy to ask their parents. I felt deprived of not having a brother or sister like my friends had. I would have done anything to have a big brother or even a big sister to discuss things I didn't want to talk about with Mom or Dad. But that was not to be. However, I did have GOD, Jesus Christ, and the Holy Spirit and my conversations, especially with Jesus, brought me much satisfaction. I will explain a little later how my Sunday school teacher, Mrs. Carson, deserves much of the credit for my knowing and accepting GOD, Jesus Christ, and the Holy Spirit.

Time passed, and I seemed to get healthier and started acting like a typical little boy who had a knack for getting into mischief and always getting caught. There were times that I felt Grandpa McJunkin was the only one who understood me; the only one I could talk with and share many of my concerns. He was the one that seemed to have the time and who seemed to know what I was saying, and he always had good advice as to exactly what I should do or not do.

I'm sure this was because I was his youngest grandson at that time before he and Grandma both went home to be with the Lord. I think he also may have been in his "second childhood," and he may have looked at me as being the only family member that understood him and who he could relate! I recall how he would take me out on the back steps of their "church" home where he would say something like, "In a few days, I'm going to buy a bucket of potatoes, cut them up and you can help me plant them." That kind of comment always made me feel grown-up and very important, at least in the eyes of Grandpa. Later when he bought the potatoes and started to cut them, he again pointed out to me, "When you cut potatoes to plant, be sure you always leave at least one 'eye' in each piece. Then when you plant them, always place them in the ground with the eye looking up to GOD!"

I've passed those "words of wisdom" on to several adults who indicated they were going to plant a garden for the first time and plant, among other things, potatoes. I would ask, "Do you know the right way to plant potatoes?" Regardless of what their answer was, I would always share Grandpa's way and add, "Right or wrong, Grandpa always had great success with his garden."

In many ways, Grandpa became my hero because he seemed to have time to talk with me, and at that time in my life, I never doubted anything he told me. Aside from his "knowledge" in the proper way to plant potatoes, there were so many stories he shared with me that always made me feel I was important to him. He always made me feel grown-up and a very important person, at least to Grandpa.

I recall another day he and I were out on the back steps of his "church" home when Grandpa asked, "I've never shown you my pistol, have I?"

"No, Grandpa, you haven't!"

"Well, sit here, and I'll get it and show it to you." I could hardly wait for him to return and when he did, I saw for the first time, up close, a real gun, just like the ones Gene Autry and Roy Rogers used in the movies.

As Grandpa sat down on the step beside me, he said, "Now don't ever point a gun at another person, even if you know it doesn't have any shells in the chamber. You want to remember a gun is not a toy, and you should never touch a gun until you get old enough to know what you are doing." I knew what Grandpa was telling me was the truth because Grandpa would never lie to me about "gun safety."

After that education on guns, Grandpa looked at me and said, "The last time this gun fired was when a man borrowed it saying he had some rabbits getting in his garden and he wanted to scare them away." Then Grandpa said, "I found out later the man shot another man who had cheated him out of some money." I recall looking at the gun, and my eyes probably were the size of quarters.

Today I'm not sure Grandpa was telling me the truth about the man killing another man with Grandpa's gun. He may have said what he did because he wanted me to remember all he had told me that a gun was not a toy.

I will say I never had a pistol in my hands until I was on the firing range during boot camp in the US Navy many years later.

I expect if you talked with some grownups that knew Grandpa in his younger years, they would never believe you if you said he was a very understanding and caring man. I think some saw him as a very strong-willed person. He was a man of high moral standards, and he was not bashful to let you know his view, sometimes when he was not even asked. Thinking back, I recall he had certain "do and do-not" rules we grandkids were expected to obey when in his and Grandma's home. He had rules, "without exceptions," that had to be followed by all of his grandchildren.

One rule that I recall took place in the portion of their "church" home they used as the parlor. In this room was a Victrola record player that stood about four feet high from the floor. Very few homes at that time had electricity. To use the Victrola, you had to turn the attached crank handle until it stopped, before you could play a record. The record player was "off-limits" for my older cousin Beverly and me, to even touch. In all the years after I was born, until Grandpa died, I never saw or heard anyone play the Victrola. I expect today it would sell for three or four-times what Grandpa paid for it new.

Another "no exception rule" that I recall was one my cousin Beverly, and I had a hard time obeying. It involved Grandpa's rocking chair. He had a high back rocker made of solid oak and seemed to weigh at least a ton! Grandpa told both of us when we asked him if we could sit in his rocker when he was not using it.

"Yes, but remember it is a rocking chair, not a toy. You can rock in it but don't stand on the rockers because in time you will break them loose."

However, when my cousin and I thought Grandpa was outside or taking a nap, we would take turns using his rocker. One of us would sit in the chair part and rock it while the other one would stand on the back portion, on the two-floor rockers and hang on until we jumped or fell off.

We got the message when Grandpa caught us a couple of times and hearing him say, "I've told you, kids, *not* to use my rocker as a toy, now get off and stay off!" I sure would like to have that large rocker today. I know if I could rock in it now I would still feel that roller-coaster thrill of those by-gone years.

I can still see Grandpa sitting in his rocker in front of their old potbelly stove in the winter months, lighting up his big crooked stem pipe and puffing away. What a man! At that time in my life, all his children were grown and had their own families, except Dad's younger brother, Everett. However, when any of his children were in Grandpa's home, they all still showed him respect, even if they didn't always agree with him.

Probably the one characteristic I will always remember about Grandpa McJunkin was his knowledge of the Bible. My Aunt Lora, Beverly's mom, told Beverly and me several stories about the days when she and some of the other children were still living in their "church" home. One rule they had to live by and never question its fairness was. On Sunday mornings, unless you were so sick you couldn't get out of bed, you better be up, washed and getting dressed for church.

The thought of saying, "I don't feel like going to church today!" *Never* crossed their minds, according to my Aunt Lora. Grandma would always say something like, "Now you kids need to get dressed and eat so we can get to church on time." Grandpa was a rather tall man with a huge mustache, and Grandma may not have been much over five feet tall and looked like she wouldn't weigh a hundred pounds if she were soaking wet. But she knew how to handle Grandpa, especially when he was getting a little out of line. When

Aunt Lora told us kids these stories, and knowing Grandpa as I did, I had no doubt what she was telling us was true. I felt Grandpa was right in expecting his children to adhere to his rules concerning the church. "If they didn't hear it from him, where would they hear it?" However, he may have been a little too harsh, since none of his children were active churchgoers once they left home. But I think they all believed the message that Grandpa gave them.

In many ways, GOD is saying to each of His children today—that is, "If you don't follow My rules, there will be consequences.!" Maybe Grandpa was following what he felt GOD expects from His children. If that were true, I would agree with Grandpa's firmness.

I remember Aunt Lora or her older sister, Aunt Lela, more than once, talk about one of the most impressive characteristics of Grandpa. It was a time in our American history throughout the 1930s, almost daily you would hear a knock on the front door, and it would be a door-to-door salesman. One of the items many were trying to sell was a brand-new King James Bible. Now, I don't recall if Grandpa built their front porch or if it was there when they bought the church. I do know it ran across the front of the house and had a roof. Grandpa hung a swing on the porch that became another favorite place for my friends and me to play on, knowing we better not make too much noise or break the swing.

The porch was Grandpa's favorite place to talk with salespeople. He would be in "tall cotton" when a salesman knocked on the front door and asked, "Would you like to have a brand-new Bible?" Grandpa would say something like, "Well, I don't know, do you know where I could find one?"

With those words spoken, the show had started. The salesman would explain he was selling the latest version of the King James Bible (he may have added, "complete with a concordance"). Grandpa would reply to the salesman's comment with, "Man, that sounds great."

The salesman then would question Grandpa about his knowledge of the Bible. At that point, Grandpa felt it was time for the rest of the show. He would say, "Tell you what, let me get my pipe, and we can sit in the porch swing (as he motioned to its location) and you can tell me about your Bible."

On returning with his pipe loaded and lit, Grandpa would sit down, and I expect the salesman already thought it looked like he might be able to sell this "man of interest" two Bibles. Usually, the salesman started by asking what Grandpa knew about the Bible. Grandpa would say, "Oh, a little, but I am not too knowledgeable in what it says or means." I expect the salesman is now thinking he might end up selling three. The salesman would continue picking out different passages and explaining their meaning. Grandpa, in turn, would ask a question, suggesting he didn't quite understand what the salesman had just described. This back-and-forth discussion would go on until Grandpa seemed to know it was time to burst the salesman's bubble.

After one of the salesman's explanations about a specific passage, Grandpa would say, "Well, I hear what you are saying, but I seem to recall in my old and worn Bible, it says…" And he would recite the passage. Before salesman could challenge him; Grandpa would say, "Let me get my Bible, and maybe I can find the passage we are talking about, and if I'm wrong, you might have just sold me a new Bible."

He would get up, go into the house and return with his Bible. As he sat down in the swing, he would say, as he started leafing through the pages, "Now, I hope I can find it, and I may be wrong… Oh, here it is!" He then would read the words and say, "Yep, I thought that was what my Bible said. Now, if you can show me in your brand-new Bible that it says just the opposite, I might buy it."

By this time, the salesman realized he had been talking with someone who knew the Bible and what it says. He also knew it was time for him to move on. Grandpa would smile and say something like, "Well, it's been nice talking with you and stop by again the next time you're in town." Grandpa was what many would call a "hard-shelled Baptist," even though he was not a Baptist.

Grandpa McJunkin was one of two people that played a big part in my understanding that I needed Jesus as my Savior. I viewed Grandpa as someone I could rely on to tell me the truth, and this was because of the respect he showed me at such a young age. He made me feel I had value, I was important to him, and I could have a bright future if I had Jesus Christ as my Lord and Savior.

The second person that had an impact on my asking Jesus Christ into my life was my SS teacher, Mrs. Carson (the wife of our preacher). It was because of the love she showed me and how she explained how GOD wants all of us to make a confession of faith, acknowledging that Jesus is His one and only Son and what He did for all mankind when He gave His life for all our sins; those in the past, present and throughout the future.

I remember one Sunday (quite some time before I asked Jesus to be my Lord and Savior) when I had a bad cold and was not able to attend Sunday school. On the following Tuesday, I received a postcard in the mail. I think it was the first piece of mail I had ever received, other than birthday cards and Christmas cards. The card had a little red chair on the front. Our SS class, at that time, had little red chairs that we sat in during Sunday school. On the backside of the card were the following words:

"Last Sunday, we noticed your chair was empty, and that was because you were not there.

Next Sunday we hope you will feel much better and be with us again in your little red chair!"

The card was signed, "Mrs. Carson and Your friends in your Sunday school class."

That one-cent postcard made me feel so proud, happy, missed, and so much a part of Jesus's family.

With Mrs. Carson's love and Grandpa's faith in the words of the Bible and the respect he showed me, there was no doubt in my mind that Jesus was who I needed to guide me throughout the rest of my life.

It was during this time; I was experiencing something I could not understand. I was around six years old, and I could not understand *why* I was feeling hurt and sorrow?

"What was causing it?" I only knew that it was always present when my dad drank too much, and he and Mom would argue. I now feel Mom and Dad also felt bad for their actions, in front of me.

Today I think they both knew Dad was not living the life of a good Christian and realized everyone in our small town also knew it. I believe they both felt if things changed in the future, they would do more to encourage me to go to church, and maybe they would even take me. Unfortunately, that was not to be. The only time we were all three in church together was when my family accompanied Dad, to attend the funeral of my mother. My family and I were in the same church with Dad, not too long after that, when we attended Dad's funeral. Today I believe parental love and guidance were not what my parents felt they were equipped with and, therefore, not able to show me they loved me. Today I think they did what they could, under the circumstances, and I love them very much for that.

However, at my young age and feeling the hurt I was experiencing, it was even compounded by my not understanding *why*. I only knew I had been placed in a situation, time after time, that I didn't want to be in, and it hurt me very much.

I can't speak for GOD, but I believe my parents' actions, at that time, had a positive impact in my young adult years. However, it didn't surface until after I went through more hurtful times. I'm sure my parents didn't feel the way they were living would help prepare me to handle some of life's trials in my future years. When I became aware of what the "cause" was behind Dad's drinking problem, I had a different view of him. This understanding helped me not to judge others when not knowing why they did things that are not what GOD wants His children to do.

GOD will lead us through the valleys of despair if we believe and follow Him. There may be no better scripture to remind us how GOD will take care of our needs, than the words of David in Psalm 23:4–6,

> Even though I walk through the valley of the shadow of death, I will fear no evil; For you are with me; Your rod and Your staff, they comfort me. You prepare a table before me in the presence of my enemies; You anoint my head with oil; My cup runs over. Surely goodness and mercy shall

> follow me all the days of my life, and I will dwell in the house of the Lord forever.

These words give us another example of what GOD can and wants to do for us; He only asks that we believe in His Son, Jesus Christ, as our Lord and Savior...and then obey His teachings.

Today I realize and better I understand, the financial problems my parents were having at that time. By Dad not being able to have steady work, it was causing even more pressure on him and Mom. I don't believe they realized their day-to-day problems were also affecting me. I was too young to understand how the heavy load they were carrying made it impossible for them to spend more time with me, like the more fortunate parents were able to do with their children.

I assumed most parents were encountering the same challenges and reacting the same way as my mom and dad. It was during this time that GOD started to show me that He loved me and it was during that period He opened doors for me that I didn't understand and sometimes were not aware of what He was doing. Fortunately, GOD also led me through those same doors, and as I followed Him, my life changed.

I still remember those nights, lying in bed, thinking how nice it would be to have an older brother or sister. I feel we all have a "trial period" in our lives that we must decide as to which "fork in the road of life" we are going to take. These times can be very costly if we make the wrong choice. I have come to believe if we are serious about Jesus in our younger years and understand what He has done for us, it is much easier to want Him as our Lord and Savior. Once we make that decision, we find it easier to forgive others and focus on the "plan" GOD has for us. When we follow His guidance and the opportunities He gives us; we will succeed. If we give Him praise and glory He deserves, our lives will be changed. Then, we will be more successful in our encounters in our adult life and realize the words in (Psalms 23) is a wonderful example of knowing when we have GOD, through His Son, Jesus Christ, as our Lord and Savior and His Holy Spirit within us; we have nothing to fear.

However, in those early years of my life, I didn't understand the "causes" of why my parents often did not show me the love I wanted. The Holy Spirit later showed me the load they were carrying made it hard for them to do what I feel they wanted to do. The number 1 cause and reason for many hurtful times in those early years of my life, always centered around Dad's drinking problem. Later, I found what the "cause" for his drinking was, and that made all the difference in how I viewed him from that time on.

Let me now reflect on some of the experiences I encountered and then explain the reason or "cause" that led my dad to do many of the things he did that resulted in "hurtful times" for me. I am not trying to justify what my dad did, but hopefully, you will see why it was easier for me to forgive him when I knew the "causes" for his actions.

I was around six years old when Dad's activities started to involve me. I was too young to understand the "cause" that led to Dad's excessive drinking problem. I could only see his actions and feel the hurt it made in my life. I could not understand why it was happening. "What had I done to deserve those hurtful times? Why was it happening, especially to me, Dad's only son?" I know today I was too young to understand what was going on. But GOD was about to show me the cause that gave me the desire to forgive my dad.

The cause for Dad drinking was *not* because he liked to get drunk: Mom did not tell me the real reason until I was older and in high school and could better understand the reason. She felt, at my younger age, hearing the reason could cause me to have even more questions as to why Dad drank so much. (I'll explain this in more detail in chapter 4.)

Dad was known to be one of the town's best "three-ball billiards players." When he said he was going downtown and play some pool, Mom never said too much because when she heard Dad say those words, she knew it would only take a few more words from her to hit his hot button.

I don't recall exactly how old I was when the activity started that included me. As I look back on this time in my life I see it was the beginning of so many hurtful moments that would impact me, and I asked, "What did I do to cause it to happen?" I had to have been around six years old at the time. When Dad left the house at a time he had not been working because of bad weather, a pattern of events began to take place that would involve me. Mom and I both knew what was going to happen—that is, from the pool hall, Dad would go to the beer hall. I also learned my involvement in these events would start shortly before supper time.

It was around that time, and Dad had not come home, Mom would say to me, "Go down to the beer tavern and tell Dad supper will be ready in half an hour." Now try to envision the small town we lived in was one that almost everyone knew everyone else by their first name. Since we only lived two blocks from Main Street, Mom was not sending me on a mission trip as if we lived a mile from the business district. We lived in an area in which I was familiar with. My safety was not at stake.

However, my charge was not one I looked forward to doing. Even at my young age, I felt sorry for Mom and usually only asked one question, "Do I have to?"

She would say, "Yes, and tell your dad he needs to come home now."

The two-block trip was one that seemed like two miles. I knew what Dad was going to say—that is, "Tell Mom I'll be there in a few minutes."

Then I would say, "Mom said you need to come home now."

"After already having several beers, Dad would look at me and say, in a firm voice, "Go on home and tell Mom I'll be there as soon as I finish my drink." I would turn around, and as I left the beer tavern, I would slowly walk back home, knowing what Mom would say when I gave her dad's message.

Often, I would have to repeat this routine a second time, and then Dad would start getting upset, with Mom and me. He would tell me to go home and tell Mom he would be there in a little while and not to send me to get him again. I would return home, and give Mom the message. She would tell me to go ahead and eat, and then she would go into the bedroom, and I would hear her crying. I couldn't understand why these things were happening.

Today as I reflect on what was going on in my life at that time, as a six-year-old, I see GOD was about to show me the first of several vital lessons in life that we should all understand—that is, "Life is too short to waste time disliking anyone."

I must add, "That is sometimes easier to say than to do!"

When Dad finally arrived home, I knew it would only be a few minutes before the fireworks would start. If Mom was still in the bedroom, she would come out and say, "Your food is probably cold."

Dad would take a bite and say, "Yes, it needs to be warmed up."

Mom would take it, and depending on what it was; she would either pour it in a pan or place it in a skillet on the open fire of the stove.

Then she would turn around and say, "Why didn't you come home when Lloyd Dean told you supper would be ready in a half-hour?" (Mom always referred to me as "Lloyd Dean" during these situations since Dad's first name was also Lloyd). With Mom's question, the battle was on. I usually went to a chair some distance from the table where Mom and Dad were arguing and continued to watch what was happening.

I never realized at that time, with all the "four-letter" words an oilfield driller knew and used, I never heard my dad use the Lord's name in vain. I give Grandpa McJunkin credit for this because he was a "black-and-white" believer in the Bible—that is, the Bible means what it says and when it says, "You shall not take the Lord's name in vain." It means exactly that. I believe that Dad recalled many times what Grandpa told his kids about honoring GOD's Word and I expect Dad, like I have many times, said in similar situations, "Please forgive me, Father."

I have come to believe that it was because Dad didn't feel he had the right to advise me about my future, knowing he went to high school four years as a freshman. When I think of the differences in ages when Dad was in junior high and playing on their high school football team, and, against teams that had twenty and twenty-one-year-old players, I can only assume he was a pretty good "running back." Probably one of the reasons I liked sports was because of the stories I heard about Dad being a good football and baseball player.

Many will say, "Well, you shouldn't have had to go through what you did at such a young age." That might be true, but I like to think GOD used those experiences to condition my life so, when I encountered those same temptations, I would be able to handle them, hopefully in a better way than Dad did.

I'll address this later and share some of the things GOD did through my early married life. But first, I want to refer to the point I made on the "Preface" that states in part, "I have never done anything good that GOD has not enabled me to do." Even before I accepted Jesus Christ as my Lord and Savior, I believe there was not even *one* thing I ever did or accomplished that was halfway good, that I did on my own. GOD used me, first to show me what He could do through me *if* I followed His commands. Second, to show others how GOD can use anyone to accomplish anything He desires, regardless of what people feels the person's capabilities are.

I will also share how there was a time in my late teens and early twenties when I drifted far away from GOD's teachings. But by the Grace of GOD, I returned, and I'm proud to reveal what He has done for me after forgiving my sins, and they became forgiven history.

The lesson I have learned in life is, to GOD all sin is equal. In other words, GOD does not judge our sins as being big, middle size, or small. In His eyes, when we sin, we have disobeyed His commands. So when I think of Peter denying knowing Jesus, I realize, when he drifted away from following Christ's teachings, there were consequences and many lost blessings. But if we have Jesus Christ as our Lord and Savior, He will forgive us, if we ask Him, yet we will still have to live with the consequences, knowing all the blessings GOD had for us during the times we turned from Him, we have lost all the blessing He wanted me to have. He had for us, He would have forgiven as did Peter and as You and I will when we sin.

Once I knew I had been forgiven and was back in the good graces of GOD, I felt I needed to reassess the ground rules I was following that had separated me from GOD. I believed, as His Word says, that He had a plan for me and He still does, but what was that plan? Was it to be the president of our nation, a world-famous person, or the creator of medicines that would cure all kinds of diseases? The answer was, we are expected to put GOD, His Son and Holy Spirit, first in our life, over family, church, job, friends, and we are to put GOD ahead of "ourselves." When I focused on putting GOD first, I found He would take care of all the rest.

Some would ask, "You advocate putting GOD ahead of your own family?" You got it! There are two reasons why I don't hesitate in saying that. First, He demands us to do it, and Second, He was the one who gave me His Son and Holy Spirit, then He gave me, my family, my church (His Word), and (on down the line). That includes giving me my life (two times!), and later you will see that I feel He gave me life a third time on January 9, 2001.

When I was three months old, it was GOD who gave me life a second time, not Dr. Newman. If you believe in a different sequence in thanking GOD—that is, first Him (and His Son and Holy Spirit); then human life, family; the church (His Word); and then salvation. If you believe some other scenario, I think you are in for a lot of disappointments. I tried it, and as soon as I moved GOD from being number 1 in my life, it was as if the Holy Spirit said, "Okay, call me if you change your mind." At that point, old Satan moved in and said, "Do I have a life of fun and good times for you!" I'll talk about how Satan can seem to be, later, when I discuss my teens and beyond stages.

Let me continue by explaining how I discovered we seem to have specific actions in one stage of life that helps us accomplish things but when we move to a different stage of life; we find that action not only doesn't aid us but, it becomes a handicap. For example, before I started school, I discovered at that stage of life if I wanted something like another slice of mom's apple pie, and she said, "No," I found if I started crying and stomping my feet while begging for another slice of pie; I often would get it. However, I found when I started the first grade, that same approach would make me look very foolish in the eyes of my teacher and, it would also bring about a lot of laughter from my classmates. The older we get, the more critical it becomes for us to recognize that what worked for us in one 'stage of life," usually will not work in the next stage. The differences in these "stages of life" seem to be most noticeable when we start our "formal education" stages.

That is when we often spend as much time with our grade school teacher and Sunday school teacher as we do with Mom or Dad. If we are still trying to get what we want by stomping our feet and crying, we find we can be in big trouble very fast. I thanked GOD for showing me the futility in trying the 'stomping and crying" act, once I started school. I saw things like "stomping and crying" in front of the teacher, and in front of my first-grade classmates, would not get the results I wanted. It was made clear to me when I saw you don't challenge the teachers and expect them to yield to your "demand." One of my classmates "challenged" the teacher one day, in front of the class. His action resulted in the teacher taking a twelve-inch ruler and told him to place his hand on the desktop, palm down. Then she whacked him on the back of his hand several times. (Today if a teacher did that, they would be looking for a new job!) I like to think that experience of my friend convinced me, crying and stomping my feet was no longer going to get me anything like it did in my preschool days.

If we believe GOD has a plan for us, why don't we try to do our best to accomplish what He wants us to do? I had found things in life seem much more comfortable when I asked for help from my Lord and Savior. When GOD helps us, we should thank Him and always give Him praise and glory for his blessings. When we try to do things without GOD's help, we will find life is not a "bed of roses." It's all up to you and me in how we act as we get older and still are accountable for our actions, not just to the world, but more so to GOD!

GOD shows us that He never stops loving or using us, even when we get older. He may give us different talents and ask for different things from us, but He will never ask us to do anything that He has not given us the skill and ability to do. For example, around the age of eleven, I felt I "knew" everything. However, it was about that time I realized, "There is more to life than eating, playing and sleeping." I found I could do other things, and I felt GOD wanted me to start doing them and giving Him the praise and glory. Sometimes, we find this out the hard way.

I was about eleven when GOD opened my heart as well as my eyes, and I made the most important decision I have or ever will make. It was at that time GOD reminded me how Grandpa McJunkin and Mrs. Carson (my SS teacher) were the two people that played a big part in my knowledge of GOD's Word, and I needed Jesus in my life.

Grandpa McJunkin and Mrs. Carson knew GOD, and they convinced me GOD loved me. At that time, I didn't understand why many things were happening in my life, e.g., what my parents were going through. Looking back, I know GOD was telling me it was time for me to come to Him and accept His Son, Jesus Christ, as my Lord and Savior. (See Appendix C. I'll share with you in the following paragraphs how, at eleven years old, I felt GOD's Holy Spirit gave me the conviction to tell, not ask, my parents what I was going to do the following Sunday in church.)

To sum up what I have covered above and what it led to

On July 7, 1946, I repented of my sins before our congregation at the First Christian Church in Toronto, Kansas, and gave my life to GOD and asked His Son, Jesus Christ, to be my Lord and Savior. I was baptized the following week on July 14, 1946. But I'm getting a little ahead of my story.

I was eleven years old when I invited Jesus Christ into my life as my Lord and Savior. I wish I could say my parents were strong and active Christians and took me to church and Sunday school each Sunday, but that never happened. What I experienced during this time in my life, I feel was the power of GOD's Holy Spirit. The decision I needed Jesus in my life as my Lord and Savior did not come from by my mom or dad. As I said earlier, the credit goes to my Grandpa McJunkin and my Sunday school teacher, Mrs. Carson, both of whom had the Holy Spirit within them. I believe my parents had accepted Jesus Christ as their Lord and Savior, but because of the load they were carrying, they seemed to be trying to take care of their needs without asking for GOD's help. I'm not sure that was true, and I hope it wasn't. I will explain this in more detail in the following chapters.

Their parental love and instruction that I did not receive were not factors in my decision. I believe my parents did not understand what they were doing was having a hurtful impact on me. They were not aware GOD would use this experience to prepare me to handle some of life's trials when I was older. He led me through situations during that time in my childhood and gave me the strength to get through more difficult events over the years that followed. I did not enjoy many of the happenings, but I always felt GOD would take care of me, and I felt my parents did love me.

One of the most important lessons we need to learn early in life is responsibility. As we enter this stage in life, we enter a time that GOD and society both start holding us more responsible and accountable for our actions. When we don't show we are responsible for our actions, we find life starts being more unforgiving. I felt that I needed Jesus Christ as my Lord and Savior and start being responsible for my actions to Him for what He did for me on the cross at Calvary.

Let me describe what led me to show my church, my parents and myself what I firmly believed and was going to do, and no one was going to change my mind—that is, first and foremost, I was ready to accept Jesus Christ as my Lord and Savior. Being only eleven, going on twelve, I can't recall any other time when I "firmly" told Mom and Dad what I was going to do—period!

It took place when we were bringing Dad home from the hospital in Eureka, Kansas, after having his arm reset from breaking it in the oil field. I was in the back seat and leaning over the front seat between Dad and Mom when I announced, "Do you know what I'm going to do next Sunday?"

Mom replied, "What are you going to do?"

"I'm going to go forward at the invitation and accept Jesus Christ as my Lord and Savior."

One of the few times Dad ever entered a conversation between Mom and me was that day when he said, "Well, you better know what you are doing."

My reply was, "I do, and that is what I'm going to do."

The following Sunday, on July 7, 1946, I took that step of "faith" and walked to the front of our congregation, and made my confession of faith, acknowledging I was a sinner and asked Jesus Christ into my life as my Lord and Savior. There is no doubt in my mind that I believed what I did that Sunday morning, was from my heart. I must admit I didn't understand what it all meant, but I had faith in GOD that His Holy Spirit would show me, and He has and continues to reveal the truth in GOD's Word.

On the following Sunday after church, I was baptized in Lake Fagan, about a mile from town. Mom and Dad did not attend. Years later, I felt they regretted in not attending my baptism, but since they knew their influence did not influence my decision, and they might have felt their input didn't have any impact on the situation or right to attend. I forgave my parents when I married and started realizing the pressures that married life can present. I expect they felt if they had come to my baptism, many of the people (possibly some even in our church family) would say words of "judgment" then or at church the following Sunday.

I find it easy to tell others I have forgiven Mom and Dad for all those hurtful times in my life and I give praise to GOD for bringing me through those times of not understanding why certain things happened. My *faith* in GOD became stronger over the following years, and my love for Jesus Christ gave me an inner feeling I had never experienced before. Faith in GOD and His Word is a significant part of my life today. I must say the more I follow His teachings, the stronger my faith grows. I have since experienced many positive results when following GOD's Word. Albeit, the hurt in my past reminds me not to judge others. Even if we know the "causes," we still should not judge others. But "knowing the cause," we should look for ways we can help the one who is causing our hurt, so they will not want to be judgmental. I know many things my parents did were not right and did hurt me. I feel I was experiencing a lesson in life that we all learn sooner or later—that is, "The world we live in can be very hurtful at times, and we often don't understand why, but that's when our faith in GOD will make all the difference between giving up or going to Jesus in prayer for understanding."

Those experiences indirectly helped me understand that if I wanted something, I should work for it, and earn it through my efforts or accept the fact if I didn't get it, life was still going to continue. I also learned at an early age and even more so as a young adult, "If you don't have the money to pay for it, quite often, you don't need it, and with only a few exceptions, you should not borrow money to get it." Borrowing money when it creates problems in being able to care for your family is something we should not do, especially early in life.

I found life did go on, and before I knew it I was looking at the things I was doing in junior high and asking myself, "How are Mom and Dad going to be able to help me take care of my needs in high school?" The earlier we understand we can not expect our parents to give us everything we want. We need to learn this vital lesson in life, and know if our parents bought us everything we asked for while we are living with them, they would be conditioning us to expect them to continue their act of "giving" after we finished high school.

If my parents had bought me most of what I asked for while living at home, "What would I do if I wanted a new car so I could use it to find a job and move out of my parents home?" This request would seem no different from their paying for me to go to summer camp, buying me new clothes when I asked, and paid for those things that I didn't need but because some of my friends "had them." If my friend's parents bought them a car, why shouldn't I get one? What would I do if I married and didn't have a steady job, but my bride and I decided we wanted to buy a house? Why wouldn't I think Mom and Dad would insist on taking care of all the initial costs and anytime we were a little short on cash, they would have no problem in making the monthly payment(s)? They have always taken care of those types of things while I was living at home." Why would they change, after all, I'm still their son!

However, if Mom and Dad told me, "Son, you are old enough now to take care of those things you want. We may be able to help you out on things you need or have to have, but you will have to take care of your day-to-day expenses and responsibilities." Would I have been mature enough to tell myself, "If you can't do it, or pay for it, then you don't deserve to have it." That challenge never arose because I knew my parents didn't have the money to continue taking care of me the way they did in my younger years.

Some young people may react by saying to their parents; "I can't believe you are serious; after all, I'm your child. If that is the way you are going to act, I'll show you I don't need you. And we (my wife and I) will stop coming over during the week for dinner in the evenings."

Who would be at fault if this situation developed as the above suggests? Would it be the parents, the children, or both? As a child, we need to recognize; usually, each person or family unit is responsible for taking care of their own needs shortly after they finish high school or college. However, they may ask their parents to help them monetarily to take care of something they need, with the understanding, it would be a loan and repaid within a reasonable period.

As parents, we need to think twice before creating a pattern in the eyes of our children in their preteen and teenage years that Mom and Dad will always take care of all their needs that their children have, while they are living at home. When their children graduate from high school or college, Mom and Dad will continue writing a check when their children want something they would like to have. I've seen families get to the point they stop speaking to each other when Mom and Dad either run out of money or realize their children are taking advantage of their love for them. If it continues, it could lead to real hurtful problems in the future, for both the children and parents.

Based on what my parents couldn't do for me at my young age, I knew they would not be able to buy me big toys like a car. I could blame my parents for not doing what the other parents seemed to do for their children. Or I could start earning money and buy the needed items myself. The lesson I learned at that early age taught me many things. I found that if I had to spend my hard-earned money, many of those things I wanted, I didn't need. I also learned another valuable lesson. After I had started mowing yards and making money, I didn't spend it immediately. As my bank account grew, I found I analyzed my needs carefully and quite often decided, "I don't need that new shirt, and when I do need one, there may be another one that I like better than the first one."

My first business venture in taking care of my finances came when I started mowing lawns. Later I bought a paper route and delivered the *Topeka Daily Capitol* newspaper to the homes and businesses in Toronto. It was later when I sold some of my US savings bonds that I bought during my earlier grades in place of buying candy with the money I received for my birthday or at Christmas. Our school sold victory stamps that could be exchanged for a $25 US bonds when you had purchased enough stamps. I decided to sell some of those to buy a Whizzer motorbike at the end of my seventh grade. I had ridden my regular bike each day, delivering my papers on a seven-mile route. Notice I said, "I decided to sell some of my savings bonds. The reason Mom or Dad didn't say "No" was because it was my money! I later sold both my paper route and my motorbike for more than I paid for them.

During my early age, I showed my parents and me; I could do things that many felt I could not do. My newfound *faith* in GOD also guided me in my needs and gave me a feeling I would be able to handle more of my financial needs as I entered high school. I know today it was GOD's guiding hand that kept me aware of my financial capabilities. I was doing things very few kids my age was doing in our town. I'm not saying they couldn't, but they weren't, and maybe the reason was, they didn't have to. Some of them didn't have to work, but I looked at it as, "I have a job and I'm making money, and I feel better knowing I don't have to ask my parents for everything I wanted or needed." In buying my paper route, I realized I now had a year-round, money paying job. My additional job enabled me to put more money into my bank account that my mother helped me open in our local bank. I feel the Holy Spirit was showing me something had to be a real need before I would even think about writing a check. Today you can ask my wife if I still have that trait of *not* spending money just because we have it and I can tell you what she will say! Without knowing it, I was now "diversifying" my investments and being responsible for how I was using GOD's money. Even at that young age, I realized it's all His money, and He would be observing how I was handling His money.

In no time, I was making "big money." Well, maybe the phrase "big money" is a little exaggerated, but making fifty cents total for mowing two small yards in one day and a dollar and a half for mowing a large yard on another day, compared to making nothing, I felt I was making "big money."

I soon found I could buy a "milkshake" each day after mowing and still have money left over. Before becoming a "young" businessman, I had to ask my mother to buy me a milk shake, and often she said, "No!" Now I decided when I could get a milk shake! Good or bad, I think those milk shakes may have prevented me from losing weight doing all that mowing! "You think?" I like to believe GOD was showing me the wisdom in saving—that is, "Save for retirement starting with your first paycheck." I admit that thought never crossed my mind, even in junior high, but I sometimes think GOD may have planted the seed when I realized I had my bank account and the money in it was money I had earned by work I had done.

During all this activity, I became interested in the Boy Scouts, and I attended most of the Scout meetings due to the encouragement I received from my three "buddies" (Hody, Meredith, and Hoyt). After joining, we all focused on earning our merit badges and going on to that next level in scouting. These types of activities seemed to be more challenging when I moved up to my freshman year in high school. At that time, I felt I was preparing myself to be able to handle most of the "social" financial needs of a high school boy.

With the two jobs I had between my seventh and eighth grades; I would never have believed that by the time I graduated from high school, I would have experienced no less than four additional jobs, each providing more income than the combined income of those first two jobs. I didn't realize it at that time, but my good friends and I were all viewed within our community as "good boys." Our families were quite different in so many ways; I expect many people said, "I don't understand how those four boys became such close friends." Hoyt went to the Presbyterian church and had an older sister and a younger brother, Meredith went to the Methodist Church and was an only child, I went to the First Christian Church and was an only child, Hody didn't attend any church regularly and had two older brothers and a sister. Toronto, at that time, had a population under one thousand, and there were no Baptist, Catholic or Jewish churches. However, we had seven churches, and four would be considered in the Pentecostal denomination today. These four were all very small in membership but had a faithful attendance by their members.

I think all four of us boys were entering a stage of life that we were starting to realize, Mom and Dad won't always take care of us like they have, up to this point in our lives. Before and during my freshman year in high school, Hody had a job cleaning the theater, Meredith mowed lawns, Hoyt worked on his dad's farm, and I mowed lawns and delivered newspapers. Looking back, I sometimes think that may have had something to do in bringing us together. A lot of the boys in junior high and starting high school did not have jobs. Also, many lived on farms, and they would challenge anyone who suggested they didn't have a job and I know Hoyt would agree even though his parents lived in town, he worked on their farm.

Chapter 4

Moving Up to High School (and Beyond)

Make peace with your past so it won't screw up your present.

[But] let the one who boasts boast in the Lord. (2 Corinthians 10:17–18)

For it is not the one who commends himself who is approved, but the one whom the Lord commends." This verse reminded me each time I was able to get a better job in school and save more money, that it was GOD who gave me the job, and I knew He was observing how I handled the money I made, from the jobs He provided.

Preparing for high school

The summer following my eighth-grade graduation, I experienced a change from the previous years when I mowed yards and delivered newspapers. In preparing for high school, I advised the people I had mowed for, I would not be mowing yards anymore. I sold my paper route and started working at the furniture store on Friday and Saturday each week during the summer and on Saturday only, on a year-round basis. I found this schedule enabled me to make more money at the end of the year than mowing yards six days a week during the summer months.

In starting high school, my life seemed to change in almost everything I did or wanted to do. Things I never gave a second thought, now became very important. I was still mindful that I believed in GOD and Jesus as my Lord and Savior, but now I realized, more than ever before, that I had to also believe in myself. I knew if I left everything for GOD to give me, I would not accomplish much. I realized that GOD expects us to be responsible (and accountable) for what He has provided.

I didn't understand all of this on my first day as a freshman, and I can't tell you the exact time I became aware of the importance of being more responsible and accountable I may have become mindful of the significance of these two words as I became involved in different activities as a high school student. I believe it was not just one event but a combination of several things that started me to feel, "I am going to be doing things as a freshman that I've not done before."

Near the end of my eighth grade, I took advantage of an opportunity to make more money for my soon-to-be "high school freshman year." I accepted a job offer at our furniture store on Fridays and Saturdays, that proved to be the right decision. The owner was also the town's undertaker. He did the embalming and preparation of the bodies in another room, separated from the furniture area.

Before I move on to my high school days, I want to say a little more about my new job at the furniture store during the summertime when I worked on Fridays and Saturdays. I received a call from Francis, the owner, on a Wednesday, asking me if I could also work on the following Thursday because he had to take care of some business at their funeral home in Yates Center that his father and brother operated. I said I could since I didn't have anything to do that day that I couldn't do later. Francis had given me a key to open the store shortly after I had started working for him, so this didn't pose a problem.

It was still early in the morning when I arrived at the store on Thursday. I went to the back room where we kept the floor sweep and getting a scoop full; I sprinkled it over the floor. As I started sweeping it and the dirt to the rear of the display area, I glanced out the front window and noticed a crowd gathering in front of the café directly across the street.

As I was watching the commotion, Francis, who had not left for Yates Center, came rushing in and said, "Mr. Sanders (not the real name) just shot himself!" Mr. Sanders and his wife owned the café. They had several children and were a lovely family and was well-liked in our community. Francis rushed to the garage behind the store to get the ambulance to pick Mr. Sanders's body up and bring him to the preparation room as soon as the sheriff and county coroner finished with their investigation. When the investigation completed, Francis brought Mr. Sanders's body to the back of the building about the time his brother arrived from Yates Center to help him bring the body to the preparation room where he also helped with the embalming.

The next morning, Friday, I opened the store and started my routine. As I mentioned earlier, the preparation room was in the rear section of the store, where we kept the floor sweep and other cleaning supplies. As I went to get some floor sweep, so I could have that out of the way before any customers came in. I never gave it a second thought when I noticed the "slab room" door was open since the only time we kept it closed was when Francis was in the process of embalming a body.

After getting the floor sweep, I glanced up, and there was Mr. Sanders's body laying on the slab table. I remember dropping my broom, but for some reason, I held on to the scoop of floor sweep and moved "briskly" back into the furniture room. It took me several minutes to settle down from my unexpected shock. After a few minutes, I returned to the back room and closed the door to the "slab room." I also recovered my broom and finished sweeping the floor.

When Francis arrived at his usual time, I told him what had happened, and he laughed and said, "I remembered when I got home that I forgot to close the 'slab room' door. I should have called you and asked you to close it when you came in this morning. We both laughed at what had happened, and he returned to the backroom to finish taking care of Mr. Sanders's body. About an hour later, Francis came out and said, "I do need some help, but if you don't want to, I understand. I need someone to help me lift Mr. Sanders on to the table where I'll finish preparing him, once the family decides how they want him dressed. I said I would if I could lift his feet. He laughed and said, "You got it."

A couple of weeks later, Francis asked me, "Now that you have been alone with a dead person, have you ever thought you might want to be an 'undertaker'? Because if you think you would, I believe I could get you in the school in Chicago or St. Louis." I told him I felt the money would be useful, but I wanted to join the Navy since it looked as if the fighting in North Korea was escalating and could become World War III. I knew that being an 'undertaker' was a well-respected profession, but I'm still not sure I would have been able to finish the schooling required to get a license! Francis laughed and said, "You would do great. If I could adapt, I know you could."

As the hot days of summer started, I began working at a gas station. I continued working at the furniture store on Friday and Saturday when Francis had to be out of town. The owner of the gas station agreed with this arrangement since the gentleman (former owner of the gas station) agreed to work at the station when I was not available.

The owner of the gas station also owned the ice house that was next to the station. My job included working at both units. During the summer, I delivered ice to the homes (M-F) that were still using iceboxes versus refrigerators. On an average day, I delivered between five hundred and a thousand pounds of ice in blocks weighing twenty-five, fifty, or seventy-five pounds. I was the last "home deliverer" of ice in Toronto. That distinction plus a nickel could have bought me a five-cent Coke! When the demand reached less than one hundred pounds a day, it became unprofitable to deliver to the homes. No one complained because it seemed "icebox days" were history. One summer the gas station and ice house owner, 'rented' me and his new flatbed Ford truck to farmers to pick up bales of hay in the field, haul them to their barns and stack them inside. He let me "hire" another boy to help me load and unload the bales of hay.

Often it would be over a hundred-plus-degree temperature inside the barns. I don't recall what I made on those jobs, but I do recall I made twice as much as my helper. I also received an additional four dollars a day for driving the truck. I recall that at the end of the day I knew I had done a hard day's work, but the money I was making eased the pain and I was always ready to repeat the routine the next day. I felt I was becoming more "financially independent," as I began my high school years. Today I think, some of my motivation may have been from the trust others showed in me by letting me drive that new full-sized Ford truck on the highways and giving me the authority to hire another boy to help me who was paid by the truck owner. I felt, even at that young age, GOD was leading me to recognize my responsibilities and accountabilities.

The following is an example of why I enjoyed my new jobs, even though they involved hard work. The owner of the ice house had an agreement with the owner of the local "beer tavern" to store their pony kegs of beer in the ice house until they were needed. The driver of the beer truck, out of Emporia, made a delivery to the beer tavern once a week. He would leave a couple of kegs at the "tavern," if needed, and the extra kegs he would bring to the ice house. The driver always insisted on taking the kegs inside and placing them where they would not be in my way. I assumed he did this to get in out of the heat of the day. I found out later that was not the real reason.

One day the owner was not at the tavern when the kegs were delivered. The lady that was taking care of the tavern didn't know about the agreement the owner had made with the driver. When the driver asked if she needed any kegs left at the tavern, she said, "No, there is one already connected."

The driver said, "Okay, I'll leave them at the ice house." I guess she agreed and that is what he did.

After arriving at the ice house, he unloaded the kegs, as was his routine. When the owner returned and found there were no extra kegs left at the tavern, he decided to come to the ice house and get another keg. The driver of the beer truck was still there, inside his truck rearranging the kegs for his next stop. When the tavern owner pulled up, he opened his car trunk and said to me, "I need one of the kegs." Since this was his routine, and I was always ready to show him and any customers that were there at the time, that I could carry a pony keg of beer from the ice house and load it in the trunk of the car. I don't recall how much one keg weighed, but I would guess it was between seventy-five and one hundred pounds. I had gone into the ice house and was on my way out when I heard the voice of the beer truck driver say, "Put that keg down right now." I looked at him with a surprised expression, as I set the keg on the ground.

I no more than set the keg of beer on the ground and stood up when I saw the driver turn to the tavern owner and say, "I never want you to let that "kid" lift those kegs again." The owner, with a look of fear, asked, "Why, he's being doing that for months." I don't care what he's been doing; he is not old enough to lift that much weight. His bones and muscles have not developed, and if he continues to do it, he will have back problems later in life. If you want to store the kegs here, you lift them, out of the ice house and into your car trunk. I mean it, the boy does not lift them, understand?"

"Okay!" the owner replied.

Let me explain why the owner was not about to challenge the driver. The driver had won the title of Mr. Kansas a couple of years earlier and advanced to the Mr. America competition, but he did not take that title. However, when you looked at him, you knew he was not someone you wanted to engage in a test of strength!

After a day of having this kind of fun, regardless if I worked at the gas station, ice house or in the hayfield all day, I would come home, take a shower, get dressed and then I, with one or more of my friends, would drive to Yates Center and roller skate until it closed around ten o'clock. We would sometimes stop at Woody's Truck Stop, on the way home for a coke and sandwich, and then head for home. I would get to bed around 11:30 p.m. Then around 5:00 a.m. the next morning I would get up and go through the same daily routine. Today the only thing I can do, of those activities, is to get up at 4:30 a.m. and go to the bathroom and then go right back to bed. I still think of those earlier times as, "The good old days," however, I do have some back problems, for what that's worth. I now know the truck driver said what he said—not to show off, but it was for my benefit.

By this time, I had sold my motorbike because Dad let me use his Ford Model A coupe to deliver my papers. It wasn't too long after that; I sold my paper route for more than I paid for it a few years before.

I recall, during this time, I bought a sports shirt that I liked and a pair of socks that were popular at that time that Mom probably wouldn't have bought me, because of the bright color of the socks. I say that because of what she said when I brought them home. I think her words were, "You aren't going to wear those socks to school, are you?"

They were bright neon colors, and I replied, "Yes, all the high school boys are wearing them."

It would have been more accurate if I had said, "All our basketball team was wearing them."

We did get some comments from our schoolmates as well as from some of the teachers. When we went to another school to play a basketball game and walked into their gym, with our bright socks showing, we also got some comments that were not intended to be complimentary. However, we viewed their words as signs of envy and marched on as if we didn't hear anything. Buying a few of my clothes was a new experience for me because, before my newfound wealth, I could only hope to receive one shirt at Christmas time from Mom and Dad. My parents still bought me clothes when I needed them, but now I also bought some of my clothes. Through it all, my bank account kept growing, and I would have told you that I genuinely did believe that, "GOD is good all the time!"

At that time, GOD showed me I could work at multiple jobs at different times during the year and make more money than mowing yards in the hot summertime. These were times when I could be working in the hayfields one day then working at the furniture store or the gas station and ice house the next day. Wherever I was working, I was usually working Monday through Saturday each week during the summer months. Some of these jobs didn't come about until my sophomore year. As a freshman, I often recalled the "importance" of fulfilling the work activities I had committed to, in mowing yards. Those didn't compare to my new job at the furniture store on Friday and Saturday during Summer break before my freshman year. It was even more noticeable when I added additional jobs when I started my sophomore year that required planning as well as the willingness of the job providers being flexible on some of the days I would be working for them. However, this multijob arrangement lasted throughout my final three years in high school and often became somewhat demanding on my part during the school year when I would get a call to see if I could work on the weekend.

With all these good things happening, I was still encountering some hurtful times due to my dad's drinking problem. I was nearing the age that I knew I would be tempted to take a drink and smoke a cigarette some Saturday night. That was when the farmers came to town and did their shopping for the following week. Many of my friends were farm boys. "Get the picture?" I'll share a stupid "self-confession" I was guilty of, to show how easy it is to take Satan's bait without thinking what we are doing. I'm not sure, but I may have been fourteen when these temptations first presented themselves.

My friends and I knew we couldn't buy beer or cigarettes, but, we also knew we could get some of the older boys to buy them for us. And "I yielded to temptation, and I knew what I was doing." I know today it was only by the grace and love of GOD that kept, all of us from getting hooked on cigarettes and beer. It may have been the "Lack of a Thrill" we were expecting to get from our acting like illiterate young teenagers. I hope any young person who is reading the experience I had, would understand there were many young kids my age, at that time, that were not as fortunate. You would often hear on the news, even back in the early 1950s about young kids dying from alcohol overdose; others died in vehicle accidents because the driver was DUI, and some spent their adult life in prison due to crimes they committed while they were intoxicated. Thinking back at that time in my life, I feel it was the Holy Spirit within me that kept me from getting hooked on any of these evil temptations. And seeing what my own dad was doing had a significant impact on me, in *not* making it a habit.

Being a teenage boy, I had pride in some of the things my "Dad" did when he was my age. I even admired the fact that others viewed him as someone who was willing to stand up for his beliefs and was ready to defend them physically. To me, this was the reputation,

Mike, his best friend, told me Dad had throughout the county! Dad had the reputation of a fighter. As I mentioned before, I never saw my dad in a fight, so I would like to think as he grew older and married, he realized fighting wasn't the best thing for people to remember about us. I know those events in my early life could have led me down that same pathway. Maybe Dad felt the same way because, when I asked him in my junior year of high school if I could help the next time they moved their oil rig from one location to another; so I could make some money to have when school started. Dad's reply was firm, "No, and as I've told you before, I never want to find you working in the oil field. That is work for someone that doesn't have a good education or a good job." Those words were among the most definitive words of guidance Dad ever gave me. Later, remembering those words also made me feel Dad did love me.

Now was also the time that Mom felt I was old enough to understand why Dad drank.

The cause for Dad drinking was not because he liked to get drunk. It was always related to an act of nature. When the drilling crew finished a well, the crew would load the heavy equipment on the beds of the trucks, ready to move early the next day. With the trucks loaded, it usually gave them time to get to the new location and set up during the day and be ready to start drilling in their new location with the evening shift. However, if it rained all night or heavy snow fell, all plans came to a halt. The trucks would not be able to get out of the field in which they had just finished working. They could not move more than a few feet, and they would be stuck. They had no choice but to wait until the ground dried or the snow melted so they could drive out and continue to their new location. They would take all day to get set up so they could start work the following day. However, often days would pass before they were able to move the trucks.

Mom told me Dad couldn't cope with the fact he wouldn't be bringing any money home until they were able to move to the next location. She tried to tell him they would get by with the food she had canned and the money she made from ironing clothes. She told me that Dad had too much pride to depend on her income. In a small way, I understood how Dad felt. He probably felt all the people in town would look at him as a failure who couldn't provide for his family. Unfortunately, in a small community like Toronto, that would have been the feelings of many of the people.

Dad knew if he didn't work, he didn't get paid, and if they didn't have any money, he couldn't buy food for his family. What made matters worse, Dad felt, he couldn't do anything about it. I expect, more than once Dad asked himself, "Why did I continue working in the oil field, knowing someday I would be married and have a family? If only I had looked for a better job when I was younger, one with a future. If only I had done that, the problems I'm experiencing today would not exist, at least to the degree they do."

It was at this time the entire picture became clearer to me. I soon realized Dad's excessive drinking was caused by his not being able to work and making the money he knew they needed to pay the bills. I'm sure many people in town, were quick to say, "So he went out and spent what little money he had, on beer?"

To those "judges" I would only ask, "Have you ever been in a like situation of feeling helpless in not being able to take care of your family?"

What Dad did was not the right, but since he felt he couldn't do anything about the problem, drinking at least clouded his mind for a brief time. It enabled him to "blot out," for a few hours, the fact he was not taking care of his family the way he wanted. That did not justify his actions, but I now believe it was not done to hurt Mom or me. It was also during these times in the oil drilling business; if you didn't work, you didn't get paid, regardless of the reason. I don't remember Dad complaining about these setbacks in front of me, but now I understand it was a time he didn't want to discuss these facts, especially with his six-year-old son.

If we have no control in solving a problem and feel we must live with it, we often make bad decisions. Dad was in that situation each time they needed to move locations and couldn't, because of the weather.

I know Dad, in later years, regretted not finishing high school. He knew all of that was history that he could not change when He found himself, not only responsible for taking care of himself but now that responsibility included a wife and a small son.

Now that I had found out the primary cause for Dad's drinking problem, it seemed to him he felt he didn't have the right to advise me about my future. Dad's oldest sister, Lela told me when I was in high school, that at the time Dad left school for good, he was considered by many in town to have been one, if not THE best athlete, in playing football and baseball, that had ever attended our high school. Dad's friend "Mike" told me similar stories when I worked for him in my high school years. I'm sure on my hearing about Dad's athletic skills was a motivation for me being active in sports.

Our school had discontinued its football program when I reached high school. However, we played baseball, basketball, and a couple of years, we had field and track. I didn't set any records in junior high, but, in high school, I was on the traveling squad my sophomore year in all three sports. I was on our varsity baseball and basketball teams my junior and senior years. I was also captain of our basketball and baseball teams my junior and senior years. Now, before you think I'm bragging, I must explain how that all came about.

First, our high school was not the largest school in the county, but it was not the smallest either. I did have a basketball scholarship offer from one of the state junior colleges. However, it came with a condition—that is, if I would also try out for their football team. This offer also came with a try out for a scholarship to Kansas State University after graduating from junior college. However, the proposal also brought about the second time Dad voiced his view concerning the opportunity to play football.

He said, "You may think you're tough, but being tough and being a good football player are two different things. Kids who have played high school football four years have learned how to make a tackle and how to absorb a tackle. If you go up against these top players in their respective schools, you could end up in the hospital before you played your first game."

I don't think I believed Dad, but today I feel what he told me was his way of saying, "I don't want you to get injured because you aren't prepared to play that type of sporting event." Whatever Dad's reason for saying what he said didn't make a difference because I had already decided I was going to join the Navy with my friends, Jim and Ed.

As I grew into young adulthood, there were times I would assess what was going on in my career and then ask what came to be my "reality check question"—that is, "Is the life I am living today (and the job I have) what I want to be living and doing five years from now?" The first time I asked myself that question was near the end of my "hitch" in the Navy.

I asked myself this question more than once throughout my working career when I realized I had more responsibilities than just providing for myself. That question proved to be a motivator, during the years after finishing my "hitch" in the Navy, getting married, and starting a family. We need to acknowledge that accepting the status quo will often prove to be an unwise decision. When the demands of taking care of our financial obligations, and unforeseen surprises, we tend to think, "Does my job enable me to take care of those unforeseen needs?

If you have never asked yourself the above question because you felt it was not relevant in your life, I challenge you to ask yourself the following question, "Am I convinced I would be willing to make sacrifices and work for the changes that will make my life better *before* it is causing problems for my family and me?" I have seen families lose their home, their marriage, their children, and still not be willing to "seek and find" a better way of life as a "responsible adult." I have talked with young boys and men while I was in "prison ministry" and every one of them was sorry that they didn't do what they knew they should have and could have done before they got in trouble and sent to prison. "Getting a good education and a good job was always at the top of my list," one young man shared with me who was in a juvenile prison unit. It was his, "Should I, could I, would I list?" But as he put it, "I was not willing to put out the effort to do what I knew I needed to do." He was about seventeen or eighteen years old, nice looking, seem to have a friendly personality, but he was in prison, and he acknowledged that when he served his time in prison, he would be viewed as an "ex-con" by many. What a shame, and he knew being an ex-con was not a plus on a resume!

Remember what I said when I was mowing yards daily during the summer and had a paper route year-round? I felt I had arrived; it couldn't get any better than that? The fact I was twelve or thirteen years old, living with my parents, I had *no* real financial obligations; my evaluation of my life was, "It looks like my future is going to be a bed of roses!" Once I realized I was no longer twelve or thirteen years old, not living with my parents, and I now had growing financial obligations, married, a father, with yearly increasing financial responsibilities; I knew mowing yards and delivering newspapers would not be enough.

Fortunately, GOD showed me very clearly and very early, I needed to recognize the need to start planning before the time these needs existed if I was going to be able to take care of my future responsibilities. I knew my future needs would be for more than myself. I would probably have a family and other obligations that required money. That was when the above question came to mind about being satisfied five years in the future with my current lifestyle, and I had to be honest with myself when I answered my question. Sadly, I must admit, "I never considered the above responsibilities while mowing yards. Remember, I could afford a milkshake each day and still have money to put in my bank account! Being twelve years old, I felt I had it made, and for a twelve-year-old, I was doing pretty good. However, before I knew it, I was seventeen, eighteen, and a then a twenty-one-year-old veteran, discharged from the Navy and starting a whole new life experience, and I needed to get my "ducks in a row now."

Often, when we fail to address these "adult life" situations, the day will come when we realize the five-year period will be ending tomorrow. That is when we start to realize those guidelines of yesteryear are not what we can use to take care of our future. During my eight to twelve years of age, I felt everything I "knew" about life was right because much of what I knew, I learned from the older boys in town and I thought they wouldn't lie to me. It was not until I was in the early teens that I realized, "There is more to life than eating, playing and sleeping. I recalled the feeling I had when I was going into high school, and GOD pointed out that I must be aware of the importance of being Responsible for the things I do or should do as I get older. Later, I had a flash-back to the feeling GOD placed on my heart when I started high school. He showed me that there comes a time we must not only be more *responsible*, but we must also be more *accountable* for our actions. We must ask ourselves, "Are these two elements a part of my lifestyle today, as I move from one stage of life into the next?"

Asking myself the above question has helped me to understand *why* my parents, especially my dad, did what he did during my early years of his life. Dad felt he couldn't do anything that would change the problem because he chose to continue to live the lifestyle and do the things he had been doing since from his young teenage years. There is no doubt in my mind that my mother and father both loved me very much from the first day I was born until the day they went home to be with our Lord and Savior. I have forgiven them both for every time their actions hurt me and made me feel not wanted and all alone. Today I feel my parents never did anything with the intent of hurting me, and I feel Dad asked himself more than once, "*Why* was I so sure I couldn't do something besides working in the oil field?"

I believe that it is essential we know and understand the "causes" surrounding the actions of others; especially our parents, close family members, friends, and even coworkers. Only then can we hope to understand their actions. Knowing the causes may enable us to help them see the wrong they are doing versus our judging them.

In the following paragraphs, I would like to share a period in my life that caused me to react in ways that seemed justified because they were very hurtful at the time. I realize they were usually activities I did not understand why my parents acted a certain way, especially my dad. Today I know it was because, at my young age, I was not able to understand what was going on or "Why" it was going on? And my real question was, "Why was it happening to me?"

I believe GOD's answer to me then and today is, "It was to make you realize I gave you the strength to get through each valley of despair you traveled, so today you would understand, you were never alone. I wanted you to know I always had your hand in mine. I wanted you to look back at those times and hopefully see, it was My Son, Jesus Christ, who led you to the mountain tops on the other side of your pain and sorrow. I wanted you to believe what I did for you then, I will do for you today and all the tomorrows if you follow My Son's commands. Most of all, I want you to understand today, what it cost My Son for you to have eternal life."

I will never be able to repay GOD for the blessings He has given me. There is no doubt in my mind; He knows that as well. I'll address that point in chapter 9 when I talk about how GOD enabled me to do and accomplish things that I would never have felt possible.

Whoever you are and whatever you've done in your past, there is nothing impossible for what GOD can do through you and for you. If we have faith and hope in Him, there is nothing impossible when we follow His commands and follow His Word. We should always remember the one thing that pleases GOD more than anything else is our *faith* in Him and our belief in His Son, Jesus Christ, as our Lord and Savior.

We need to remember what GOD told (Jeremiah in 29:11) and realize He is telling you and me that same message today. We need to follow what the old hymn says, "Trust and obey, for there is no other way." GOD will lead the way, but we must follow and always give Him full credit for the blessings He gives us. If we follow His guidance, He will give us the will and the opportunity to be successful in what we do. However, we must always give praise and Honor to Him as we travel through life. When we do this, He will bless us. When we don't, and later ask for forgiveness, He will forgive our sins, just as he did to David, *but* we will not receive the blessings we could have received during the time we turned from Him. Those blessings will be gone forever.

GOD tells us to forgive others that have wronged or hurt us. As time passed from being a preteen to a teenager, I realized it is only "by the grace of GOD" that we understand we can not hold on to those views we had in our preteen years that often got us what we wanted. They are not absolutes, and we can not continue to use them, as we grow into and beyond our teen years.

Dwight L. Moody is quoted as saying (as only he could say), "No man is living that can do the work that GOD has got for me to do. No one can do it but myself. There ain't no one else."

I have found there are, however, specific procedures, beliefs, and rules that are spelled out in GOD's Word that, if we refuse to abide by them, having a successful and meaningful life is virtually impossible. The underlining pathway to attaining a satisfying and fulfilling life is believing His Word tells us we must follow His commands. I'm sure I will make this point more than once in the following pages, but it has proven to be so true in my life from the time I started school until the time of this writing. I can't emphasize too much how GOD has impressed on me the importance of following and obeying His Word.

It is Satan who brings ideas into our minds that suggest GOD's Word (Bible) is a book of lies. Sometimes GOD allows things like this to happen via a person we think is our friend. But His Word makes it very clear that He does not judge us by one another and He has not given "man" the authority to judge each other, He alone has that power. When we let Satan influence us, we have set the stage whereby we will never feel the real love and forgiveness of GOD.

One example of my not knowing the cause for my dad's drinking in excess led me to assume the reason (cause) was his weakness or unwillingness to stop drinking. Not knowing the real "cause" resulted in a bad relationship I had with my father during many of my teen years.

In starting high school, my life seemed to change in almost everything I did. It was at that time I realized GOD was telling me I now had to be "responsible" for *my* actions.

Feeling this, I seem to have a flashback to my early junior high days when I was mowing yards and feeling pride in making money by working for it for the first time in my life. Mowing yards became a motivation for me to mow as many yards as I could and make even more money that would enable me *not* to be dependent on my parents to buy things I wanted or needed. As I've pointed out earlier, I did not look for the easiest jobs, but I looked for jobs I could do if I was willing to put forth the effort to do them. The effort was not always easy because until halfway through my eighth grade all the yards I mowed were with my parents two iron-wheeled push lawnmower. If you can find one of these mowers today, try using it to mow your yard each week next summer. When I started mowing, I was not yet in high school, and many times the grass was so high I would push the mower about two feet, back up and repeat it, making about six inches headway. But I stayed with it until I finished mowing the yard. Those were the days my milkshakes tasted good at the end of the day.

Speaking of buying things with my yard money, along with the milkshake, I also continued to purchase US savings bonds to go with those I had bought in my earlier school years by buying a ten-cent stamp at a time until I accumulated enough money to buy a $25 bond. This activity took place during the end of World War II.

I say the above to point out that when I decided to spend some of my "hard work" money, during the following school year, I knew what it cost me to earn that money. Mom and Dad also knew what I had been willing to do to earn money to buy the bonds. They knew when I was ready to spend my money, to buy something I wanted and felt I needed, I also knew what it cost me.

Today many young people seem to feel GOD, our government, even Mom and Dad, are responsible for taking care of their needs. They don't realize He owes us nothing (but, we owe Him everything), our government consists of men and women who have worked, and many fought to make our country what it is. Our mom and ad sacrificed many things. It was their hope we would become responsible and accountable human beings. We need to accept the responsibilities of adulthood and start doing our share to make America the great country GOD has enabled our forefathers to build. Many gave their lives so that others could enjoy the freedoms of our Constitution. We must realize that it is GOD who gives us a better understanding of life and an awareness that people will not always recognize us for what they see we do that is good. Knowing and believing this, we must also remember it is only GOD who has enabled us to accomplish the things we have achieved; it is as simple as that.

GOD is the only one who can judge and give us the power to resist the temptations Satan puts in our pathway each day. An excellent verse to recall when others judge us is the one Paul said to the Corinthians, and I will reference it several times throughout the following chapters:

> I care very little if I am judged by you or by any human court. Indeed I do not even judge myself. It is the Lord who judges me. (1 Corinthians 4:3–4)

GOD led me to realize there would be a lot of exciting things happening as I began my freshman year that made being in high school a new and exciting experience. We had several students coming to Toronto to finish high school from the country schools that only went through the eighth grade. I don't recall knowing any of them, and it gave me a feeling of "importance" when one of them would ask me where the restrooms were, or, where Ms. Burkett's classroom was for Constitution 101 was, and many other "important" questions that the new freshman didn't know the answers, but I did.

I laugh when I realize how little it took to make me feel I was a big and important high school student when knowing where the restrooms were, and one of the new students had to ask me for directions. As I think of those events today, I realize that being a high school student was recognizing the challenging courses I had to take, and different teachers were teaching most of the classes, each having a different personality and a different teaching technique. I soon realized that being a freshman equated to having very little influence or power over anyone. I was soon to become aware that only GOD has the authority and control over all of us but, so does Satan, to the point we let him. Over the following years in high school, both GOD and Satan's power would be factors I would encounter. However, when we follow Satan, he will always bring harm and failure into our lives, and I encountered both more than once when I made the wrong choice.

Overall, my freshman year turned out to be nothing to write home about. I wasn't too far into the year when I started feeling about the same way I had felt in going into junior high. One thing I remember that was different from my grade school years was having a "study hall" period during school hours. I was surprised to find out you didn't have to spend all your time studying when you are in "study hall." As I look back on that "freedom" today, I realize I took advantage of that reality, and in the end, I was the "loser" for not studying more and talking less; with others who thought they were entitled to do the same.

At that time, I was about to see, GOD was now going to present me with changes and opportunities in school and beyond school:

I can't say much about my freshman year except it came and went. It was after I started my sophomore year, that I broadened my horizons and became even more interested in Boy Scouts and girls. I recall I was still a little suspicious of girls, as far as going on dates. I can't remember how old I was when I joined the Scouts, but I had been attending Scout meetings for some time. I remember my close friends, Hoyt, Meredith, and Hody were in the Scouts before I was old enough to join. I would participate in the games they would have, as well as the training and testing periods during each meeting. I became more interested in scouting with each meeting I attended.

It was during this time that, things started moving faster: As I look back, many of the experiences I was encountering were indications of events that would continue for the rest of my life that involved what we may call challenges and responsibilities in life's journey. They differ only in name, size, location, and environment. For example, when I played basketball and moved to the varsity team from the JV team; I soon recognized this was a challenge that could bring more attention to me and provide more opportunities in school and more recognition from the people who came to the game each week. However, it also meant I would be responsible for practicing with more determination and focus on being a "team player." In later years I would be offered various promotions within management that equated to various features my previous jobs did not have. They always involved an increase in salary, and usually, they included certain "perks" that didn't exist at my former level. It also meant I would have more responsibilities than I had in my previous position.

Each opportunity came with new challenges. I would have to evaluate the advantages and disadvantages of what I was told would be a promotion. They each offered new and more challenges, and they came with additional demands that did not exist in my former position. However, I could reject the offer and continue, "as is" or I could accept what the changes offered and expects. The decision was always mine to make, and I needed to think about the new requirements as well as the new opportunities and ask myself, "Is it worth it?" and "Am I willing to live with the results of my decision?"

I believe the attitude GOD led me to accept in my younger years led me to view scouting as being very high on my list of priorities during my high school days. It followed me during my tour in the US Navy, and throughout every opportunity, I had following my discharge. In each step along the way, in each job, I had the opportunity to say, "I want to stay where I am, I don't want to take on more responsibility, or I could say *yes*, I want the new job, knowing it will require more effort, time, and results than the job I would be leaving." The "challenge and responsibility" function for me will be talked about in more detail in chapters 9 to 10.

I could remain a Boy Scout at the Tenderfoot level and not accept the challenge and responsibility for success that was required to be an Eagle Scout. Some decided to enjoy scouting as a Tenderfoot. My three good friends (Hoyt, Hody, Meredith) and I chose to "go for the gold," and you will see the results of that decision, later in this chapter.

At the first meeting after I was old enough to join the Scouts, I not only joined, but I passed my Tenderfoot test at the same meeting, and that made me feel I was now a member of one of the best young boy's organizations in the world. My three close friends and I took scouting seriously. We worked on passing the tests for the required merit badges to qualify for the next level in scouting—that is, Tenderfoot, Star, Life, and the big one, Eagle. I don't think any of us realized at the time, but by being serious on passing our merit badge tests, we were conditioning ourselves to be willing to do whatever was required to move onward and upward to that next level in scouting. If future years this same factor proved to be true—that is, the decision was ours to make as to how much we were willing to do to be a success at the next level.

Those same opportunities, requirements, commitments, and results were what I needed to consider in each stage of life I've encountered; including each job I had, and each level of education I chose to attain. None of these would have been successful endeavors had it not been for GOD placing something or someone in my life at the right time that was the encouragement or a motivator for me to continue. I must say that after I married, my number 1 encourager/motivator has always been my wife, Sondra.

In my high school years, I attended all the Scout meetings unless I was sick, or we were out of town visiting relatives. With the motivation I received from my three "buddies," we all focused on earning our merit badges for the next level in scouting. These types of activities seemed to be more challenging when I entered my sophomore year in high school. It almost became an obsession with me to attend every Scout meeting. The activities were fun and exciting, but a little more challenging, now that I was in high school and occasionally had evening school events that I did not have in my grade school years.

I remember going to scouting camps a couple of years during the summer months, and they were a lot of fun. They provided those of us from smaller towns that didn't have YMCAs or certified instructors in areas like "lifesaving" to be able to pass specific merit badge requirements that required licensed certification. I passed my swimming and lifesaving merit badges under a qualified YMCA swimming instructor that was on staff at a Scout camp I attended. But when I found new and better jobs than mowing lawns and delivering papers, I had to limit the number of summer camps I went too so I could take care of the job commitments I had made. I found this was also teaching me another lesson in life.

In adult life, we must prioritize events in our daily life to be able to succeed in our job and be able to take care of the needs and desires of our family the way we want. The requirements for more effort and sometimes more money to accomplish is often part of the solution.

While still in high school, I was faced with a decision that caused me to look at the big picture. Two of my close friends, Hoyt and Meredith, had signed up to go to the Philmont Scout Camp. At that time, Philmont was felt by some as *the* ideal Scout camp to attend. I also wanted to go but, I was working at the gas station and ice house that summer and the owner told me he would have to find someone to take my job (permanently) if I was not there. His situation was valid because he had a full-time job on the railroad and couldn't do both jobs. Giving up these two jobs and the money I was making to help me when school started was too much to give up. After all that had passed, I soon forgot about the missed opportunity to go to Philmont, and it was a nonissue, especially when school started that fall and I had enough money for the activities I wanted to do or needed to do.

Shortly after I officially became a Boy Scout, my parents took me to Chanute, Kansas, where one of their clothing stores sold Boy Scout uniforms. I mention that because I know, it was a real sacrifice for my parents to spend the amount of money it cost them to buy my complete uniform including pants, shirt, hat, belt, neckerchief and merit badge sash. I don't recall ever feeling prouder than the first time I wore my Boy Scout uniform in public, with my merit badge sash that displayed the merit badges I had earned at that time.

I soon found it was going to cost me and my "buddies" more than just having the desire to be an Eagle Scout. It was going to demand we stay focused, dedicated, and determined. One event that comes to mind was a lot of fun but required our commitment as well. It involved passing our camping merit badge test. I may be a little off on the days, but I think we had to sleep outdoors for a week (roughing it), sleeping outside the niceties of the city environment, and cooking at least our evening meals.

At that time, we felt this would be a "pushover" since Meredith's dad had a large tent, almost the size of a circus tent. We pitched the tent in his backyard and were planning on sleeping in it all summer. We then decided to go to a place we often went swimming; on the banks of the Verdigris River for one week to pass our camping merit badge requirements. We felt it too would be a "piece of cake." As I recall, everything seemed to be going as planned as we staked out a location that was clear of rocks and weeds. We each had or borrowed a "pup tent," and I think it was Meredith's mother who had a huge iron pot that she cleaned out for us to use. It looked like the ones women used to heat water over an open fire to wash their clothes back in the Pioneer days. "This was going to be a fun-filled week." On the first night, we brought water from home to fill the pot. I don't recall what we put in the pot, but after the water finally became hot enough to heat the food, we ate it. We felt we couldn't wait any longer. We were tired and hungry, so we ate the "luke-warm" stew and tried to get a good night's sleep. I might add, we did this each of the remaining six nights, and none of us got food poisoning, and we seemed to eat enough not to be hungry the next morning.

The following day a couple of us were telling one of the men in town about what we were doing and how long it took to fix our evening meal.

He laughed and said, "You boys need to talk with Snakes Estep, he knows how to prepare a pot of good mulligan stew."

We looked at each other and said, "What do we have to lose?"

When you are desperate, you often do silly things. I'm not sure all of us went to Snakes' house, but when we knocked, he opened the door, and there was Snakes holding a can of beer in his hand. Everyone in our small town knew Snakes liked his beer. After explaining our problem, Snakes said, "I'd be glad to tell you how to make mulligan stew." He invited us in and told us to grab a chair as he proceeded to say to us, "You cook the meat first and leave it on the fire to keep it hot. Next, you take any vegetable you can find and throw it into the pot of boiling water and let it boil until you see the cut-up potatoes are starting to get soft and look like they are about ready to dissolve into potato soup. Then you pour in the 'already-cooked meat,' stir until everything is well mixed."

We looked at each other, and I recall Hody saying, "That seems simple enough, we'll try it." We thanked Snakes and started to leave when he said, "Oh, you mentioned I have a reputation of making good mulligan stew. "What I just told you, plus one additional ingredient is how I earned that reputation."

I think we asked in unison, "What is it?"

Snakes said, with a big smile on his face, "The reason I didn't mention it was because you boys told me you are camping out to earn a Boy Scout award, and I don't want you to do anything that would keep you from getting that award. I'm pretty sure you boys wouldn't add my secret ingredient anyhow, so I think I'll tell you what it is."

Being typical young boys, we said, "We won't use it."

"Well, after all the cooking and mixing has been taken care of, I pour a pint of Jim Beam whiskey into the pot and stir it a little more."

I think it was again Hody, who said, "Oh, we can't do that."

Snakes said, "I know that, so fix it as I first told you and let me know how you make out." We made the stew, without the one ingredient, and it lasted the rest of the week.

Everything went well, with a few minor problems, but nothing we were not able to handle. The week passed, and still, none of us got food poisoning, and as I recall, we all earned our camping merit badge. We were willing to do what it took to accomplish our objective. All of us enjoyed scouting, and we continued working on the remaining required merit badges. Hoyt, Hody, Meredith, and I were all focused on earning that next level in scouting. I still recall after I earned my life (rank), saying to myself, "I am going to be an eagle scout, and nothing is going to stop me."

I soon found how dedicated a Boy Scout had to be if he wanted to become an Eagle Scout. We earned some of our merit badges when attending Boy Scout camps in the summer months. As I mentioned earlier, that was when I qualified for my swimming and lifesaving merit badges, since the lifesaving badge had to be certified by a qualified instructor.

Being a Boy Scout teaches the principles that obtaining success in scouting are often similar to obtaining success in adult life. Both usually involve the assistance, help, and encouragement of other people. GOD expects us first to thank Him for enabling our accomplishments, and second, thank those who helped and encouraged us in being successful.

Scouting and other activities did become more challenging when I became a sophomore. Time was flying by, and my three "best" friends, and I were having a great time enjoying life, school, and scouting. As I think back to the comment I made earlier—that is, in all stages of experience, we encounter opportunities to better ourselves. However, to do this it requires our commitment and a willingness to do whatever is needed to succeed (within the rules of honesty). We also can say, "No, I am satisfied with what I have, and I don't want to change." I feel this is something GOD established for us to show others as well as ourselves, what we are willing to work for and sacrifice to be successful. Life holds the need to sacrifice in many areas from one generation to another, and it is true in scouting. They both require support from others—that is, family, friends, or coworkers, and in some cases, all three, whether we recognized it or not. These factors are made known to us by GOD, to show us what He has provided and what it cost His Son who died on the cross, so we can understand the cost of being successful in GOD's eyes.

On February 7, 1950, in our small town of Toronto, Kansas, a first of a kind event took place. For the first time in its history, as far as we could determine, a Boy Scout Court of Honor was held to present the awarding of Eagle Scout rank and medals to two of its hometown boys. Aside from their names being different, they were typical teenage boys who each had a goal and were willing to do what was required to accomplish their goals. Their names were Hoyt (Bill) Black and Lloyd McJunkin.

No two boys were happier that evening in Toronto than Hoyt and me. Today I'm quick to tell people about my experience of becoming a Christian. There have been very few years go by since that date in 1950 that I have not also had that same opportunity to tell someone that I was not only a Boy Scout, but I also became an Eagle Scout. If the people show an interest, I tell them, since I retired, I have my eagle medal on display in my den at home where it is to this day, not too far from my framed baptismal certificate. Both of which I am very proud of and love to talk about what led to my obtaining each of them.

I am proud to talk about being a Christian and an eagle scout and some of the costs I incurred in obtaining and living up to their standards in the world we live in today. I like to tell them of the hurt and pain we often experience but having Jesus Christ as our Lord and Savior makes all the difference in our journey through life.

I was very proud a few years ago when I had the honor to award and pin my grandson, Sean Fuller, with his eagle scout medal during his court of honor.

God is good, all the time.

In chapters 5 through 9 (following) I have given examples of the above experiences involving challenges and responsibilities in more detail throughout the different stages of my life after I finished high school. Some of them may remind the reader of similar type events that took place in their life.

I mentioned in the "outline" I used in chapter 1 that I would elaborate in more detail on some of the items I would be talking about in later chapters. One I would like to give a little more detail on, is why I found going to a small high school had both advantages and disadvantages and the lessons I learned from my experience in going to Toronto high school. By the time I was a sophomore, I was on the varsity traveling baseball team. I was given this opportunity, not because of my outstanding baseball talent; it came about when our varsity catcher was hit on the nose and broke it.

He decided he did not want to continue playing baseball.

Coach Huntington asked, "Who would like to try out for the catcher's position?" The event we all saw the day before was fresh in our minds, so it was no surprise when there were no immediate volunteers.

My dad had been a catcher in high school and later played post-high school ball on the hometown team. When I told him, what had happened to our catcher, he said, "When a catcher gets behind the batter in a game or at practice without his mask on, he is asking for trouble."

He went on to say, "In all the years I was a catcher on the high school and the city teams, I never saw or heard of a catcher being hit in the face while catching, however, we were often hit on the mask while wearing it." So when the coach asked for volunteers the following day, and no one stepped forward, I said, "I'll give it a try." The result, as a sophomore, I was the varsity team catcher. "Yes, I agree, it was by circumstance, not by proven talent. I did, however, have to prove I could do the job as time passed."

As for basketball, I played on the JV team during my sophomore year, and the coach seemed to think I was not too bad. He may have felt, "Compared to the rest that was playing on the JV team, I didn't look too bad." Whatever he felt, I did get to play in a few varsity games that year when it looked like we had the game, "in the bag."

Since we lost several good players from the previous season by their graduating, our coach was looking for new players in my junior year, and I was selected to be a starter on the varsity team. Before our first game, the coach asked the team who they wanted to be the team captain since last season's captain had graduated. I was surprised when my name was given, and several others seconded the nomination. I became the new team captain of our basketball team that day in my junior year. Several of my good friends were seniors and were varsity starters. There is no doubt they had a lot to do with my becoming the new captain! I also maintained the role of captain on the basketball and baseball teams during my senior year. I say all of that to say, if I had been going to a larger high school, I might not have even been on either team, let alone being team captain. Although it didn't make our Woodson County newspaper, I felt it made Mom and Dad proud, and that made me feel good. It was not until I was a senior and had become more active in our church youth programs that I realized being the "captain" on both baseball and basketball teams was not an indication that I was a super athlete," it was more to show me what GOD can do with those who are not necessarily "super talented." I've wondered if He did it to see how I would react. I feel even more humble now, especially when I saw the talent our daughter Stephanie displayed in riding her horse in "English rail jumping" competition. Or, the ability our son, Grant, showed in high school wrestling and football in his sophomore through senior years. He later played football in college. Our oldest daughter, Vicki, didn't go out for sports, but she showed her talent in the academic area. It was much higher than I showed in school, especially in my high school days. When I see many of the young children today, in high school, who look more like professionals or graduate students at the college level, I wonder, "What happened since my generation graduated?"

I recall some "wise guy" asking, "Do you think it is because they all had more talent and 'smarts' than you had?"

To make the above point even more clear, I was also president of our senior class. People that knew me then might say "Well, since we only had ten students in our class and only two of them were boys, it was not a big deal that he was voted to be class president." I sure wouldn't argue their point one bit, but I did feel honored. I remember I was very nervous when I gave the "president's speech" at our banquet. That is somewhat ironic when I've heard people say, during my career with AT&T, "If you want someone to speak out, ask Lloyd, he always has an opinion or view." I think that may have been said sometimes, not intended as a compliment. I developed that trait while going to college, and I'll share how that came about in chapter 9. But that, like many other things, is history today.

Reflecting on my life during my preteenage years and then throughout high school, I am humbled when I realize what GOD had planned for me. Even when I accepted Jesus Christ as my Lord and Savior, many people that knew me probably said, "He will never amount to anything. How could he with a father that he has?" I recall there were times while I was in high school. I probably was thinking about the same thing." Today as I reflect on my life during those years, I always come up with the same feeling. I wonder what GOD thought when He saw how Dad was living after Granddad and Grandma had raised him and his brothers and sisters in a Christian family environment, that only lasted for Dad until he was in his teens. You will see that GOD knew what the "cause" was that led to Dad's drinking. He also knew how that was going to change.

It seemed Dad had turned away from GOD's teaching when he was still in his midteens and started to live a life of drinking and fighting. I wonder if GOD, when I was born and knowing the lifestyle Dad was living at that time and also knew how I was going to drift away in my late teens and early twenties, said, "I'm going to teach both of them a lesson they will never forget. From this, they will both stop their sinful lifestyle and start living the life I've wanted them to live. He would show me (in my early twenties), and Dad, because he had lived most of his life drinking, fighting and cussing, GOD would let him continue, knowing he would have many hurtful times throughout his life remembering the times he ignored Grandpa McJunkin's warnings. GOD knew Dad would continue to ask himself, 'Why didn't I follow some other profession?' Now it is too late." I think GOD also knew, in Dad's final years, he would repent of his sinful lifestyle and stop his drinking and cussing and become the nice man that Mom married. Satan was also impacting my life. I had friends in the Navy who never yielded to these temptations, and a couple of them were on their second hitch in the Navy.

I view my life has been a good example how GOD can take someone that is not the best, in his/her environment and put them in, a position to show them and others the truth in the words of Jesus when He said, "God can do all things!" We must trust and believe and then follow His commands. In all the recognition and enjoyable experiences, I have encountered, I have tried to put my life in proper perspective and not think, "I am the best that has ever been."

"We need to accept recognition with thankfulness, first to GOD and then to those giving us the help and positive acknowledgments."

I recall a situation I experienced in either my junior or senior year in high school. I was never singled out as one having musical talent. I always wanted to play the guitar but never learned. I wanted to be a good singer but was never asked to sing a solo (well I was once). I never showed any talent in singing, and I never took lessons. I do recall one year in grade school at our annual "all school's day event." The country school kids were invited to take academic tests in reading, math, and other subjects with students in the same grade level at our school. We also had sporting competition in the fifty-yard dash, basketball free-throw, baseball distance throw, and one-person sack race. On the night of the awards, there would be a boy, and a girl from each grade in our school (1 through 8) and each of the country schools represented in that year's competition, to sing and another group to recite a poem. The competition would be by grade, and there would be one boy from each grade, and one girl from each grade compete with the same grade levels from all the country schools, plus our school. I think I was in the sixth-grade when I was selected to be the "boy" singer from Toronto's sixth-grade class. I have no idea why I was given the opportunity unless none of the other boys in my class would accept the invitation. There was a first, second-, and third-place ribbon awarded in each grade level for a boy and the same for a girl. I tell this, to show GOD has a sense of humor when He arranged for me to win the second-place ribbon in the sixth-grade boy singing event.

As time passed and after Sondra and I married, she will kid me about my singing, and that starts our in-house debate.

I always point out, "I don't want to brag, but you know I sang in competition in my younger years and probably should have pursued a musical career in singing."

Her reply was, "I don't think so."

To which I say, "You know I have a ribbon to prove my talent as a singer."

Then Sondra reminds me, "Yes, you told me it was a second place ribbon, and you thought you might have been the only boy in your class that agreed to sing."

I reply, "I think that was because the other boys knew I was a good singer!"

She closes the debate with, Whatever."

I then have the last word by saying, "To show GOD has a sense of humor He arranged for me to win the second place ribbon in the sixth-grade boy's singing contest and who am I to refuse GOD's gift?"

I don't know if I still have the ribbon anymore, but I don't brag about my singing talent to anyone (except my wife) and then only as a joke. If I were to be asked today if I would sing one of my favorite Hymns next Sunday in church, I would quickly say, "Thanks but I don't want to embarrass myself as well as anyone that knows me, by singing a Christian hymn in public, especially a solo! That was the extent of my musical talent until I reached high school). I'm not sure how many boys were asked to sing that year from my sixth-grade class, but, at that age, I was thankful and proud to accept my second-place ribbon.

I think it was during my senior year in high school GOD gave me another opportunity to display my musical talent or lack thereof. Our marching band was invited each year to participate in the Emporia State Teachers College annual "high school band day." That year, our band's bass drum player became ill the week before the event. Our music teacher asked me if I would play the bass drum for the band. She was not the same teacher that asked me to sing in the sixth-grade, as mentioned above. The thought of wearing one of our band uniforms was exhilarating, plus I would get to see all the other bands and then watch their homecoming football game. What an opportunity! Then reality set in, I suddenly realized I didn't know one note of music from another. When I told the teacher I couldn't read music, she said, "Don't worry, all you need to do is hit the drum with the beat of the music we are playing, helping the band members keep in step with each other as we are marching." With the promise of our being able to practice for the next three days, I reluctantly agreed.

Over the next three days, we practiced in the morning and the afternoon, and I was feeling somewhat confident that I could fake it and maybe people would say, as we marched by, "Look at how well their bass drum player can play!" (Just a passing thought.)

About thirty minutes after arriving at the Emporia football stadium, our teacher returned from checking us in and informed us a change had been made so they could honor one of their graduates who was currently the marching band director at Ohio State University.

She said, "This year we will march onto the field from the north end, parallel to the home team sideline. As band number 1 passes the director's platform at the fifty-yard line, their bass drum and cymbals players will peel off just after passing the platform. Band number 2 bass drum and cymbals players will peel off just before they are even with the director's platform. Each band will follow this procedure when approaching the director's platform—that is, odd numbers pass the platform, and even numbers peel off before they come to the platform. She then told us we would be number 7 (odd number) band. Band number 1 was from one of the Emporia high schools and was familiar with the procedure. Their bass drum and cymbals players will peal out of their band as soon as they pass the director's platform. We will follow this procedure as we pass the director's stand and the bass drum and cymbals players from band number 5. Lloyd, all you do is watch where the bass drum and cymbals players step out in band number 5. You and our cymbals player will step out as you pass band number 5 bass drum and cymbals players. Okay?"

I think I gave a faint, "Okay!"

Before we lined up to march out on the field, our music teacher came up to me and said, "Since we won't be marching as much as we thought we would, if you don't feel comfortable in keeping time with the music, just fake it and not hit the drum. Okay?"

"This sounds good to me."

When it came time to line up in the sequence we were assigned, all eyes were on band number 1. As they announced the school it represented was Emporia Central High, the crowd stood and applauded. This procedure was repeated as each band marched on the field continuing with band number 2. When it came time for announcing where band number 7 was from, I felt pretty much at ease. As we marched on the field, I felt the music had a simple beat, and I was feeling great knowing all eyes were on the Toronto Trojans marching band! I could see band number 5 and their bass drummer. I felt things were going to work out even better than I expected. At the right time, and in the right place, our cymbals player and I stepped out of formation and stood next to band number 5 bass and cymbals players. We were all told to be facing the director's platform. Everything was going smooth, and I was starting to enjoy the event.

As the last band was in position, the president of Emporia State Teachers College presented the graduate of ESTC, as the current marching band director at Ohio State University. The president said a few more words about this day and how it was being dedicated to their visiting graduate who would be directing the bands this year. The crowd applauded loud and long. Then silence; as the director climbed to the top of the platform, raised both arms, made what I thought was a strange movement with his hands and as he brought them down the bands began to play in unison. I felt I was doing an excellent job of coming so close to the drum head but not hitting it. I noticed the beat sounded smooth and the music was very easy to follow. Since things were looking professional, I said to myself, "You should show them how you can handle the bass drum." And away I went—1 and 2 and 3 and 4, 1 and 2 and 3 and 4. Before I knew it, I was pounding the drum skin, thinking our music teacher may want me to take over the bass drum for the rest of the year. When suddenly, it was 1 and 2 and 3 and 4 and then no drum and no drum and no drum and no drum. Well, that was not exactly what happened. I guess it was shown that way on the music sheets because every bass drum in every band was silent, except one! The director from Ohio State University looked down the row of odd number bass drums to his right, as did each bass drum player starting with band number 1, then number 3, each turned and look to the base drummer next to them to see who was still beating. Well, my mother didn't raise any musical geniuses, but she didn't raise any dummies either. Just as the number 5 bass drum player turned and looked at the number 7 bass drummer (yours truly), I quickly turned and looked at the number 9 bass drummer as if to say, "Was that you?"

"Can't you read music?" I'm not sure the director knew who it was, but I expect he took a good story back to Ohio State University and shared it with some of his talented musical friends.

On our return to Toronto, our teacher apologized for not telling the band and especially me, that the director had also modified the music a little. The point in all of this is, we should recognize our ability and how it matches up with others that may have more talent than we do, in some areas. Even though we may attain the same levels, titles, and position in our respective location, companies, or activities, we should not feel better than we know we are. We should never suggest we would have received the same honor if we were attending a school or working in a company much larger than the one we are presently attending or employed. We must always look at the big picture and put what we see in proper perspective—that is, in this example, by me attending a smaller school, I should not feel I would have been given the same opportunity if I had attended a much larger school. I hope I have always acknowledged the awards and thanked those who made them possible, but not feel I was so talented that I would have received the same recognition in any other school or location. The importance of keeping our focus on the big picture of our life is something we can all learn and benefit. We should be thankful for what we have received and be sure to thank GOD first and then thank those who gave us the acknowledgments, but never suggest by words and actions that we are the greatest person that has ever lived! Only Jesus can claim that title.

Let's now move on to a different subject—one that also took place during my senior year in high school. It was an event that was very meaningful to both my Mother and me because it turned out to be the end of our hurtful days resulting from my dad's drinking. Even though Dad was raised in a Christian family and church, the oil field lifestyle dominated his life during the years I was living at home. When I entered high school, my dad was still drinking. It was not until I was told by Mom around the start of my junior year, the real reason Dad drank. She felt if she had told me before, then I either would not understand or maybe not accept what she was saying. When she explained that Dad had a lot of pride, and when he was not able to work due to bad weather, he realized there was nothing he could do to change the situation. Then as the days turned into a week or longer, he became aware that if things didn't change soon, we would not have anything to eat. In Dad's mind, he could not do anything to change the weather, and he couldn't accept the fact he might not be able to feed his wife and son. So he tried to remove the pressure of being a "failure," and spend some of the money he had, to erase the reality of life. Drinking did that, and for a short time, it worked.

Dad felt he could not do anything outside oilfield work because that was his only occupation since his midteens. The fact was when the weather conditions prevented them from moving the equipment; it resulted in him not being able to work. And when he didn't work, he didn't get paid. The adage, "No work, no pay" took on a different meaning for Dad. He looked at things as, "No work, no pay, no food." I became aware of this problem, but not the cause, when I was around six years old and could only watch what was going on, thinking, "Why is Dad acting this way? Is it because of me? What did I do?" I only knew that when Dad drank, it was when he was *not* working. "Why would he do that?" It seemed Dad would never get drunk when he was working. I recalled Dad seemed to get drunk for no apparent reason, and, then he and Mom would argue because of him being drunk.

It never dawned on me, at my young age, that Dad never drank when he was working. The only time I recall Dad having too much to drink was when he was not working due to weather conditions, and he had not come home for supper. I knew when he did come home, he and Mom would start arguing as they always did. It was on a night we were playing Buffalo (one of our major competitors in our basketball district). I should have already been at the gym, but I was so mad that Dad was not home and Mom and I both knew why. I told Mom I was not going to play that night and she said, "Don't say that. I'll tell Dad how you feel when he gets home." I replied, "No, he will probably come to the game, and I'm not going to be embarrassed by everyone seeing him drunk." I remember Mom starting to cry and said, "Please go, and I'll not say anything to Dad when he comes home."

She no sooner said those words when we saw Dad pull in the driveway. He sat in the car for a few minutes, then he opened the door and slowly got out. He wasn't as drunk as he had been in the past, but he still had too many beers to be driving.

As Dad walked into the kitchen where Mom and I were, he looked at me and asked, "Don't you have a game tonight?" I replied, "Yes, with Buffalo."

"Well, why aren't you at the gym?"

"Because I'm not going to play."

"Why aren't you going to play?"

"Because I don't want to see you make a fool of yourself." With that, Dad looked at Mom and said, "What have you been telling him?" Mom replied, "I haven't told him anything, but we both knew you would be drunk when you came home."

The next few seconds went by so fast I don't think any of us knew what happened until it was over. I saw Dad move toward Mom. I had never seen him hit her. It seemed even before I knew what I was doing, I grabbed Dad around the neck and pulled him to his knees and said, "You better not hit Mom." He got up, looked at me, and said, "Don't ever do that again." I replied, "Don't you ever act like you are going to hurt Mom." As he turned and headed toward the bedroom, he said, "You can go to the game because I am not going to be there." Mom said, "Please go and play tonight." I told her I would if she felt she would be okay. She said she would, and I did play that evening.

I want to believe that event, as bad as it was, proved to be the turning point for Dad to turn over a new leaf in his life. Then, within the next few days, I saw what GOD could do when we start living the life He wants us to live. Dad's boss, Charlie Barker, was also on the school board. Charlie asked Dad if he would be interested in being the school's custodian within the next two years.

Our longtime janitor, John Cogan, had informed the school board he planned to retire in two years and would like to have time to train his replacement. Dad probably felt he was not qualified, but he still said, "Yes." (See Appendix G.)

As it turned out, it was a little more than a year and a half later when the job was made available to Dad. I had graduated from high school and was in the Navy when I received a letter from Mom saying Dad had started his new job as the school custodian. She was so excited and said, "I don't think Dad has had anything to drink since he was offered the job over a year ago." She later told me he was a different man. I think Dad felt he now had a good job, and regardless of how much rain or snow fell; he would be working each week (and working inside). When I came home on boot camp leave, I could see the difference in Dad. He was the nice man that Mom described him to be—when he was sober. Today I do not doubt that GOD orchestrated that series of events at a time and in a way that only He could.

I never saw or heard of my dad being drunk again from the day I left for the Navy until his death some twenty years later. I know he never returned to the church, but I feel he always believed (knew) he had Salvation through his belief in Jesus Christ as his Savior and by the Grace of GOD. I am sure Dad asked Him for forgiveness more than once during the falling away time in his life. I know Mom, and I forgave him, and I believe GOD did too. It was then I thanked GOD for showing me the real "cause" for Dad's drinking, and I asked forgiveness for my "judging" him based on what I saw versus not knowing the "*cause*."

I feel Dad lived many hurtful years when he let Satan lead him into drinking to minimize the hurt he was feeling inside. The feeling he would not be able to provide for his family the way he wanted, no longer existed I admire my mother for staying faithful to her marriage vows and not leaving Dad. As for me, I have forgiven Dad for the times I couldn't understand why he did what he did. I praise GOD that, even during those days of his falling away, my dad never physically struck my mom or me. It is sad when people "judge" others by what they "see" rather than try to determine the cause for their actions. They seem to find it easier to judge others than try to help them.

However, as I mentioned earlier, the initial Korean War was being viewed as becoming World War III. Several weeks before my senior year came to an end, I and two of my friends, Jim Ross, and Ed Sherman, drove to Emporia, Kansas and talked with a Navy recruiter and returned home, ready to head to San Diego for Navy boot camp. Ed and Jim were both over eighteen. I was still seventeen, and my parents had to sign for me to be accepted.

Mom said, "No."

Dad said, "He's old enough to know what he wants."

Mom said, "No."

I added my two cents and said to Mom, "If you don't sign for me to go into the Navy now, they will draft me as soon as I'm eighteen. I will be given a rifle and a shovel and sent to Korea." I think that was the "tie-breaker" because Mom said, "If you are bound and determined to join the Navy, and Dad wants to sign for you, I won't stop you."

I now realize my parents didn't have the money to send me to college, even if I was there on a scholarship. I know Dad didn't want me to end up in the oil field, and Mom knew there were no real opportunities for a meaningful job in our hometown. I was okay with that because I wanted to join the Navy. So a week after Jim and I graduated, we along with Ed, left for Kansas City to take our physical and start a new way of life that would prove to be somewhat different from what the movies portray. Looking back, I know we would not have experienced the adventures, excitement, and the schooling we received during that same period if we had remained in the small town of Toronto, Kansas. "Thank You, Father, thank You!"

PART 2

Chapter 5

Anchors Away and "Stand Back World"

As I start chapter 5, I recall events in my life that took place after I left home as a seventeen-year-old boy and the things I encountered over the following seventeen years. In my first seventeen years about all the kids I knew were those I had known most of my young life. They were kids I went through grades 1 through 12. Some were my cousins, and others were longtime friends from church.

The following seventeen years started with my four-year "hitch" in the US Navy, where my daily contacts included new friends, shipmates, and no biological family members. My *new* contacts included a different kind of "family"—that is, people I had never known before and they were from various states throughout the United States. And they were all *new*. Many proved to be good friends, even though I only knew them months versus years, they became people I recall and also wrote about more than a half century later. In the Navy, you learn right out of boot camp, or maybe a service school, if that is your next assignment, you usually are assigned to a ship. Sometimes, before your four years are over, you are assigned to another ship. At each of these locations, you meet new people. You find some become good friends. Then they also get reassigned to a new ship or Naval base. Shortly after they leave, new Sailors replace them from another ship, and the process seems to start over. I found this wasn't all bad, because I was able to meet shipmates from all over America. I found my school years in Toronto, Kansas, was somewhat unique in that it was very different from some of the schools my new friends attended. They came from Omaha, Nebraska, Dallas, Texas, or a small town in Arkansas whose school was much different from my school in Toronto. Some of the differences were minor, and others were unbelievably different. In the beginning, I recall feeling like I had left what I thought was a typical small-town school and was now living in a different country where they spoke English, but their schools were very different, and some spoke with a funny accent.

The readers of chapter 5 and beyond, will be reading of my experiences after leaving home one day as a high school graduate and the next day finding I was in an environment foreign to me. As I think back to that time, I see it was the start of learning about "life in the real world." It was a time I realized I needed to start thinking more seriously about my future.

The following chapters cover that time in all our lives when we hear, see, and are tempted to experience things we had not encountered while living at home with Mom and Dad. I want to point out to my grandchildren and other young people in their preteen and early teen years, how important it is to have Jesus Christ as their Lord and Savior and know He will never change or leave them. However, if they listen to Satan, they will often unknowingly ignore GOD's Holy Spirit, and that is when they become vulnerable to the evils of the world. Even at an early age, there are so many things Satan will use to tempt them. He will try to lead them down the road to Hell and make it seem they are on their way to "fantasy land." I found having Jesus as my Lord and Savior was the only way I could cope with and overcome the many temptations Satan offers. Satan can appear very tempting, especially when we leave Mom and Dad and their protection. He is a "pro" in making sin look like a "picnic in the park." He can make sin appear attractive and will try to make us feel our yielding just once is not going to turn us into making it a habit. He will even suggest, "What harm can there be if you try drinking or drugs just once? That is not going to make you an addict." If a young person (even some not so young) does yield to these temptations once or twice and also if they don't have Jesus Christ as their Lord and Savior, "It's not going to be so tempting and hard to refuse, and I can say *no* any time." That may be true, but statistics show more tend to yield vs refuse, and they do get hooked.

However, if a young person has Jesus as their Lord and Savior before they leave home and family, they will know they have GOD's Holy Spirit within them, and that can make all the difference when they come to the fork in the road of life. They will find it much easier to take the road that will take them to the "Pearly Gates" of heaven versus ending up in Hell with no way to escape, throughout all eternity. It's also a time we can show GOD and ourselves, our real faith in Him. It will show Satan that he is messing with someone who knows GOD through His Son, Jesus Christ, and Satan knows GOD is someone he has *no* power over! Most importantly, it's a time when young and old alike must answer to themselves: "Do I know and believe I am a child of GOD?"

"Do I believe GOD loves me and will protect me?" These are questions we all must answer when Satan is tempting us. "What will be your answer?" Do you have Jesus as your Lord and Savior? GOD's Word says Jesus is the only way to GOD the Father. In John 14:6, Jesus states,

> I am the way and the truth and the life. No one comes to the Father except through me.

What will your answer be? At that point, you realize when we die and stand before the White Throne of judgment and are asked, "Why should you be allowed to come into heaven?"

"What will your answer be?"

Hopefully, younger members in my family and other youths in their age group, who read the following chapters, will see the impact the Trinity had on me during my childhood. Without Jesus, at that age, I would have been lost, literally. Even having Jesus as my Lord and Savior, I found I still had so much to learn, on my own. Today I see in knowing GOD and having His Holy Spirit within me and Jesus as my Lord and Savior; I give GOD praise and glory for taking care of me during those times I was searching for answers. I now know I was never alone, Jesus always had my hand, even when I ignored His love and concern. I missed many blessings during that time in my life when I yield to Satan's temptations, and I will never receive any of those blessings! I know they are lost forever.

I also believe GOD gave me His promise of Salvation on (July 7, 1946) that all my sins; past, present, and future were forgiven the moment I made my confession of faith and invited Jesus Christ to be my Lord and Savior. I believe, GOD knew I, like all humanity, would still sin in the future, because we are weak. When we yield to Satan's temptations, we will not receive GOD's blessings, but He has already forgiven all our sins. He will not give us His blessings when we turn from Him. When we fall away and don't serve GOD, He will not bless us. What sinful act could ever be more significant than a blessing from GOD?

Our Salvation is not taken away each time we yield to Satan's temptations, but we will not receive GOD's blessings while we continue to yield to Satan. "I believe Jesus Christ is the only begotten Son of GOD the Father, and He sacrificed on the cross for the remission of our sins. I accepted Jesus Christ as my Lord and Savior, and I believe GOD has forgiven me of all my sins."

It is ironic realizing when chapter 5 time frame was taking place, Ed, Jim and I along with thousands of other young men and women had joined the military to defend America when our country was fighting North Korea. Today some sixty-plus years later, as I am writing chapter 5, we hear on the news that we could be in war again with that same North Korea. Today I am too old to return to active military duty, but many in my family are at that age I was, during the initial Korean conflict in the 1950s. While thousands of our military personnel were being killed by North Korea soldiers, our government would only call it a "police action." I pray for young people today who are of an age they could be called on to finish what Grandpa and his generation were not allowed to finish. If they are called to fight North Korea, I'm afraid it will be much worse than it would have been back in the 1950s! GOD help us that will not happen.

I recall with much clarity, Jim, Ed, and me boarding the bus in Yates Center, Kansas that took us to Kansas City, Missouri, where we reported for our first (of several) physicals. For a lot of guys that had not played sports or had not been in an environment that required stripping down to their "birthday suit," the good Lord fitted them with; they were about to experience a new part of real life. We would be joining some two hundred enlistees for the Army, Air Force, Navy, and Marines. These young boys were coming to KC from all directions. Probably 95 percent of us did not know anyone in the entire group except the one or two they came with from their hometowns. We each had an idea of the great things we would soon encounter. And guess what? We found 99 percent of our "expectations" as to what we would be doing next, after we were turned into military men that day, and found out it never happened.

With that picture in mind, continue to read. On arriving in KC and taking a cab to the auditorium, where we were told we would now be starting our military life. As we went inside the auditorium, we were told to form a single line around the outer walls and then face toward the center. Next, we were advised we could talk with each other but, "Keep the noise level down."

When we were all lined up, with our backs against the four walls, our attention was directed to the door we had just entered. This time we saw a *large* man enter wearing a US Navy first class petty officer uniform. He had to be at least six feet four and had several rows of ribbons on his chest and a "no-nonsense" expression on his face. Very few knew at that time, but he would soon let us know he was First Class Petty Officer Reed who had just returned from a tour in the "war zone" near the Thirty-Eighth Parallel of South Korea. As he walked to the center of the room and, using a power-pack megaphone, he made the following announcement.

"All right, men, let me have your attention." Pause. Then in a more forceful voice, "Listen up!" The noise level dropped noticeably, "You are all here to join various branches of the US military. The first step in doing that will be a 'strip-down' examination." What did he say? "Now, from this day forward, you will hear many English words used together that initially will make no sense to you. However, I guarantee you will very quickly learn what they mean. For those of you that don't know what a strip-down physical means, it means you are to remove everything from your body with the following exception. If you are married, you can keep your wedding ring on your finger. Other than that, everything else will be removed from your body and placed in one of the baskets on the tables near you. Is that clear?" Various responses of low voices. "Okay, do it!"

I recall thinking, after boot camp was only a memory; we were starting to find out what the order of the day means from, First Class Petty Officer Reed. He was also beginning the process of breaking us down to the point we could be built up as men versus naive teenagers. Since I wasn't married, I wondered if it would be okay if I kept my school class ring on since I was proud to show it to other people. I quickly decided I was not going to be the one to ask that or any other question, this early in my career.

Immediately you could see the reactions from those who had never showered in high school along with the rest of the sports team players, or those who did not have a brother close to his age. You could also see those who were thinking, "Is he telling me I have to undress in front of some two hundred other males that I have never seen before?" (Welcome to the military world of reality!)

Over the next couple of hours, we would hear words of instruction we had never heard before. It would be embarrassing to many of those who were standing naked in front of two hundred or so strangers. We would hear comments that had sexual overtones directed at us. Why was this military man saying these things in front of young teenage boys? In the weeks to come, many of these young teenagers would see this as an introduction to the real world where "teenage boys" would have to become teenage *men* to survive. Many of these "men" in the auditorium that morning would soon be in battle zones that could claim their lives while defending the freedom of our country. Fighting a war cannot pamper or coddle naive teenage boys. You are expected to know what is going on in the world and not allow it to prevent you from doing your job. We "young boys" were being introduced to the real world. We would have to know what was going on around us at all times and be able to react in a proper way to live another day, defending the good "ole" USA. That day would be the first of many like-type days of learning to expect the unexpected and know how to react in a time of the battle.

Slowly, with encouragement from Petty Officer Reed, to speed the activities up, he said, "Let's go, men, we've got a war to fight." In all fairness to those who were having a shocking experience, I don't think anyone was breaking any speed records in trying to be the first one to get undressed. After about five minutes, with most of the baskets filled, Petty Officer Reed again, in a loud voice via the megaphone said, "Some of you appear not to know what it means when you hear, "Remove everything, except a wedding ring, from your bodies."

"Why are a dozen or more of you still wearing your undershorts?" (Embarrassment.)

Those that still had their shorts on probably felt that about 185 pairs of eyes were staring at them. Finally, after a few more embarrassing comments from Petty Officer Reed, "Everyone was "stripped down." Now, with this picture in mind—that is, two hundred young boys, all facing a no-nonsense petty officer who recently returned from the war zone off Korea and is standing in the center of the auditorium, they hear the following words.

"Well, Well, as I gaze around the room at you men, or should I say, boys, I realize the phrase, "All men are created equally is not true." (A few weak laughs, but mostly dead silence and more embarrassment.)

Then Petty Officer Reed said, "Okay, all eyes on me now and pay attention. "You will now go in single file, through this door (pointing to a door) where you will find a long table with many small glass bottles with lids on them. You will pick up one bottle, and only one. You will remove the lid and deposit a urine sample in the bottle and then replace the lid. You will then proceed to the far end of the room and give it to the corpsman, along with your name. Do you understand?"

I expect, at that moment, at least one-quarter of the guys were thinking of going AWOL. Then, to complete "the entertainment" for Petty Officer Reed, he said, "As you are walking naked, single file into the next room, do not walk too close to the one in front of you!" (More embarrassment.)

As the line started to move the petty officer walked over to the exit door of the second room and in a few minutes, looked inside and said, "What's taking so long to give a urine sample?" (embarrassment). After quite some time, all but a few had exited and were standing with backs to the wall. I don't recall any of us having a smile on our face, not knowing what was going to come out of Petty Officer Reed's mouth next. It seemed the few that were still in the other room were having trouble in being able to give a urine sample.

I say this because we all saw the petty officer look in the room again and say, in a loud voice, "Why are some of you standing facing the corner of the room, is that making it easier to give the sample? Remember, you *cannot* take a portion from someone that says he has some extra." (More embarrassment.)

After quite some time had passed and everyone was back in the auditorium, we were told to put our clothes on and stand at attention. I have since wondered why it was necessary to be naked to check our heart, blood pressure, and take a urine sample. However, that was the extent of our physical before boarding trains the following morning to various basic training camps. After we dressed, we filled out some paperwork and watched a military training film!

By this time, I realized the true meaning of the phrase, "Don't rock the boat. And who was I to question this battle-hardened sailor as to why we had to undress to do what we just did?"

After finishing boot camp, I thought back to that day in Kansas City and realized that it was a day many young boys were introduced to the real world. That day's experience was a day many young boys became aware of things in the world that Mom or Dad had not shared with them, *and* they were things they needed to be aware of as they entered the "real world" of life as a military soldier. However, the way many were being embarrassed was not the best training in preparing some two hundred young boys to fight a man's war. This was not the time or place to explain all things in life to the few that was not aware of them. Time itself would take care of that.

In 1952 the government was not flying enlisted (or drafted) personnel to their basic training camps. So after boarding a Santa Fe Troop train, the next morning, we spent the next couple of days, with guess who? Right, First Class Petty Officer Reed with all his embarrassing questions and comments. There were about seventy-five future Navy personnel and about seven future Marines on our train headed for San Diego. Early the first morning before breakfast, we were awakened from a not-too-restful night's sleep. After getting dressed, we were advised each car would have breakfast together, and no one was to eat with a group scheduled for a later time from another car.

The above schedule seemed to work okay without any confusion. After each carload was finished with breakfast and had returned to their assigned car, our good friend from K. C. met them. This time P. O. Reed told everyone to pay attention because he was only going to tell us once. Each of us was given a "stick-on" label and told to print our first and last names on the label with the felt pen he provided. Then we were to place the label on our shirt, over our heart, and leave it there until we arrived at the San Diego Naval Training Center (NTC). After everyone completed this, an unexpected event took place.

Up to this point when Petty Officer Reed talked to an individual, he would say, "You!" in a voice that demanded your attention. After we had our name tags on, all the way to the Naval Base, he would address us as, "Mr. Jones, Mr. Smith, or Mr. McJunkin, etc." What a change! Maybe this first class petty officer was a human after all! Little did we know this too was a hint of things to come.

All in all the embarrassment we encountered in Kansas City, and the train trip to San Diego went by with no significant problems. It gave us a chance to get acquainted with some of the guys that we had not met in Kansas City. On arriving at the train station in San Diego, we were transferred to buses that took us to the Naval Training Center (NTC).

Before boot camp

I was not aware until we disembarked at the NTC that we had guys from all over the country being sent to the San Diego NTC. This was because they had closed the Great Lakes NTC a few months earlier. In our Company alone, we had guys from Illinois to Texas and all over Kansas, Nebraska, Missouri, and Oklahoma.

Boot camp starts

I remember when we pulled in the front gate of the NTC, I could feel my heart beating a little faster, not knowing what awaited us when we stepped off the buses. The "future" Marines were told to stay on their bus that would take them to their new home, a short distance from our location.

Minutes after our arrival, we began to find out what boot camp was going to be. As the doors of the buses opened, we disembarked and were told to "fall in" formation ("fall in" formation, what did that mean?). By now First Class Petty Officer Reed had been joined by two more petty officers, who separated us into what they said would be our "squads" throughout boot training. Each "squad" had a number, 1 through 4. I was in squad number 3. In just a few minutes, we had been organized into what we were told would be a "company.". My two buddies from Toronto and I were in company number 422. It was about this time I was thinking, squad 3, company 422.

Are they going to expect us to remember all of this? Yes, they expected that and more. And Yes, we remembered.

During our days going through boot camp, we drilled on the parade field, and in classrooms, we were taught and tested for things soon to come. For endurance, we spent time in the swimming pool, gas chamber, or some other "not too pleasant places." Much of our daily activity involved competition with three other companies. Occasionally we would enjoy a few rest periods. When these came about, it enabled us to talk and get to know each other and start developing a sense of team effort.

While all this was going on, we were given additional information like, "As soon as you get 'squared away' as to what company and squad you are in, you will be marched down to building 0245 and issued your 'sea bag' (which I found included all my Navy clothes)."

"Next, you will be fitted for the proper sizes and will leave that area wearing a pair of your Navy dungarees."

"You will wear dungarees as you're training uniform, including the GI underwear, socks, and shoes you receive today."

We were then told, "You must decide if you want to wrap your "civvies" and send them back to "Mommy" or you can donate them to a "welfare store," and we'll see they are delivered."

"After that, you will be marched to your barracks and be assigned a bunk and locker. From that point on you will always have your 'white hat' on your head whenever you are outside your barracks, and it will be squared on your forehead (versus on the back of your head), there will be no exceptions or excuses for not wearing your white hat and wearing it properly. Is that clear?"

"Yes, yes, sir, okay."

We were still showing we didn't know or understand all the Navy vocabulary.

"This afternoon at 1300 [1:00 p.m]? You will receive your first free government haircut. The petty officer that was giving this information also added, "You might be thinking how you want it cut and be sure you tell the barber before he starts, otherwise he might leave it longer than you want." (That will be the day!) He went on to say, "And tomorrow morning, after breakfast at 0600 [6:00 a.m.]? You will receive a couple of shots, not from a bottle but by way of a needle with a square tip at the end! Ouch! After receiving your shots, you will be marched to the parade grounds and start your training on marching in formation, plus a few other 'fun' things."

At this point it dawned on me I didn't even remember what we were going to do in the next hour, I guess I was banking on the hope no one else could remember all we had been told and I felt sure they would not court-martial the entire company.

Things were going too fast, and nothing so far was what I had expected. On arriving at the NTC, I expected since we arrived in the morning, by noon, I would have my dress Blues and have an over-night liberty pass. I had it all figured out how my two buddies from Toronto and I would step off the bus in downtown San Diego and would have to shove the young ladies out of the way so that we could walk down the sidewalk. Boy, that was a pipe dream that never came true in San Diego. There seemed to be more Sailors downtown on a weekend than there were back on the base.

Keep in mind the above instructions and schedules were given to us in the first few hours after disembarking from the busses. Maybe by design, but I think, at that time, we were all so tired, confused and mentally exhausted, that if anyone in a Naval uniform gave us an order and led us to carry it out, we would follow. At a point, we felt things couldn't get any worse; they did.

The agenda for the immediate future had been outlined, and some of it had been completed. Thinking we would now be able to go to our barracks and take a nap, the surprise of the day happened. We were still in our civvies and standing at ease and in formation, when one of the first class petty officers said, in a loud and firm voice, "Attention on deck!"

To my left, I saw a man wearing what I later found out was a chief petty officer's uniform, coming toward our company. At that time, I didn't know if he was an enlisted man with an impressive looking uniform or an Admiral. The closer he came, the more I felt like, "This guy looks too old to still be on active duty in the military." When he was in front of us, and directly between squads 2 and 3, he stopped and did a "right face" and slowly scanned, what looked like, each face in our company.

After what seemed like an hour, he turned his head from side to side and announced, "I'm sure glad we had men to fight World War II and not a bunch of 'knuckleheads' like 'youse guys' or we would never have won the war." (I found out later, those words were Brooklynese for "you guys.")

He continued by informing us, "I fought throughout World War II, I served on one ship that was torpedoed and sank, I was on another ship that was in the war zone, under enemy fire, for days at a time. We were attacked by the Japanese Kamikaze suicide planes over ten times, and through all of that, I never had any doubt that we were going to be the victors, and we were." And let me tell you why I felt that way. It was because every crew member on our ship was a *man*! Someone I knew I could depend on to do his job and do it bravely and professionally."

"I've been retired for almost a year. I had returned to my wife and family in Brooklyn, New York, and was enjoying the peace that all our World War II military personnel had fought, and many died for, so we could live a life of peace once again."

"Six weeks ago, I received a letter asking if I would be willing to be activated and train recruits for the battle that was increasing in intensity in Korea. Thinking about what I had seen and experienced in World War II, I knew I had to do what I could for the young men that would be asked to do what thousands of my brothers and I did."

"But as I stand here this morning, I don't see a company of men, I see a bunch of 'knuckleheads' who look like you don't have the brains to come in out of the rain, let alone fight a war to save our country from defeat. I may have to think it over as to why I should waste my time trying to train a bunch of "kids" that appear not to have the intelligence of a baboon when I could be back in Brooklyn enjoying my family and friends? I may tell the base commander that until they can give me some men with (Bs) and brains, I'm out of here."

As that point, he turned to the first class petty officer and said in a loud enough voice that we all heard clearly.

"I don't want to see any more of these 'knuckleheads' today. I feel like I'm about to throw-up." As he walked back into the barracks, I think most of us thought we had seen the last of this "true war hero." You talk about feeling low; we felt lower than low. Then, to make matters worse, the first class petty officer said, "Well, I hope you guys are proud of the impression you made on Chief Wargo, a man who was awarded more medals for bravery than probably all of you will ever see." He turned to one of the other first class petty officers and said, "March these characters down to the uniform shop so they can get their sea bags, although I agree with the chief, they probably may never deserve wearing a US Navy uniform."

I expect if anyone observed us on our way to get our sea bags that day, they too would agree with the words we heard from Chief Wargo. Some of us may have felt, "Maybe we were a group of 'knuckleheads.'"

Even before they blew "revelry" the next morning, I was awake. I was thinking about the words; I heard Chief Wargo say the day before and thinking about the impression we made on him. I remember getting out of my bunk, going into the latrine (restroom) and finding at least nine or ten other guys up and shaving. No one was saying anything. The "downer" of yesterday was still fresh in our minds. "What more discouragement could today bring? Many years have passed since my boot camp days, but I know it seemed twice as long as it was. I know we spent around four weeks out in the desert area at Camp Elliot—a World War II training camp the Marines used during part of their basic training. I remember thinking it was so far away from civilization that if you had a midnight to 4:00 a.m. security watch, you could look 360 degrees around your post and not see any indication of human life. To give you an idea of life at Camp Elliot; when we had completed our time there, we felt better in coming back to the Naval Training Center, than we felt on our first liberty.

However, a new segment of boot camp was yet to come after we had dressed and fallen-in formation, under the direction of our assistant company commander, also a chief petty officer. No one asked, and he did not say anything about what took place the day before. I expect anyone who saw us that morning would agree; we would never make it through boot camp. Then, the door of our barracks opened, and there was Chief Wargo. As he stepped down the four or five steps to the "grinder" (the area where companies practiced their marching drills), not changing the expression on his face from the day before, he walked to the front of our company and asked, "Are 'youse knuckleheads' ready to become sailors?"

In unison, we shouted, "Yes, sir!"

"Then I want you to show me."

And that started the first day of boot camp under the guidance of Chief Wargo.

Boot camp has officially started, now we were going to see what it is like:

At the beginning of boot camp, the tallest man in each of the four squads became the four squad leaders of company 422. If a squad leader had any demerits in inspection, he would go to the end of the squad, and the next tallest in that squad moved up to be the new squad leader. I think it was at the end of the third week our squad had gone through three squad leaders, and I, at five feet ten inches, had been moved into that position in squad 3. (By the grace of GOD I was still the squad leader of squad 3 when we graduated.)

As I recall we spent one or two weeks at the Naval Training Center (NTC) and then headed for Camp Elliot where we found how cold it gets in the morning hours in parts of California. I can't recall anything that was good or from our perspective, even beneficial about Camp Elliot. During the evening and night watches, we had to wear our heavy, winter, Pea Coats because of the cold temperature.

I recall one morning I had the 4:00 a.m. security watch, it was so cold, even with my gloves and Pea Coat on I didn't think I was going to make it until I was relieved by whoever had the misfortune of standing the next watch that day. As I think back to that time, I think the only reason we spent time at Camp Elliot at the beginning of boot camp training was to break our resistance down a little more so when we returned to the NTC; we would think we had returned from "hell" and arrived in "heaven."

After we finished our "endurance testing" at Camp Elliot, we were scheduled for service week. Service week was a week that each company was assigned to serve in the chow hall and serve the other companies their meals for a week. I don't think any of us were looking at the "big picture" at that time. We could not believe what had happened. For the first time, the Navy was allowing us to decide what we wanted, rather than telling us what we had to do. Since we were all new boots,' we were allowed to choose when *we* wanted to return to the NTC. We were asked to decide if we wanted to do our service week at Camp Elliot or return to the NTC and do it there. I guess we were all too young to know what "psychological testing" was, but that is what we were experiencing at that time.

There is no doubt in my mind if asked, "All those that want to leave Camp Elliot next week and return to the NTC, and do your service week there, hold up your hand." I expect every man in our company would have his hand reaching for the sky. As cold and remote from civilization as Camp Elliot was and we had a chance to get out of there early, only a fool would want to stay. But before we could decide what we wanted to do, Chief Wargo casually pointed out the following, "If youse guys go back to the NTC and do your 'service week,' you will be the junior company, and you will be serving companies that are near or ready for graduation. You will not get any respect for the lowly job of serving them." He continued, "However, if we stay at Camp Elliot, we will be the senior company, and we will not have to stand any security watches, and we will have our choice, at mealtime, in getting the biggest pork chops."

Whether we passed the test or not, we chose to spend our service week at Camp Elliot.

Back to the NTC

When we did return to the NTC, most of our time was spent in classrooms watching wartime films and viewing the importance of knowing what our battle station was and what we would be responsible for, in case of an enemy attack. I recall before viewing some of the gruesome casualty films; the instructor told us, "If you feel you are getting sick, think of anything pleasant in your life and look away from the film." I recall playing a lot of basketball during some of those films, and I know I was not the only one.

After an hour engaged in watching actual war casualty films, they would often march us over to a mockup version of a ship's compartment. We learned how to put on gas masks and check them for leaks while wearing the mask. All the instructions seemed easy enough, and most of us thought the chances of having to use them were probably quite small. By this time, I recalled when we thought one thing, Chief Wargo would come up with an activity that called for us to prove just how easy it was to do, only to find out it was not as easy as we thought. However, with "team effort" we were able to accomplish what we were ordered to do. That was progress!

Everyone had a chance to go through the stages of fitting and then putting on their gas masks. Next, we were told to enter a mock-up of a ship's compartment, carrying our gas masks. We were told to prepare to put our gas mask on and when the command to "remove gas masks" was given to slowly remove the mask and slowly walk to the open hatch at the end of the compartment, go outside and stand in formation until everyone was out. We were also told if anyone ran or in any way did not follow the orders given, they would have to repeat the procedure until they "got it right"!

As luck would have it, there were at least four or five guys that yanked off their masks and ran to the hatch, rubbing their eyes. I felt sorry for them because they had to repeat and follow the orders given. Even those of us that followed the orders received enough burning sensation to know, "When told to do something a certain way, do it!"

It seemed like we were doing these types of activities each day after returning to the NTC. If not engaged in types of "on-the-job learning" activities, we were out on the parade field marching, trying to reach a level of perfection so we would be chosen the number 1 company over the other three companies we competed.

There was one major reason, during boot camp, that kept us from being number 1, and I think it made everyone ask themselves, "I'm either going to be a team player or I'll be viewed as someone that always wants to do everything, My way—that is *not* be a team player." This gradual "attitude change" came about over days after our company had been formed, with one exception. One guy that seemed to have decided he wanted to do everything his way was the guy from the Chicago area who claimed to be a member of, as he put it, "a tough gang." He was the one individual in our company that had demerits taken off during inspection almost every day. His demerits would be the result of a dirty rim on the inside of his white hat, or his uniform was not wrinkle-free. Even though company 422 started as the top company in our group of four, when this guy started having demerits every day, the spread began to narrow between our company and that of the number 2 company.

Chief Wargo called we four squad leaders into his office one day after morning drills, and inspection and his message went something like this. "Men, I know you want to remain in first place in our competition with the other three Companies. We all know we aren't doing too well at that and we are running out of time. Our situation reminds me of what we did during World War II, aboard ship, when we had a screw-up like Seaman Recruit Carver (not real name) is doing in our Company. The petty officers in the department the "screw-up" was in decided they had enough, and they would give him a shower with a ki-yi brush. (This was a hard-bristled brush issued as part of our sea bag and used to scrub our dungarees.)

As the chief dismissed us, he said, "I'm not telling you what to do. I've only told you what we did in World War II."

As we left the chief's office, one of the squad leaders asked, "Do you want me to get the brush?"

We all agreed.

When he returned, with the brush, we checked to see where the "troublemaker" was and decided our plan of action. He was sitting on the lower bunk at one end of the barracks. We decided two of us would get on the far side of the bunk he was facing, and the other two would do the same on the back side of the bunk he was sitting on. The plan was, when he stood up, we would pin him in between the two double bunks and take him to the shower. We also noted we had the rifles we used in marching drills, hanging parallel to the floor, on the frame of both sides of the top bunks. We knew we had to make sure he did not get hold of one of them.

We appointed Squad Leader Jackson to tell Carver, who was in Jackson's Squad, we wanted him to come to the "latrine" (Navy word for the *restroom*). When Jackson told Carver what we wanted him to do, Carver said he was not going anywhere and stood up and grabbed the rifle from the bunk next to him and said, "And none of you jerks are going to take me." With that, the four of us pinned him between the two sets of double bunks. The squad leader on my side of the bunk Carver had been sitting on, and I dropped down and grabbed Carver at the waist and pinned his arms and held him until the other two could disarm him and then, kicking and screaming, we escorted Carver to the shower.

Once there, we gave him a choice of taking the brush and giving himself a Ki-yi shower, or we would do it. He paused a few seconds and then said, "Give me the D-brush because you guys aren't going to do anything to me." With the shower running, he took off his shirt and started brushing up and down until the blood began running down his arms. I don't know if he thought, in our seeing the blood running down his arms it would make us feel sorry for him but, if that was what he was hoping for, he was in for a big disappointment. Carver left the shower that morning, knowing if he didn't get his act together and become part of our company team, he would not have control of the brush the next time.

When the chief came in the next morning, he noted Carver's arms and said, "Don't you know the brush is for scrubbing dirt out of your dungarees? It looks like you've used it to scrub the dirt out of your arms, let's hope you did a good job."

With that said, he turned around and walked out. The shower seemed to do the job, and as I recall, Carver had only one demerit taken off throughout the rest of boot camp and, as the scars on his arms started to heal, he began to become a team player. I think what happened to Carver showed him and the rest of our company, in training for war, you seldom are given a second chance if you messed up the first time.

I know many people, most of whom never served in the military, might say, "The military will ruin a person and cause them to start drinking, smoking and doing all kinds of sinful things."

There may be some truth in that statement, but if the person was raised in a Christian environment and saved, I have a hard time believing the military would have the power to influence, even a young eighteen- or nineteen-year-old man to permanently change his life that way, especially ending up with it being a habit after he left the military. I would not go so far as to say every young Christian man that was in the military never yielded to temptations, but when they returned to civilian life if not before, they often left those temptations behind them. I must amend my statement somewhat, because I recall a couple of Christian boys (men) that, as far as I knew, never yielded to those temptations while they were still in the Navy. Speaking for myself, I can only give GOD the praise for watching over me and forgave me the times I failed Him. I'll address my experiences later in chapter 5 when I'm sharing my experiences after being assigned to my first ship.

When the end of boot camp arrived, our company 422, was awarded second place, mostly due to the performance of two people—that is, the self-proclaimed "gang member" of a Chicago street gang who, near the end of boot camp started being a "team player." However, he had received such an excessive number of demerits in personnel inspections; the damage had already been done. The other guy that caused our coming in second place was an uncoordinated guy that never could figure out how to "stack rifles" on the parade field. These two guys probably accounted for 98 percent of our company's demerits. Most of us felt without the two people that received demerits almost every day; we would have nailed first place without any problem. I think the importance of having "teamwork" as an objective of everyone in our company, was realized when we found out the guy that had some mental problems received a "government convenience discharge." The Navy made a mistake by accepting him when he enlisted. Hopefully, due to his short stint in the Navy, enabled him to get government help later that he may not have been able to obtain on his own.

Radio school

Returning to the NTC after my boot camp leave, I was glad to have been assigned to my first choice of schools. I had listed radio school as my school of choice before going home on a week's leave. In finding, I had been given my first choice of schools, and it was taught at the NTC in San Diego. I felt like everything was coming together nicely. I had become familiar with the NTC and had been able to go into San Diego a couple of times on one-day weekend liberties, and this made me feel I would not be a stranger to the location of my next assignment in the Navy. It was about that time I started feeling, "Life is good" and "Navy life is also good."

In learning the code in radio school and "letting it run in my ears and out my fingers, was not as easy as my typing teacher in high school used to tell us how we would know when we had mastered the art of typing." I found that having to learn the code and then translating it into an alphanumeric character, *then* letting the character flow from my head and out of my fingers and hit the right key on the typewriter, added significantly to printing a meaningful message that had to be acted on, sometimes in the heat of battle. However, out of our class of forty starters, thirty-six of us graduated.

On completing radio school, if any of us wanted to change the ship or station assignment we had been given, with someone in our school class, of equal rank, that also wanted to switch, we could. I didn't have any problem with my assignment to an LST whose home port was San Francisco. Being a young kid just out of high school, I never gave a second thought to try and get a better assignment than the LST. However, the day after the "assignment posting," another seaman apprentice asked me if I would be willing to swap assignments. His reason was, his home was San Francisco, and his assignment was an LST out of Norfolk, Virginia.

He told me, "I will never get to spend any time with my family when we are in home port if it is on the East Coast unless I take leave."

My response was, "Sure, I'm from Kansas, and I'm not going to be able to spend time with my family regardless of where my home port is."

We made the swap, and at the end of school, most of us were heading home for a week's leave. Since my home was between San Diego and Norfolk, Virginia, I was able to take advantage of adding my "days in transit" to my ship and extend my week's leave by three days.

I did wonder several months later if I did the right thing in making that swap out of radio school. How would I react if anyone said, "Oh, you didn't have to go into any battle zones?" Most often anyone that would ask such an irresponsible question is someone that was never in the military during peacetime or a time of war. But I hoped I would recall what a chief petty officer told me one time after I reported on board my first ship.

He said, "There has never been an enlisted man or woman who voluntarily joined the military with the condition they would only join if assigned to a location that had beautiful beaches and not a lot of military personnel. Like it or not, if we joined it was for wherever our country wanted to send us, train us and school us in whatever field they felt we could best serve."

I know many military men/women would respond to the above question with something like, "I assume you never were in the military but stayed home and let mom and dad pay for your college, and never joined the ROTC to qualify yourself for a commission. So tell me what you are doing now that you have the freedom of choice, that was made available by those who did serve?" Hopefully, those that did serve (including myself) would not feel they need to respond to such an "irresponsible question" with an equally "irresponsible answer"!

My first cruise

I was soon to find, in the military, being in a life-threatening situation is not always confined to being in a war zone.

My first cruise took place on March 1953, shortly after I graduated from radio school in San Diego and assigned to the USS *LST* 1144. When I reported aboard ship, it was just coming out of dry dock in Portsmouth, Virginia. Arriving at the Portsmouth dry dock piers and reporting on board my ship, I was escorted to my sleeping quarters, located my bunk and locker and started to unpack my sea bag. I hadn't completed doing that when the PA system came on. The announcement I heard came somewhat as a surprise. It stated, "We will be coming out of the dry dock in two days and spend about a week at sea, checking the operational readiest of our ship and then head to Davisville, Rhode Island. There we will bring aboard supplies and head for our destination port in Argentia, Newfoundland."

I was still unpacking my seabag and stowing my gear in my locker when a third class personnel petty officer told me that Lieutenant Browner, our communications officer, wanted to talk with me. The PO escorted me to Lieutenant Browner's cabin where he welcomed me aboard ship. He then told me he wanted me to go to the galley where they would be giving "seaman" tests in about an hour. I remember he laughed and said, "Being fresh out of boot camp, you should have no trouble passing the tests, and you may be the only crew member that received a promotion the first day they reported aboard the ship!" About three hours later, I was Seaman Radioman McJunkin. (Thank You, Father!)

I remember thinking, "Great, this ole boy from the Midwest can now say, 'Today I, R, a real sailor boy.'" Remember I had just turned eighteen and couldn't wait to get out on the high seas and feel the salty spray from the ocean on my face. I was ready to "single up all lines and get underway, right now"! Little did I know what awaited the crew and me in the coming days.

First, I found the salty ocean spray was not a skin softener plus the rolling and the up and down continuous motions of our ship in rough seas, was not like a relaxing vacation cruise. In the next few days, I started looking at things as they were. I thought about those words in the announcement I heard the first day I came aboard the ship. I wondered how the married guys reacted when they heard, "In two days we would be leaving and spend the next week at sea." What did their families think when they received the news? What were they going to do over the weeks the ship would be away? Who was going to take care of the needs of the kids that called for "Dad" to handle? But that was not my problem, and I'm sure this was not the first time it happened to our married guys who knew how to handle the situation.

I'm not suggesting the Navy is the worst branch of military service there is for a married man because I've heard that same story from former members of the Army, Air Force, and the Marines. I think it takes a certain personality, commitment, love, and a strong relationship with GOD on the part of the wife *and* the husband, to make it last. However, aren't those the qualities that are necessary to make a marriage last in a civilian marriage? Enough said."

Getting back to my first cruise and finding out GOD can get your attention, even when you are "at sea." At this writing, I still remember with much clarity, some sixty-five years after the events that took place between the time we left Davisville, Rhode Island, arrived in Argentia, Newfoundland and returned to Norfolk, Virginia.

When we pulled into Davisville, Rhode Island, and being a radioman, I didn't have many duties while we were tied up. So a fellow radioman and I took off to "check out the city." After the first day, we both agreed it seemed to be a beautiful place to live but not anything to brag about if you are taking a one-day Navy "liberty."

Fortunately, we were only there a couple of days, and then we were on our way to Argentia, Newfoundland, and experience the scenery on our short trip in the North Atlantic waters. What I first thought was humorous, turned out not to be so funny. The lead radioman (Third-Class Petty Officer Brooks) told me before we left dry dock that he would get seasick when the ship was underway for a long time. He said if I agreed to take his watches when we were in rough seas, he would take all my watches when we were tied up. He was married, and I was single, and I recall thinking, "Man, this is an offer I can't refuse."

"So out of the kindness of my heart and to show what kind of guy I was, I accepted his offer!" (Do you believe that?) However, we no more than cleared the Chesapeake Bay, before he said, "Can you take over, I'm feeling bad." I didn't have any problem with that since it would be my first "real" radio watch at sea. Right off the bat, I found that copying code in a rough sea is not as clear and easy as being in the classroom in San Diego.

The other thing I became aware of was some of the messages you receive at sea would not be pleasant. The message I'm thinking of did not come on my first watch, but on the second day when we received a warning of a possible hurricane developing in the North Atlantic just a little southeast of Newfoundland. As the day wore on, the reports worsened, the ocean waters became very rough, and our ship seemed to be moving in all directions, including some that seemed to be taking us backward. On top of that, I found it was almost impossible to sit in my chair in front of the typewriter and copy code when the chair wanted to slide all around the steel deck. It was practically impossible to distinguish a "dit" from a "dah" in the coded message I was trying to copy through the static caused by lightning. (In the 1950s the transistor had not been developed and electronic technicians will understand what I mean by that statement—that is, vacuum tube equipment used during storms equals static and can make it very difficult to distinguish the difference among "a dit, a dah, and a pop of lightning," when you are copying code in the middle of a storm! At that time, I just wanted to get tied up to the pier in Newfoundland.

As we came within sight of the pier we would tie up for the next four or five days (that was what our orders called for at that time) we noticed the winds were becoming more forceful. With the aid of a Navy tug, we began some very slow and cautious maneuvering until we finally made it. ("Thank You, GOD!")

Little known to us, the real show had not started. The next morning the storm intensity had increased even more. Chow call for breakfast had sounded about thirty minutes earlier when suddenly, our ship made one of the loudest sounds I've ever heard. We then seemed to be lifted out of the water and again come down with another loud noise. I had already gone through the chow line and was sitting at the table discussing our trip and the current storm with some of my shipmates when this happened. We all looked at each other with that, "What in the world is taking place?"

What had happened was a fully loaded civilian cargo ship was coming in to tie up at the pier in front of us, and with the heavy seas and dense fog, all their navigation gear went out, their radar, sonar, radio, etc., at the last few minutes; nothing was operating. The captain indicated later; they thought they were parallel with the pier versus heading straight into it. But guess what was between the dock and their ship? You're right, our USS *LST* 1144. I still have the pictures of the hole their bow sliced open in the "port" side of our ship. It went right through the steel plate and into the crew's sleeping quarters. The opening measured twelve feet vertical and just above the waterline, three feet wide and about four feet into the main deck. By the grace of GOD, everyone had left for breakfast, and no one was in that area when the collision occurred.

We had been scheduled to unload our cargo and head back to the States at the end of the week. I don't recall how long we were there, but it was longer than originally scheduled. A "temporary patch" was welded over the hole, hoping it would hold until we returned to Portsmouth. I don't think those words gave any of the crew a feeling of relief. However, that was the condition of our ship when we "up-anchored" and headed south, still on the outer edges of the hurricane. The storm seemed to be worsening, and the thought of going back into those forceful waters with a "Band-Aid" on the side of our ship did not give us a warm and fuzzy feeling. Over the next few days, we never heard the phrase, "I had a good night's sleep last night."

While we were still tied up to the pier, and starting to prepare to get underway, our lead Radioman had been copying our messages during the hours we were to receive traffic. I knew Petty Officer Brooks had to be getting tired, so I went up to the radio shack early and told him I would take over because I couldn't sleep with all that was going on. I remember his reply, "Thank you, man; I don't know if I'm going to make it."

"Hey, give me the headset and try to get some rest."

"Thanks again, I owe you one."

"Forget it." With that, he was off to his bunk!

When I saw that it was about ten minutes before I would be receiving incoming messages, I made a preliminary frequency check of our ship's receiver and found we seem to be getting as good of a signal as could be expected. With a blank message sheet in my typewriter, I was ready to copy "FOX" (code).

Each ship has a unique four-letter ship identification. Ours was NKHE, and those "call letters" were what our duty Radioman would be waiting to hear. It seems strange that I remember our call letters over half a century after the last time I used them, and I doubt if I could tell you what we had for dinner yesterday evening.

When I heard our call letters, I knew I would begin typing the words in English that I heard in code. I had already noted we did have some messages, so I started paying a little more attention. Then, instead of hearing NKHE, I listened to what I first thought was someone playing jokes on us. Then I realized you don't play those kinds of jokes in the military unless you are looking for a court-martial, but, there it came again...or in English. It was SOS, SOS, SOS, followed by a ship's name, then its coordinates. I waited until I heard them a second time. I recall one of the instructors in radio school telling us about the message we never wanted to hear, and the odds were, we never would hear, was a distress SOS message. I pulled the message sheet out of the typewriter and yelled for the Chief Quartermaster, who was in the next compartment. When he read the msg., he asked me if I was sure I had received it correctly. I don't know why I was so firm in my answer, but I replied, "Yes, I am."

He said, "I'm taking this to the captain." And off he went to our captain's quarters.

The SOS was coming from a Norwegian freighter that was being split apart at midship by the hurricane. We found out later that its skipper, as I recall his name was Captain Cook, had ordered his crew to abandon ship because it was starting to sink, but he refused to leave. He was later ordered by the owners to leave, and we understood he did. I don't know if the "rules of the sea" then are the same today, but at that time, if all the crew leaves the ship and it does not sink, it's up for grabs by the first ship that secures it. At that point the ship and its contents become theirs. I'm sure that is why the captain had refused to leave the ship until he was ordered to leave.

Our chief quartermaster determined the damaged ship was not that far from our location. In the meantime, I forwarded the sinking ship's SOS, and its location to all ships at sea, per standard procedures. We found out there were two US Navy destroyers who were about as close to the ship as we were. When our captain heard that, he decided that there was no way we would be able to get to the ship before the destroyers could, especially with that "Band-Aid" on the side of our ship.

He was right because we heard later most of the crew was found and saved. We never heard if the skipper was one of them, but that event made the headline news for several weeks. I kept a copy of the SOS we forwarded on our military frequencies to ships that may be close enough to help in the rescue of the crewmen on the sinking ship. I kept it for years, but in our many moves, while working at AT&T, I think it must have been lost somewhere along the way because I haven't seen it in quite some time.

We now became more aware of what the odds were for our USS 1144 to get underway and arrive safely back in the Portsmouth naval yards! But orders are orders and we "singled up all lines" and headed south. As the storm grew in intensity, tension grew among the crew. I could go from the radio room into the navigation area that was just forward of the radio area and have a panoramic view from midship to the forward portion of our ship. We observed the canvas covering some of the gun mounts, flapping in the wind as if it was about to rip the guns off their bolted mounts.

We could also see the seaman, secured around his waist with a line attached just outside the "hatch" (door), closest to the "temporary patch." If you can picture this poor Boatswain Mate, in full winter gear, face covered with only eye holes to see through, on his hands and knees with a lantern tied to his wrist, and moving slowly, as he looked for any irregularity in the seam of the patch on the deck area. I'm not sure how comforting it was to him, knowing he would be relieved in an hour!

We knew before leaving that *if* the movement of the ship caused the seam to crack even a little, without further warning, "the entire patch, on the deck and down the side, could 'pop off' in seconds." The results of that occurring was not a pleasant one for the entire crew, especially the poor Sailor at the end of the rope, on his hands and knees, checking the patch for any indication of a split.

To this day, I can't help but feel some of our crew, for the very first time in their life, "Had a little talk with Jesus," along with the rest of us that talked with Him every day. I am sure there was not one-person on-board ship that would have said, with conviction, "GOD had nothing to do in our having a safe return to Portsmouth."

As for me, I believe it was by the grace of GOD that we made it back safe to Portsmouth and never lost one crewmember.

Sometime later I was talking with a retired World War II Navy chief, and I shared our experience in the hurricane and the feeling many of our crew members had, knowing that in a split second if the patch started splitting, our ship would sink in record time. We knew there probably would not be any survivors, being in hurricane waters, especially if we would probably not have time to send an SOS with our ship's name and coordinates before we sank.

The retired Navy chief said, "I can identify with what you are saying. I served on a Navy ship during the final days of World War II. Like you and your shipmates, we were once caught in the destructive winds of a hurricane. Before the hurricane, my ship had several engagements of being fired on by enemy airplanes and enemy ships. Even though we didn't have a temporary patch on the side of our ship, many of us felt less safe in the hurricane winds constantly pounding us for several days and nights, than we felt when exchanging fire with German naval forces, usually only during the daytime hours."

After arriving safely back in the States, I made several exciting cruises on the LST 1144, including going to Port-Lyautey, Africa, French Morocco, Ponto Delgado, the Azores Is, Vieques Island, Havana, Cuba and several ports along our eastern coast of the USA.

When the USS *LST* 1144 was due to be decommissioned, I was ready to move on. With my twentieth birthday behind me, I was prepared to meet new shipmates, see, and visit places that many have only read about in books. And that is what I was about to experience when I received my orders to a ship whose home port was outside the USA.

My second ship was PC 486, and I reported on board in March 1954. Homeport was on the Pacific side of the Panama Canal. On reporting aboard ship, within a couple of weeks, we took an R&R cruise to Acapulco, Mexico. We saw the world-famous "cliff divers" dive from the cliff into the water just at the right time that the tide was coming in and the water was deep enough they would not hit bottom and possibly be killed. We also went through the Canal several times and once up the Eastern side of Mexico, to the Gulf and on to Key West, Florida for a week of war games with the US Air Force.

We often went by way of our ship to some of the surrounding islands of Panama that had interesting history and sites to visit; courtesy of Uncle Sam. Being on the PC 486 turned out to be a great duty because we seemed to be going to an exciting place every couple of weeks. I will say some of the married crew had their families living off base in Panama, and I'm not sure they were as thrilled as their Navy husbands. However, we did take the families that wanted to go through the canal to the Atlantic side once while I was on board. As I recall, our ship went through several times.

Our ship was stationed at Coco Solo, Canal Zone on the Pacific side of the canal and was the only ship with any fighter power in case the Western side of the canal came under attack in an attempt to damage the operation of the canal. While I was there, we were on alert status for several days and went to general quarters once in search of a possible sighting of an unidentified submarine from either Guatemala or El Salvador. The two had been exchanging fire between each other due to border problems and were on the brink of war. There were indications that either of these two countries might attempt to damage the canal to draw attention away from what was going on North of the canal zone. Knowing all the central American countries would be focusing their attention on Panama and not be concerned or interfere with the activities between Guatemala and El Salvador. However, this proved to be a false alarm, and we resumed our normal operations aboard ship.

I was on the PC 486 when the United States was operating under a long-term lease with Panama to maintain, manage, and police the Panama Canal. The contract has since expired, and Panama is responsible for the canal's operation.

In September 1955, after deciding not to "ship over." I received orders to report to the US Naval Base in Brooklyn, New York, for separation. On September 13, 1955, I was released from active duty to serve four more years on inactive reserve status. I saw and learned a lot about "life in the real world" during my active service in the

US Navy—some I benefited from, and some I've asked GOD for forgiveness.

I experienced both good and bad times during my tour in the Navy. I give GOD praise for giving me the wisdom to distinguish between the two, and I asked forgiveness for the times I ignored His input. I've asked forgiveness for the bad decisions I made, and I know He has forgiven me. I still thank GOD for His mercy and grace He showed me during those times I failed Him. "GOD is good…all the time!"

Chapter 6

Put the Anchors Away and Help Me, GOD! I Need a Job!

There is nothing on this earth that pleases Christ so much as our *faith* in Him.

After graduating from high school as a seventeen-year-old teenager and finishing a tour in the US Navy, I found myself a twenty-one-year-old Veteran. For the first time, I realized in those few years in the Navy, I had seen more, done more, and experienced more things, events, and happenings than some people experience in a lifetime. Even when my ship was tied up at a pier, we were always taking steps for getting underway to a different place and often to a different country. It was an exciting and challenging time, not knowing what awaited my shipmates and me at the next port. All of that is now history, and I realized, I'm on my way back home in Toronto, Kansas.

When the plane landed in Kansas City, Missouri, I had a "flash-back" thought. I recalled this was where my Navy life began some four years earlier and now I was ending it by returning to Kansas City after receiving my active duty discharge and catching a taxi to the Kansas City, Missouri, bus station. As I boarded the bus for Yates Center, Kansas, I couldn't help but wonder if the bus I was boarding to end my active military duty, might be the same bus I boarded four years earlier in Yates Center to start my military duty in the Navy. I told Mom and Dad what day I would be coming home, but since

I didn't know what time that would be, I told them not to plan on meeting me in Yates Center. I knew, wearing my uniform, and carrying my sea bag, I would be able to get a ride home on Highway 54. As I was writing this chapter in 2019, I thought, "I'm not sure a serviceman today, in uniform, walking on a highway like Highway 54 and needing a ride would be a smart thing to do."

Being a young boy from the heartlands of Kansas, I remember thinking it didn't seem like four years had passed since Ed, Jim and I boarded the bus in Yates Center that took us to Kansas City and the US Navy. I recalled during those four years and the many things I had experienced, places I had seen, and training I had received; and I asked myself, "Did I experience all of that in just four years?" I knew for sure I was no longer a seventeen-year-old boy; I was now a twenty-one-year-old Navy veteran, and it seemed between the two trips between Yates Center and Kansas City; a lifetime had passed.

I recalled some of the thoughts I mentioned in chapter 2 and realized I was now at a time in my life; I needed to get my act together concerning my future. I knew "my future" was not just for next week; it was for the rest of my life. GOD showed me how much I needed Him, through His Son, Jesus Christ, to lead me step by step, in following His plan for my life since; I didn't have an idea!

I had not thought much about my future during my time in the Navy. Now I'm asking myself questions like, "What if I get married, and we have children?" I realized these, "what if's" would not always be satisfied with money. I knew I was starting a time in my life that I, and I alone, would be responsible for what I would do and the decisions I would make. Mom and Dad, and their house was only the place I lived when they were responsible for me. When I arrive back in Toronto, and their home, I need to understand, "It was only for a short visit. I could not remain there waiting for someone to come along and offer me a job. I knew it was time for me to start spending more time with GOD and talk to Him about what His plan was, for me. I needed to get back on the road of following His guidance, via His Holy Spirit versus trying to do things my way and going to Him when I was going down for the third time. I then realized I would not be able to take care of my needs without help. I knew He was telling me He would help me if I asked for help and had the faith He could show me what I needed and enable me to do what was required. I realized trying to do it myself, was no longer an option. At that point, I knew I had to follow GOD and His plan for me!

The reality that I was no longer a dependent of my parents, but I was now accountable to GOD and the world for my actions, and I needed to put Him in the "driver's seat" of my life and do it *now*!

Much of what I addressed in chapter 2 was designed to show the things I felt important when I was younger than twelve and then during my high school years. Today as an adult, I see many young children don't care about things like "family history." When my Grandpa McJunkin let me know he was more than willing to share this kind of information with me, I felt he was showing me respect, and he thought I was important to him and our family. I can't help but think many of our children today feel the same way, but some don't recognize it, and others don't know how to express their feelings. Some young people get tied up in false beliefs about our Lord by listening to Satan's self-pronounced profits espouse the falseness of Christianity, the Bible, and GOD Himself. These false concepts will prove to be a major heartbreak for both their Mom and Dad when they see their daughter or son not only pick up on what they observed at home, in their preteen years, and now they are refusing to listen to their parents, not only about the Lord but life in general. They feel they *know* the truth, and it is not what Mom and Dad want them to believe. All too often, many of the Grandpas and Grandmas in the twenty-first century are still working and are not living down the block from their Grandchildren like I was fortunate to experience. Another situation that often exists today that was not as prevalent in my preteen years is, the "one-parent" family. Most often, the one parent is *Mom*, and she is a working mother who is struggling to keep food on the table.

So who is at blame? We can start at any level in our society where we have allowed ourselves to become, led by Satan's demons who sometimes are in our schools, jobs, government and even in certain groups that operate under the banner of a "church." Not to point to any of these groups specifically, but young parents today have a real challenge. I believe in many ways, parents today have a much more massive load to carry than when my wife, Sondra (Grandma), and I had at that stage in our lives. I don't want to imply we did everything right; we were far from being perfect when starting our family. What I am suggesting is we believed, we had Jesus as our Lord and Savior. Today we believe the Bible tells us He wants us to come to Him when we need help and not listen to a so-called friend who has no credentials in knowing what the Bible says. We know we have Jesus as our Lord and Savior because of His words to Thomas,

> I am the way, the truth, and the life, NO ONE comes to the Father, except through ME. (John 14:6)

Many young parents today have never heard those words of Jesus, and neither have their children and maybe neither will ever hear them if Christians remain inside their four walls on Sunday morning and throughout the rest of the week in being a follower of Jesus.

The Bible shows us GOD will not force us to take that step of doing what we know is right. He created us with intelligence enough to make those kinds of decisions ourselves. What GOD will do is *judge* each of us in how we use what He has given us to serve Him in all aspects of life, including rejecting Satan's temptations.

We must pray for our preteens and teenagers to be more responsible for their actions and decisions. They must realize they can no longer blame Mom and Dad for their not doing a better job of teaching them the right things in life. We must pray for our teenage children to see and know what is right and what is wrong. Some may ask, "Why?" We must be able and willing to tell them how their eternal life is at risk. These are things many young people don't seem to think about today. Some don't seem to understand they will be held accountable for their decisions once if not before leaving Mom and Dad's home, Mom and Dad will be judged on how well they performed as parents. If Mom and Dad do not tell their teens and preteens, who will?

If teenagers are *not* attending the church, SS class, and youth group activities while they are still living with their parents, they have two strikes against them already. They should realize the truth in the previous sentence and take advantage of still living at home and attending church on Sunday mornings.

"Mom and Dad do you understand, time to tell your children is running out?"

The following chapters cover a part of my life I thought might be of interest to some of the readers, hoping many of them will still be in their teens or early twenties. I pray it will show what I was willing to do to fulfill my hopes and dreams for the tomorrows of the future, especially when I realized what the alternative offers. I've shared some of my experiences (and mistakes) of the past with some of my grandchildren, and beyond. It was with the hope; they might see life when they are on their own is *not* always a bed of roses. I pray those in my family and other young people that are living in this span of life will see the impact GOD, Jesus Christ and the Holy Spirit can have on their daily walk. All of us must strive to understand what and why we believe the things we believe. We will never be perfect in this world, but we should never quit or give up expanding the understanding of our faith and hope in the Trinity.

GOD will lead us as long as we follow. We have to show GOD (and ourselves) what we are willing to do to understand and receive what the Lord wants to give us. Without Him, I would be lost, have no objectives, and probably be depending on the world to take care of me! Many young people nearing the end of their teens have turned from GOD and His commands, and some will end up in jail or prison. If they admit their sins and ask for forgiveness, He will forgive them. Young people need to understand in choosing to live life without Jesus Christ as their Savior; they will find society is not as forgiving as GOD when it becomes known they served time in jail or prison. This truth alone should be a motivation for teens not to do anything that could put themselves in the position of saying, "I didn't mean it" or "I'm sorry." These are no longer acceptable excuses if you are in your upper teens or older. Having Jesus as your savior will help you in making the right decisions.

I think back to a time in my younger years and realize I had drifted away from GOD and the church. Satan was trying to convince me I didn't need to hear a preacher or be in a Sunday school class on Sunday, but the Holy Spirit convinced me I did. It took some time before I accepted the fact, there is no other way than following GOD's will, and there are not many ways better to know and understand His Will than in His church and Sunday school on Sunday, hearing and studying His Word (Bible).

I recall the many times GOD allowed me to do His will, and I turned away. It was as if I was looking at a giant balancing scale. On one side was all the bad things I had done and missed opportunities to do good, and they were piled quite high. On the other side of the scale was the counterbalance side with the good things I had done in my twenty-plus years of life at that time. The gage was not anywhere close to balancing the bad side. Then GOD seemed to be saying, "While you have focused on the few good things you've done for me, I've been looking at the other side. If you would start focusing on the negative things in your life to ensure you will not repeat them; they will start to fade away."

"You will soon notice the good things on the other side will increase in weight, and the bad things will diminish." GOD then impressed on me: "Only you can make the decision, and whatever it is, YOU will reap the benefits or live with the consequences, throughout eternity."

GOD pointed out, "I do not waste My time listening to excuses and reasons for your failures because you and I both know the truth. When I see you didn't use the talents I gave you to glorify Me, it showed your lack of faith in Me. If this continues, you will find the truth when you come to the fork in the road of "eternal life." You will choose the one that looks more attractive, knowing you will not be able to change. You will have selected the "road" that will take you to your eternal life. The beauty of its entrance is quickly burned away by the fires of hell, and you will then realize, You alone made the decision. It was like having the picture of your life displayed in front of GOD, and you realize it was accurate, and you could not challenge any of what He was seeing."

Today as I think of those terrifying moments we were in the hurricane, that lasted day after day until we were almost back to the States, I can't help but think GOD was showing us He was going to bring all the ship's crew back safe. I feel today, GOD is now telling me my days are a "dwindling few." In some respects, my past was as if I had been on a fast train traveling to so many places and yet to nowhere. My life had been moving so fast, and I was trying to take in everything I could without slowing down. Now it will soon be over and, "What do I have to show for it?"

"Were there more meaningful things to life than what I experienced?" Since the hurricane experience was over a half a century ago, I sometimes smile when thinking about the fear, faith, and finality of our return to the good ole USA. I wonder if GOD may have been giving, at least to other Christian believers and me; a *real* salty baptism in the power of GOD Almighty to remind us to "keep the faith" when we encounter these kinds of events in the future. Whatever it was, I will always remember each day and sleepless nights of our return trip, praise GOD He brought us all back in one piece!

All those memories—some good, some bad, and some were just memories—and I remember thinking, "What are those memories worth today?" I recall feeling a cold chill down my spine, thinking, "What am I going to do tomorrow morning?"

"What am I going to do tomorrow that will impact my future?" I'm not sure if I asked GOD that question then, but if I didn't, it was not too long after returning home, that I did.

Today I see GOD was going to let me become aware of the actual reality in my life; before He would start opening doors of opportunity that I never conceived was possible. He had a plan for me, and He knew how that plan was going to evolve. Unfortunately, I did not! He also knew the lessons I was going to learn because of some of my previous bad decisions. As I was walking West on Highway 54 outside the city limits of Yates Center; I started to see what I had tried to do on my own. I felt the presence of His Holy Spirit within me, saying, "Are you now ready to follow your Lord and Savior?" It was as if I was again standing in front of the church congregation that Sunday morning when I gave my life to Jesus, only this time GOD was asking, "Now, are you ready to be my servant?" I give praise to Him for never giving up on me, and I thank Him for everything good in my life from that moment I invited Jesus Christ into my life as my Lord and Savior back in July 1946.

Reflecting on my going into the Navy, I realize I had not matured in my Spiritual growth in serving GOD through His Son, Jesus Christ. Satan planted seeds of excuses in my mind that always seem to blame the small church I was a member, before going in the Navy. Wrong! When I joined the Navy, I knew when I did things that Mrs. Carson (my SS teacher) had taught me were wrong, and I knew they were wrong.

I had not developed the faith and hope at the time I joined the Navy to stand up against all those temptations. I feel GOD was saying, "I have a plan for you, and when you get your act together, you're going to feel bad when you realize all the blessings you missed." And that is what happened. However, I truly believe that I would have never grown in faith if I had remained in Toronto, Kansas, where my environment would not have changed. GOD knew that, and I feel He let me try to do it my way until I understood I couldn't; then I would see how much I needed Him and how much He loved me. He knew His plan for me would come about, and when it did, He knew I would realize how much time I had wasted in trying to do it my way.

I missed out on a lot of blessings in my early life. But I do not doubt that GOD gave me His promise of eternal life with Him that morning when I stood before the congregation, confessing my sins and asking Jesus Christ to come into my life as my Lord and Savior. One of the things that even today amazes me is how He operates. I know He does not wear a wristwatch! Time to our Lord is nothing like it is to man.

I was aware of this even before I became a teenager, but I didn't understand it's significance. GOD gave me an insight into the value of doing certain things, like saving money, in my preteen years. After being discharged from the Navy and many years later, I saw how the Lord led me to save some of the money I had worked for versus spending it on things I didn't need, just because "I had the money to do it." Even today, He shows me the value of planning for that emergency with the money Sondra, and I saved or invested for a significant need. After my separation from the Navy, I found, "I had some real needs," and I also found I had the money to take care of them. "Thank you, Father." I was beginning to see the beneficial result of my earlier savings.

I recalled a time before I finished boot camp, and I had made new friends and heard all kind of stories of how other young men my age lived during their school-age years. I realized, for the first time that, "My family was poor, and I was the son of a 'poor' family, compared to many other young men my age." However, I never thought of my family being poor. GOD showed me when my family could not buy for me what I wanted; He showed me the value of earning and saving money that would enable me to take care of the "things" I needed in the future. It was then I often decided I didn't want to spend my money to buy all of those beautiful "things." And guess what? I found that life continued. Throughout our married life, with the help of my wife, Sondra, we have been able to handle our financial needs, savings, and investments by including GOD as our number 1 financial adviser.

In my retirement years, I kid Sondra when she says, "I don't have a blouse to go with these slacks or skirt, and I saw one at the women's fashion store that is a perfect match." Even though I kid her about shopping, I admire her for her shopping wisdom. If it is something, she or I need she looks for quality first and then looks for the best price. Again, I think back at those early years when I knew my parents didn't have the money to buy me everything I wanted. I knew if I wanted something, I needed to work for it. In working for my money, I found I didn't need some of those things Dad and Mom were not able to buy, and I decided I didn't need to spend my money to buy them. And the sun continued to rise in the east.

After I returned to civilian life, the above "habit" remained a part of my lifestyle. The first car I bought was a one-year-old Ford, and I paid cash for it. It was also the last time I bought a secondhand family vehicle. Years later, I did buy an old pickup, for a couple of hundred dollars, to go between home and work when I was a supervisor in Boone, Colorado. I sold it for what I paid for it two years later.

The second car, a Mercury, the third car, a Ford were both new and paid for with cash from my earlier savings.,

I did take out a short-term loan from the AT&T company credit union and paid it off early by double paying the payments with the money we were saving when we were starting our family. We could have paid cash, but Sondra was expecting our first child, and I chose to take a small loan with very low interest just in case she had some problems with her pregnancy that had to be taken care of at the time they occurred.

From that time on we bought no less than eight new cars and pickups including Ford, Chevrolet, Mercury, Lincoln (demo), and a KIA. We paid for each of them with cash we had saved or invested. I remember when my job required me to wear a business suit, I only had one such suit. In no time I had four suits and four pairs of dress shoes, all paid for with cash. I know the above sounds like I am bragging, but it was just the opposite, it was all do to the guidance of my Lord and Savior.

Somewhat to my surprise, I found it rather easy to continue to save money after I returned to civilian life. Once I started working for the Santa Fe RR, I saw it was *not* that hard to save a portion of my paycheck each week. It may have been my Scottish blood, but I have never felt I needed to find a way to spend money because I had more than my cost of living demanded. Each time I would save some money, the results were the same as the first time—that is, I had the satisfaction that I had more money to take care of an unexpected need than I had the previous month. That was a comforting feeling I had not experienced before.

Before starting my job with the Santa Fe RR, I first decided I would go to college under the GI Bill, after my tour of duty in the Navy but I soon found I could not adjust to college life and all those "children" in my freshman classes! It was then I decided I needed a job *now*, and if college was in my future, I could always do it then. Believe it or not, this decision turned out to be a blessing as you will see later. I was interviewed in Topeka, Kansas, by members of the

Santa Fe RR personnel department and was offered a job in the city of Fort Madison, Iowa. I accepted the job offer and after my first two weeks on the job, if someone had asked me what I thought about the location, I probably would have shrugged my shoulders and said, "At least I have a job."

I was again going to learn a lesson that we all should learn as early as possible in life. All Christians would agree that GOD knows everything. We also need to recognize that He expects us to use the brain He has given us, especially when we are talking with Him. In chapter 7, you will see I did need a job, even if I had remained in college. However, I failed to acknowledge the other things I would need once I found a new job.

In my moments of need, I assumed, "GOD knew all the other things I would need and would automatically take care of them. I just wanted Him to guide me to a job and then take care of everything else." I'm about to reveal how GOD showed me He has a sense of humor in teaching us know-it-all humans the facts of life.

It is somewhat amusing now, but soon after I arrived in Fort Madison and began my "GOD-given" job with the Santa Fe RR, I soon encountered something that proved *not* to be the most enjoyable and pleasant experience I would have in that city. When it happened, I did not recognize it was an experience He may have been planning for me for some time. When we don't think through our needs and ask the Lord for all we require, we can encounter some disappointing results. In His time, He showed me Fort Madison, Iowa, was the place He had chosen to provide me both good and great things I needed then and throughout the rest of my life.

Chapter 7

A New Job—In Fort Madison, Iowa

No one is in charge of your happiness,
but GOD first and you second!

As I indicated in chapter 6, GOD opened a door of opportunity for me by giving me what I asked for, a job.

GOD was now going to show me some of the good things and some of the not so good things I would experience in the months following my move to Fort Madison. Some of these may be of value to the reader if he or she is starting on their own and recently began thinking what their total needs will be, especially if they feel their relationship with GOD is not what it should be.

After I had been on my job with the Santa Fe RR for several weeks, I felt things were not turning out the way I had expected. On my arrival in Fort Madison I checked in with Mr. Banks, our wire chief. He informed me he had arranged for me to rent a room at a boarding house that many of the train crews used when they had a layover from Chicago or Kansas City. That was good because I never even thought about a place to live. I immediately noticed the men on the train crews were all much older than me, and they were in and out in one night. Other residents in the boarding house consisted of a group of single women…all in their seventies and eighties! I think "the straw that broke the camel's back" (and my view of where I was sleeping each night), came one evening when I was about to go out to eat.

I heard a knock on my door and when I opened it I saw it was the elderly lady that I had seen go in and out of the room next to mine. With a smile on her face, she asked, "Would you like to come over to my apartment for a cup of coffee and we can watch the *Lone Ranger* show, together?" Just getting out of the Navy and having heard about all the come-on pitches, I must say, I was in shock at what I had just heard. For a moment I couldn't think what to say in reply to her question. I'm sure I probably stuttered as I was searching for an answer, and finally, I muttered, "I'm sorry, but I have a dinner engagement, and I'm already a little late." Her reply, "Oh, I was so looking forward to the two of us spending the evening together and get better acquainted. Maybe tomorrow?"

As I recall, I didn't eat that evening but spent the rest of the day and several following evenings, looking for another place to live. It was sometime later that I realized I did not specify in my prayer for a new job that I would like to be close to the Kansas City or Wichita areas. I guess I just assumed GOD knew I wanted to stay close to either of these two cities and, at that time, I sure didn't understand why I had to end up in Fort Madison, Iowa!

GOD answered my request as I asked it—that is, He gave me a job, albeit in Fort Madison, Iowa. I would later find out the job was only a tool to get me where He wanted me, for a different reason that had nothing to do with my position on the railroad. Although I didn't know at that time, I soon would be leaving Fort Madison with a gift from GOD that would prove to be far greater than any job I would ever have.

After starting work in the "relay office" with Santa Fe, I remember one of my first instructions from the wire chief (Mr. Banks) was, "Be very careful saying anything you might be tempted to say to or about anyone that works here. The same thing is true when talking with people at the diner. Odds are the person you are talking with is related to the person you are making a comment about, who also works for the railroad." The dinner was an eating place across the tracks from the "relay office" that catered to the railroaders. I found what Mr. Banks told me was right when I heard one of the other operators commenting on someone and the person he was talking with said, "Oh, he is Jack Simmons's brother-in-law, and he works down at the "switching terminal."

This experience reminded me of how GOD's Word is obvious, in that He is the one and only judge of humanity. Even though I had accepted Jesus Christ as my Lord and Savior, the advice Mr. Banks had shared with me, caused me to think about how I had drifted away from serving GOD the way I should. And I knew I needed to focus on getting back on the road of righteousness, where He wanted me to be.

Aside from not being too impressed with my new job, I was somewhat disappointed when I found that all but one of my coworkers were married, and he was going steady. It looked like I was on my own. I knew GOD had given me another opportunity by providing me a job; at least that's what I thought at that time. I don't know if it was the experience I had in the Navy or the fact I was the youngest operator in the relay office, but I kept asking myself, "Is this really what I want to be doing five years from now?" Even though the job paid a good salary, there were two "apprentices" that had more service than me. One had over two years' service, was qualified, and still didn't have a permanent job. I kept telling myself, "I'm making good money, I'm single, and I don't have any loans to pay off, so don't complain."

There were, however, a few somewhat humorous moments that made life bearable at work. One centered around our wire chief (Mr. Banks). He was a "gung-ho" believer in the Santa Fe RR. He didn't want anyone to talk to the operators when they were copying "train orders." That was a good rule because the railroad cars all had different ID numbers that were about seven or ten digits long. If even one car number was wrong, it could cause a lot of problems if it arrived in the wrong location.

One of my first assignments in the relay office was with (Sally), the lady whose responsibility, among other job assignments, was to ensure the new operators were trained to get the "train orders" delivered timely and properly for the train crews to pick up on time at the designated "pickup boxes." One of the crew members would often be in the area when the apprentice dropped off their orders, and this would allow them to meet and get to know each other.

Sally's work location was directly behind the wire chief's desk. If there were any questions about an order, the wire chief was only a step away and available to answer any questions. Soon after starting my training on the "order desk," I noticed all the "train orders" were signed by "Louie." One day, curiosity got the best of me, and I asked Sally, after picking up an order to be taken to the "pickup box."

"Who is this Louie? Does he work here?"

Sally quickly put her "trigger finger" to her lips and pointed to Mr. Banks! At that moment I felt I probably was working my last day for the Santa Fe RR.

The name Louie just didn't fit the looks or personality of Mr. Banks. I never did find out how he acquired the name unless it may have been his first name. Mr. Banks also had a unique habit of referring to an apprentice as "young man." Now, even though I was a few years from drawing Social Security, after spending a tour of duty in the Navy, I didn't exactly feel it a compliment to be called, "Young man," even though I was only twenty-one at the time. But it came with the job, and I didn't let it get to me, especially knowing the other two apprentices were older than me.

Mr. Banks wore glasses, and whenever he was talking with one of the operators, he had a habit of looking "over" the top of his glasses. The glasses did seem to give him a certain amount of "domination" over their conversations. Once when Mr. Banks had gone to the restroom, one of the operators, who also wore glasses, slid them to the tip of his nose, turned to the operator next to him and looking over the top of his glasses said, "Am I, in any way distracting you from your being able to copy a train order?" Unknown to the operator, Mr. Banks had returned from the restroom and was standing directly behind him.

I was still on break at the time, but Sally told me the next day that Mr. Banks called the operator to his desk and, looking over the top of his glasses, asked, "Do you think I, in any way, distract you or any of the other operators, in their ability to copy a train order properly?"

The operator replied, "No, sir."

With that, Mr. Banks said, "I'm glad to hear that, and you can now go back and do the job you are being paid to do."

It was about this time when I felt GOD was opening a second "door of opportunity" for me. I think this was when GOD started implementing "the plan" he had for me. First, He was going to show me why He led me to Fort Madison, Iowa. I realized He gave me what I had asked for—that is, a job. But I asked myself more than once, "Why did GOD send me to Fort Madison, Iowa?"

I had never been here, and I didn't know anyone here. The fact it was in Fort Madison was not because I requested it. Unbeknown to me, GOD was about to answer my question, and I was about to see He was going to give me the second-best gift He had or ever will give me. I need to point out the first, and the best gift GOD gave me was His Son, Jesus Christ, as my Lord and Savior. Now I'll tell you about His second gift.

My first location in Fort Madison did not fit my lifestyle. I think GOD, with a smile on His face, said, "Okay, now I'm going to give you what you need, but failed to ask me to provide. I'm going to move you to the other side of Fort Madison, across the road from the state prison." He arranged this through one of the operators at work who lived at this location with his wife and children. He knew I was looking for a different place to live and told me there was one apartment vacant in their building, and I might want to check it out. It was a two-story "barracks"-style house. Its owners were two wonderful people who had no children. Their names were Mamie and Joe Jones. On looking at the vacant apartment, I felt it would be a much better place to live than where I was living at that time.

The following will pick up at that time in my life after I had met the owners and checked out the vacant apartment. I was very impressed with it as well as with the owners, Mamie and Joe. I took the apartment and moved in the following weekend.

You will now see how GOD started to use Mamie to be more than a friend; she became a person I'll always remember. I'm not sure she realized it, but I believe GOD used her as His instrument to fulfill a specific part of His plan for me.

About the second month after moving into Mamie and Joe's apartment, Mamie, with a smile on her face, said to me one day, "Joe and I were talking last night, and we decided we might adopt you as our son, the one we never had."

I laughed and said, "Okay, Mom, so that means I don't have to pay any rent, right?"

Mamie, who was as sharp as anyone I've ever met, replied with no hesitation, "No, son, as a matter of fact, Dad and I were thinking, now that you have a good job, we might raise your rent."

In all the time I lived in Mamie and Joe's apartment, they both treated me more like their son, than a renter, in more ways than one.

I had the front apartment on the ground level. Even though I had no choice, since it was the last vacancy, it would have been my first choice even if there had been more units available. I didn't have to pass any of the other apartments to get to mine, and aside from a little noise occasionally, it felt like I was the only renter in the complex. The other renters were married couples, and most had preschool-age children. After getting acquainted with everyone, I felt like one of the family.

Things were about to start moving faster

I continued to ask myself if the job with the Santa Fe RR was the job I wanted as a lifelong career—that is, "Is this the job I want to be doing five years from now?" Each time, my answer was the same—that is, "I don't think so!" I tried to focus on the nice place where I was now living and people like Mamie and Joe, who had become good friends. For some reason, I couldn't get that question out of my mind. I felt GOD (maybe with that smile still on His face, thinking about my experience with the next-door neighbor at the boarding house.) was now opening a second "door of opportunity."

Number 1: GOD gave me a job, that was in Iowa. Why in Iowa? I had only asked for a job, and He provided me with one that was hundreds of miles from where I called home. Were there no good jobs available, closer to Kansas? GOD reminded me that I only asked for a job! I began to feel GOD was telling me, "I want you and all my children to understand there is nothing too small or insignificant to ask for My help, and when you don't, you will often see your lack of asking can bring about the lack of having all you need." I felt that was true in my life since I moved to Iowa. I was in my early twenties at that time, and I'm eighty-five at this writing, and I still remember, almost verbatim, the invitation I received from my next-door neighbor in my first apartment. I asked myself more than once, "Why didn't I ask GOD to lead me to a place He wanted me to live?" Since I didn't ask for His help, He led me to a place that would teach me a lesson. I know now I have no one to blame except myself for not talking with Him about all the things I needed.

Number 2. After I saw the error in my actions, GOD seemed to tell me, "Okay, I'm now going to lead you to a place that you will like."

And living in Mamie and Joe's apartment was more than I expected. It became a place I enjoyed coming home to each evening. The other families living at Mamie and Joe's were young couples, some with preschool children. They all seemed to have a much happier view of life than the elderly residents at the boarding house. I thanked GOD for taking care of my location problem. Now I was going to find out why Fort Madison, Iowa, was the place GOD wanted me to be. It was not just to get to know Mamie and Joe and see the role they would play in my life. I was about to experience, with Mamie's "help," something that would be a blessing to me throughout the rest of my life.

But I still had a job that didn't seem to offer me real satisfaction in its working environment or job security. I can't say for sure, but looking back at that time, I feel GOD may have been teaching me an all-important lesson in my prayer life, and He wanted this to "soak in" before I moved on.

I first realized I asked for a job (period). I didn't specify what kind or any specific location, only a job. I didn't think about what Jesus tells us in Matthew 7:7,

> Ask, and you will receive; seek, and you will find; knock, and it shall be opened to you.

At that point, I had only "asked." I then found I had to "seek" for a better place to live. Then I found GOD gave me what I needed. I felt He was showing me the importance of looking at the "big picture" as to what I wanted (needed) in my future, not just what I desired next week. As I look back at the things I asked for, He took care of each one as I asked Him. But I still had the same "job," and it was not one I felt I would be satisfied with, in the future.

I like to think GOD does have a sense of humor, and sometimes I feel He is saying to himself, "I have given humanity a brain to plan and think things out, but all too often they only look at and ask for tomorrow, not the future. To teach all humanity to trust Me, not only for "a thing," but for "all things," I want him to have. I will continue to answer their requests as they ask, knowing after going through days of frustrations and needless discouragements, knocking themselves out, thinking, "Why am I still not satisfied?" It was at this point in my life I seemed to get GOD's message, and I asked, "Please GOD, give me the job you know I need." (Bingo, the right question!) It was then He opened that second door of opportunity. He was now going to answer the question I should have asked earlier, and His answer was going to include more than just a new job, it was going to include the help I would need the rest of my life. It would be something I will thank Him to the day He calls me home.

With my move to the new apartment on "the other side of town," GOD seemed to be telling me, "Since you haven't asked me for your future needs, I'm going to provide the nucleus of those needs, but you are going to have to start working with me more than you have in the past. And remember, you owe me one!"

Number 3: GOD was now going to show me the real reason He provided me a job with the Santa Fe RR and why He sent me to Fort Madison, Iowa.

As I recall I had not been in my new home over four or five months when one day, Ms. Mamie was working in her front yard when I arrived from work. I had come to realize; Mamie was a very outgoing woman. She always had something to discuss. She was also a woman that would tell you precisely what she thought, even if you hadn't asked her. During the time I had been a renter, I feel Mamie's honestly was why we had also become terrific friends.

As I opened the door of my car, Mamie greeted me with a, "Hello, Mr. Lloyd." Before I could return the greeting, she continued, "I think we know each other well enough that we can talk frankly." I laughed and said, "Okay, what have I done that you are going to kick me out of my apartment?"

She laughed and said, "Oh no, it's nothing like that. But I've noticed you don't seem to have any friends, at least any I've seen."

I replied, "Oh, I've met several people that I consider my friends, and I go to West Point (Iowa) about every evening and roller skate." West Point was a town just a few miles from Fort Madison.

Well, that was not a good enough answer for Mamie. She continued, "One of my good friends has a daughter who graduated from high school in Marceline, Missouri, last year. Her father was transferred to Fort Madison before her senior year was over and she remained with some friends of the family. After graduating, she is now living with her family and working at the Schaeffer Pen company, here in Fort Madison. Since she moved only a few months ago, she has not met many young people. I've met her, and she is such a sweet young lady." I think I replied by saying something like, "She sounds like a nice young lady, but I'm not interested in getting serious or going steady at this time in my life." Then I patted her on the shoulder, laughed and said, "I'll keep this young lady in mind in case I'm looking for someone to take to the movie some night."

A few nights later, the same type of meeting in the front yard took place.

Mamie asked, "Do you know anything about horses?" I knew this was a set up for something Mamie wanted to discuss and it wasn't anything concerning my knowledge of horses. I replied, "I know horses have four legs, and a long tail and people even ride them. Why do you ask?"

"Well, have you ever heard of the annual Fort Madison rodeo parade?"

"No, I don't think I have."

"It's one of the big annual events in Fort Madison. Many of the Rodeo people who have not accumulated enough points to qualify for the Madison Square Garden Rodeo in New York, participate in our rodeo in hopes they can win enough additional points to qualify for the big rodeo in New York. The merchants in Fort Madison sponsor young ladies to ride horses that ranchers make available for the annual rodeo queen's parade."

"Oh, do you remember me telling you about my friend's daughter a few days ago?"

"Yes," I replied, knowing we are getting down to the real reason Mamie was waiting for me in her front yard.

"I just found out from her mother that her daughter has been selected to ride one of the horses in the parade."

"She was selected because she had a horse when she lived in Missouri and rode in some of the parades there." Mamie was on a roll, "Each horse has a number in the parade, and my friend told me the number of the horse her daughter will be riding is number 25. I hope you will be able to see the parade and this very nice young lady and how well she can ride a horse. Remember, number 25."

"Okay, Mamie, I'll try to make it, and if I do, I'll let you know my thoughts of the parade."

"I know you will enjoy the event and the parade and remember her horse's number is 25!" Well, I knew I better go to the parade, or I might find my clothes in the front yard the next day.

On the day of the parade, I was surprised at the number of people lining the street the parade would follow. I found a good location that enabled me to see Mamie's "Wonder Woman" with no obstructions in front of me. As I established a good vantage point, I heard and saw the marching band coming down the street. I'm not sure how they selected the position each horse and rider would take, but I immediately knew it was not by numeric order when I saw number 18 followed by number 5. But the search was short-lived because I spotted number 25 was now in sight. The horse was beautiful; it kept moving its head up and around and always seemed to be blocking my having a good view of its rider. Then I saw what I knew was a very experienced rider, in full control. Her calmness seemed to be passed to the horse because they both looked as if they were enjoying being in the parade. I said, "Wow," knowing I was looking at one of the prettiest, self-confident young ladies I had ever seen. Dale Evens would have been proud to ride alongside this young lass from Missouri.

On my way back to my apartment, I think I asked GOD to have Mamie be in the front yard when I arrived. As I pulled in the driveway, there were Mamie and Joe, both acting as if they had no idea the parade was over, and I would soon be coming home. I kept telling myself, "Don't let Mamie know how impressed you were with the No. 25's rider." I had no more than opened my car door when Mamie came up with a grin on her face saying, "Well, what did you think of the parade? Wasn't I right about her being beautiful?"

"Yes, you were, number 25 was one of the best-looking horses in the parade."

"No," Mamie replied with a firm voice, "I mean the girl."

"Oh, she was nice-looking too."

Mamie said, "Lloyd, you are something else. I don't know what I'm going to do with you."

Guess who I'm about to meet

Two days after my discussion with Mamie, she (unknown to the lady horse rider or me) arranged for us to meet in Mamie's home. Neither of us knew what Mamie was doing. But as the afternoon continued, Mamie found it necessary to leave us to take care of some things that, "Would probably take about an hour." I think the young lady, whom I now knew as Sondra (spelled with an *o*), was as embarrassed as I was. But as we talked about the parade and how she had been selected to be one of the riders, I found the opportunity to ask if she would like to go to the movies the following evening.

With a slight pause, she asked, "What is playing?"

Without thinking, I replied, "I'm not sure, but I understand it's an excellent movie."

"Okay, I don't have any plans for tomorrow evening."

The following days, weeks and months went by fast. Sondra knew how to skate, and we went to the West Point skating rink, almost every night it was open. The exception was when we went to a movie. Some would say it was a coincidence when we found we were both Christians, and we both belonged to the same church denomination. Today we both feel it was all part of GOD's plan for Sondra to move from Missouri and me to move from Kansas so both of us could meet in Fort Madison, Iowa! Now GOD is going to show us what He will do when we follow His commands.

Today Sondra and I both feel the above was required so I would meet one of Mamie's friend's daughter, whose name was Sondra. GOD had also sent Sondra to Fort Madison after she graduated from high school in Missouri. Now with both of us being in Fort Madison enabled her to be with her parents again after her father's transfer to Fort Madison several months earlier. Beyond all that, and our being unaware of the fact the two of us were where GOD wanted us. GOD could *now* complete His plan, involving both Sondra and me.

PART 3

Chapter 8

The Start of Thirty-Plus Years with AT&T (First Half)

Life with ATT began on January 28, 1957.

I soon found in my job, as in life, "real success depends more on our walk than our talk."

Things started to move faster when I received a call from Dad one evening. He wanted to tell me about a conversation he had the day before with one of his long-ago high school friends. His name was Royal Kerns. Royal worked for AT&T and was a manager in their Kansas City office. In this chapter, I will explain how Dad's phone call led me to an open door of opportunity that would make a significant change in the rest of my career and my life. I give GOD all the praise and glory for the many wonderful things He was going to be providing me throughout the following thirty plus years.

It was Dad's call that led me to the job I had, unknowingly been searching for, plus a bonus blessing that together would make a major change in the rest of my life. Dad told me Mr. Kerns had asked about me and what I was doing. In telling Royal, I had served a "hitch" in the Navy and was currently working for the Santa Fe RR in their relay office in Fort Madison, Iowa. What surprised me was when Dad told me he also shared with Royal the following, "I don't think he is very satisfied in his job with Santa Fe as it relates to job satisfaction and job security." The following will show why I give

GOD all the praise for the doors of opportunity that only He could and did open for me.

Now number 4 (continuing from chapter 7): After weeks and months dating each other and finding we had many likes and dislikes that were the same, as well as the hopes for our future. It was at that point I still was asking myself that same question, that had plagued me from the first month I started working for the Santa Fe RR—that is, "Is this the job I want to be doing five years from now?"

At that point, Sondra and I agreed: enough talk, it was time for action. Sondra and I took a bold step in faith that GOD would take care of us in our future as husband and wife.

We had been talking about getting married for some time before Dad's call, as I mentioned in chapter 7. Once we agreed our *faith* was in GOD, and we felt we would get married sometime in the future, we then agreed, if we thought we would get married, someday, "What better way to show our *faith* in GOD than to get married now. Trust in Him to lead us on the pathway He wanted us, as wife and husband, to follow. That evening I filled Sondra in on my conversation with Dad earlier that day. When I took her home, I proposed marriage to her, and she accepted. As I recall we had the best men, bridesmaids, and preacher all lined up in a matter of days along with all the other requirements for our wedding.

On November 24, 1956, in the First Christian Church in Burlington, Iowa, where Sondra had attended years before her family moved to Marceline, Sondra and I were married.

We spent the rest of the day in Burlington as Mr. and Mrs. McJunkin; discussing our future. We shared our hopes and desires and knew they were all based on our Christian *faith* in GOD, believing He would provide us an opportunity for a better job and a better future than our trying to make it on our own.

GOD then led me to call the AT&T number the next day, that Royal Kerns had given Dad. I didn't realize it at the time, but this was our first test of *faith* in GOD as a married couple. And guess what, I was able to arrange an interview with the AT&T district manager, Mr. Roy Middleton. I honestly don't think we were aware of the importance of my getting a job offer that we both would enjoy. Today I feel it was faith in our Lord and Savior, Jesus Christ, believing He would guide us through the rest of our lives to places and experiences we never dreamed would happen.

Significant changes were starting to happen, and life was becoming much more exciting:

The three examples I listed in chapter 7 seemed to be more evident now:

Number 1: GOD gave me what I asked for—that is, a job.

Number 2: I saw the error in my decision of not asking GOD for all the things I needed in addition to a job. So He sent me to a place He wanted me to be. There I met Sondra, and we started dating. We found we had many things in common.

Number 3: GOD was now going to show me the real reason He provided me a job with the Santa Fe RR. Why He sent me to Fort Madison, Iowa, to complete His plan that involved both Sondra and me.

Even though we didn't know each other when we first arrived in Fort Madison, GOD had a plan for us as a married couple. GOD brought us to a place He wanted us so He could complete His plan and show He can do all things, even those that involved two young people like Sondra and me.

I thought later, "How would we have felt if I didn't get a job offer from AT&T?" I don't recall exactly when and what I said, but I'm sure I asked GOD to take care of all our plans, this time, according to His desire. And I believe my getting a job with AT&T was part of His plan. Throughout the remainder of this book, you will see what GOD will do when we don't try to get ahead of His plan. Today I feel it was faith in our Lord and Savior, Jesus Christ, and our believing that GOD would guide us through the rest of our lives to places and experiences we never dreamed would happen.

I prayed for GOD to provide me a job offer with AT&T! If that came about, Sondra and I knew we would have to move and find a place to live within the Kansas City District. Once settled in our new location, and hopefully, engaged in a new and exciting job that I liked; my searching for a new job would be over. I will cover more about our married life in the following chapters and tell how GOD, through His Son, Jesus Christ has made all the difference in both of our lives.

I found my "habit" of saving some of my money while in the Navy, along with the money I saved in mowing yards during my junior high years, plus a portion of the money I earned delivering newspapers; my wife and I were about to realize the benefits of that habit. The results of my saving some of my lawn mowing money from my younger years would now enable us to pay cash for our real needs as opposed to taking out a loan and start going in debt before I had a chance to get settled in my new civilian job.

I sometimes have a "flashback" and recall when I would say *no* to our children's requests for things we knew they didn't need or would not use many of the things after the new wore off and guess what? They found jobs in their high school years and earned money to buy things they first asked their mother and me to buy. I was always proud of them when they started learning the value of "saving today for the things they might want or need tomorrow"! When they bought what they wanted, I noticed quite often; they didn't want as much. Also, when they bought certain items, they took care of them because they understood what it cost them.

I often think of those early years when I knew my parents didn't have money to buy me everything I felt I needed. It was then I realized that if I wanted something, I had to be willing to earn or work for it. I believe GOD led me through each hard-to-understand experience to show me, at a very young age, life will not always be a "bed of roses." I was told the scripture in Sunday school where Jesus told His disciples that man would never experience anything close to GOD's power when He said, "With man, this is impossible, but with GOD, all things are possible" (Matthew 19:26). GOD is the ultimate answer to all our needs.

All humanity must realize we are here on earth, *first*, to glorify GOD through our *faith* in His Son, Jesus Christ, as our Lord and Savior. In doing this, we will endure many trials and temptations. However, if we follow His commands, He will bring us through even the worst of experiences throughout our time on earth, and when it's time for Him to bring us to our eternal home in heaven, He will do that, as well. At that time, we will clearly understand the true meaning of "With GOD, all things are possible."

Thinking back to the phone call, Dad made to me that I believe turned out to be the start of GOD's plan for the next half-century of my life. I believe that all good things do come from GOD, often by way of humanity. That one additional comment Dad said to Royal Kerns on their talk the day before Dad called me, and told me what he said—that is, "I don't think he feels the job he has is one that has job security or one he is interested in." As I mentioned earlier, Dad was a man of very few words, and those last few words were not what I would expect he would say unless asked explicitly by Royal." Between Dad's phone call and my retirement, GOD has given Sondra and me so many beautiful things, including, at this writing, our three wonderful children who brought into our family more than three times three the number of grandchildren, multiple great-grandchildren and at least two great-great-grandchildren. After close to half a century later, I still feel GOD implanted those words in Dad's mind to tell Royal, and with that GOD took control. "He is always good, *all* the time if we have *faith* and *hope* in Him!"

I could understand everything Dad told Royal about my being in the Navy and was now working for the Santa Fe RR. But I can't see him saying those last few words about my dissatisfaction with the job security. Those last words were not what Dad would say because he was "truly" a man of few words. "Could GOD have put those additional words in Dad's thoughts at that moment?" Whatever it was, it seemed to prompt Royal to tell Dad that AT&T was currently hiring in its operations department. Royal then gave Dad the telephone number of the manager in the AT&T office in Kansas City and told him, "If your son thinks he might be interested in working for AT&T, and if his job in the Navy dealt with communications, he might give them a call. And the rest is history.

Hearing what Dad said, my first thought was, "This looks like a 'GOD thing' if I ever saw one."

As I mentioned earlier, I called AT&T the next morning, and talked with the district manager's secretary and told her why I was calling, and Mr. Kerns suggested I call.

She replied with, "Oh, Mr. Kerns recommended you? He's such a nice man."

"If you give me your number, we'll have one of our managers call you, no later than tomorrow." I gave her my number, thanked her and hung up, thinking I may not hear anymore from them and, should that be, I would take that as meaning, "I should stay with Santa Fe." Today I feel it was faith in our Lord and Savior, Jesus Christ, believing He would guide me through the rest of my life. It also resulted in His giving me my wonderful wife and a beautiful family of two girls and a boy. It has been a lifelong experience of living in parts of our great country that many only see on TV. We lived in places and had experiences we never dreamed would happen. That and so much more is what GOD did for me that started with a phone call.

Early the next day, I was not only surprised but felt fortunate that I was still at my apartment when the phone rang. Usually, I would have been on my way to work. When I answered the phone, I was more than surprised to hear the man on the other end, informing me he was one of the plant managers at the AT&T offices in KC.

As we talked, he said, "It sounds like you have a lot of experience that we could use in our test rooms. Would you be interested in coming down for an interview?" Without any hesitation, I said, "Yes, I would." We set a date and time that fit in with my schedule for the following Monday.

During the time I had been with Santa Fe, I had become good friends with one of the other apprentices (Bob) who also was not satisfied with his future with Santa Fe. In our discussion during the break that morning, I told him about the call with AT&T and the interview I had the following Monday in Kansas City. I no more than finished when Bob said, "You know what? I have been talking with Frontier Airlines Corp office in Kansas City about a job with them, and they told me to give them a call when I would be able to come down for an interview."

"How about me trying to arrange a meeting with them next Monday and if I can, we can drive down together?"

My response was short, "That sounds great."

Bob made a call and was able to set up an interview for two hours after mine on the same Monday. Since he was familiar with the streets in KC and his wife was also interested in getting a job, hopefully with the same company her husband would be working for, she also wanted to go with us. Bob offered to take his car, and I offered to buy the gas. We were two happy campers at that moment.

On our trip to Kansas City, we almost had a wreck. A car tried to pass us on a two-lane road going up a slight incline when another car came over the hill in his lane and forced him to swing over in front of our car. Fortunately, everyone made it without any crashes, but Bob's wife about broke my eardrum with her scream.

We still arrived in KC on time, but a little shaky from our "almost accident." Bob dropped me off at the AT&T office with a few minutes to spare. I found the district manager's office without any problems.

When I arrived and introduced myself to the district manager's secretary, who greeted me with a smile and said, "Good morning, Mr. McJunkin, Mr. Middleton is expecting you. Let me tell him you are here."

To my surprise, Mr. Middleton came out, shook my hand, and invited me into his office. After the general questions like, "Did you have a nice trip down? How is the new bride, and what does she think about the prospects of moving to this part of the country?"

My answers were equally general, but I didn't mention our almost accident. I recalled when talking to the supervisor in setting up my interview that I mentioned I had married the woman of my dreams a few weeks before. I guess this was passed on to Mr. Middleton since one of his questions related to what my wife felt about a possible move.

When I told him, "That won't be a problem since she was born and raised in Missouri."

He laughed and said, "Well, that takes care of what sometimes can cause some serious problems."

We both laughed and then he started asking about my time and duties in the Navy, where I grew up and other things I had done.

Then he said, "I understand you know Royal Kerns?"

I told him I had met Royal, and he and my dad were good friends from their high school days.

At that point, Mr. Middleton said, "Royal is one of the best managers in my district. He knows his job inside and out, and he is one of the best-liked people in the district."

With that, he said, "I've notified my four plant managers to talk with you and explain what their area of responsibilities are and each of them will give you a chance to ask any questions you may have as they show you their area of operation."

Then I noticed he wrote a few words on a little sheet of paper and attached it to the top sheet on a clipboard. He then asked his secretary to have Mr. Lane come to his office and escort me around the various plant office locations.

When Mr. Lane arrived, Mr. Middleton gave him the clipboard and said to me, "This is Chief Lane, he is our transmission chief and will take you to his department and explain what they do. If you have *any* questions, be sure to ask them. After you are through visiting all four of our plant departments, you will be brought back to my office, and we can determine what the next step will be."

As we left and were walking down the hallway, I noticed Mr. Lane glance at the clipboard and looked at the note Mr. Middleton had written. He then looked up and said, "You know Royal Kerns?"

"Yes, he is a longtime friend of my dad."

Chief Lane said, "He is a very nice man." He then took me around his area and explained their responsibilities.

In no time at all, we were through, and he said, "If you don't have any more questions, I will take you over to Mr. Brown's office."

I repeated this procedure three more times, and I noticed that as each chief took the clipboard and read the district manager's note, their next comment was almost the same as the previous chief had asked—that is, "Oh, you know Royal Kerns? He's a very nice man." I wondered later if my knowing Royal Kerns had as much influence on me getting a job offer as my experience in the Navy. I was told a few years later by one of the plant chiefs that had escorted me around his department during my interview; the note Mr. Middleton had written and attached to the clipboard said, "Recommended by Royal Kerns!"

What, if any, impact the note had on my getting a job offer, I'm not sure, but I know it didn't hurt. I later told Dad about the comments the district manager and each of his "chiefs" had made about Royal, and Dad's comment was, "Royal is a real nice man."

I also noticed at the end of each department I visited; the chief would write a comment on the "sign-off" sheet on the clipboard, before giving it to the next "chief." After I had visited each department, I was escorted back to Mr. Middleton's office.

He scanned the "sign-off sheet" the chiefs had written on, and his first statement was, "It seems you made a good impression on all my chiefs."

Then he asked, "What do you think about our operation?"

I told him I was very impressed with everything I saw and heard. I told him I had no idea the telephone company was responsible for so many different areas and types of communications that ranged from customer service to providing unique types of service and performing testing and repair of their communications equipment. He continued to inquire about why I was looking for a different job from the one I had.

I was honest with him and said, "I want a job that I feel has a future and a job that I believe I can contribute to the company's success." In later years I thought my answer might have made a good impression on Mr. Middleton because at that point he said, "If a job is available, would you prefer working in Kansas City, in one of the departments you just visited or in Wichita, Kansas, in one of their like-type departments?" I told him either one would be satisfactory, but since I was raised in a little town close to Wichita, I think I would pick it as my first choice. With that, he said, "Okay, I have an opening there, and if you want it, it's yours. Could you start around the end of January?"

"That will give you and your new bride time to take care of the various things you need to take care of in Fort Madison, the holidays will be over, and you will be starting at the end of the first month in 1957 as a craftsman, with AT&T."

My reply was quick and enthusiastic, "I am interested, and I accept your offer and look forward to being part of the AT&T team." As I was leaving, Mr. Middleton said, "If you have any questions, you have my number and give me a call."

"I will, and thanks again."

Little did I know what the next thirty-plus years had in store for my family and me. Some good and some great, and all the job assignments, especially in the plant department, were enjoyable and challenging. I did have one location that was not the greatest. However, it was short-lived, and when I reflect later on what GOD enabled me to do during that period, it was worth it all. And all I could say was, "Thank You, Father!"

Many things took place from the moment I returned to Fort Madison to the end of January 1957.

My cousin Beverly and her family lived in a suburb of Wichita, and when she found out we would be looking for a place to live, she did some searching and found a few places that she felt might be rentals we would like because they were close to where I would be working. As things turned out, Beverly was a great help more than once during our five years in Wichita.

When my new bride (Sondra) and I arrived in Wichita, with the help of my cousin Beverly, we were able to find an apartment. However, we had to share the bathroom with another family. Sondra was not too impressed with that arrangement; but, since I could walk to work, she would have the car in case she needed to go shopping. A couple of weeks later, we found a quadruplex apartment that was still within walking distance to my work location. At that point, we had our private bathroom, and everything started going in the right direction.

At the time I became an employee of AT&T, I also became aware I was going to be a father. Not long after we arrived in Wichita and settled in the quadruplex, Sondra started putting on weight, and she assured me it was not due to her eating too much food. On top of that good news, we noticed the weather started getting hot and "muggy," and we did not have "central air conditioning." This fact posed a problem for my soon-to-be mother of my first child, and it was not good news. I ended up buying a window unit that used circulating water for cooling. If you were standing right in front of the unit, you could feel a cool mist; however, if you were five feet away, all you felt was hot, humid dampness. Sondra was not used to these kinds of living conditions, but she toughed it out.

As luck would have it, when her water broke, and it was time for her to have our first baby, we no more than stepped inside the door of the hospital when the in-charge nurse saw Sondra and turned to the nurse beside her and said, "Get a wheelchair and take this woman to delivery *now*!"

My thought was, "Man, I didn't expect such good service." I remember thinking, "They are showing Sondra 'first-class service.'" I found out later when the doctor filled me in as to *why* we were getting the quality service treatment, and it didn't have anything to do with standard procedures.

After I had checked Sondra in, they directed me to the waiting room for fathers and told me they would call me when our baby was born. I remember I had just sat down and started talking with another father-to-be.

I asked him, "How long have you been here?"

He replied, "About eight hours!" He had no more said that when they announced over the PA system, "Mr. McJunkin, come to the nurse's station." I thought something must have gone wrong. When I arrived at the nurse's station, the doctor was waiting for me.

He greeted me by saying, "First, congratulations on the birth of your baby girl (Vicki Lynn). And by the way, if you are planning on having any more children, I would suggest you either leave the house earlier or move closer to the hospital. Otherwise, you might have to deliver the baby yourself!" Now I knew why Sondra had received the "fast-class (versus first-class) service."

Our second child, also a daughter (Stephanie Luann), arrived at what seemed to be a somewhat surprising time. We had just bought our first home in the small town of Haysville, a little town, South of Wichita. Haysville was also where my cousin Beverly lived. At a time,

I needed to be with my wife. I was in Kansas City, going to a company school. The baby wasn't due until several days after my school was scheduled to be over. It seemed that everyone knew that except our new daughter. Again, Beverly was there and saved the day when she drove Sondra to the hospital and took care of Vicki, our oldest daughter, until I flew home that evening. I was glad the doctor that delivered our first daughter was not the one that delivered our second. I was not ready to get another lecture about, "The importance of being an 'on-time Father' for the delivery of your children."

After the excitement settled down, everything started to take on a more desirable atmosphere. By this time, we had lived in Haysville for over a year. During the following four years, we joined the church, became involved in several community activities; I joined the Masons and Sondra joined the Eastern Star, we made some improvements on our new home and started to settle down and watched our family grow. Little did we know we would see our family grow, but it wouldn't be while I was working in Wichita, and we would *not* be living in Haysville when all that happened. However, a lot would take place before we would be leaving Haysville.

My first days in the Wichita Central Office

My boss in the central office in Wichita was Chief O. J. Hutchison, affectionately known as "Hutch." I started in the equipment maintenance department. Later I worked in the transmission department. In a short time, I became familiar with most of the equipment and its required maintenance routines. When transferring to the transmission department, I became familiar with the communication procedures we used in working with our "private line service" customers (businesses having dedicated telephone facilities).

What impressed me the most in my equipment department assignment, was the company's willingness to send its people to company schools. Before a new craftsman completed this schooling and showed they could "shoot troubles" correctly, they were always assigned to work with a qualified artisan (craftsman) on any piece of equipment having a problem. I think I attended at least a dozen different schools, all dealing with various types of telephone equipment. The more I learned, the more I enjoyed my job.

Over the two and a half years I worked in the equipment department, I also became qualified on performing "acceptance testing" on new equipment that our Western Electric installers would be installing. My new job was exciting, and it gave me a lot of personal satisfaction in knowing what I had accomplished during the workday. I'll cover this more in chapter 9.

One thing I missed in many of my later assignments, even when I was in management, was the lack of an "accomplishment feeling" at the end of the day. The management-level jobs I held later were important assignments and interesting, but quite often the best story I could share with my family was, "I had a three-hour meeting this afternoon with Bell Labs." I'll expand on this part of my career also in chapter 9. Starting in nonmanagement and being promoted to management, I learned the adage "Don't judge a book by its cover" was also true among many AT&T's jobs—that is, "Don't judge a person's job by where it is in the hierarchy of the company." I had seven management promotions throughout my AT&T career. I always felt my job as a craftsman gave me as much or more pride and a feeling of self-satisfaction and value to the company, like many I received in my various promotions in management. My management jobs were relevant in "decision-making" to keep our company competitive and to move forward, but I never lost sight it was the installing, operation, maintaining, and excellent customer service of the craftsmen that made and retained the quality of service AT&T provided. The children of "Ma Bell" started with its craftsmen.

After I had worked in the equipment department for about three years, I had the opportunity to transfer into the transmission department. Since I had performed "acceptance testing" on most of the equipment in the test room. Working in the transmission department gave me a better appreciation of a different function of AT&T—that is, working with our customers.

I soon found the transmission department and the equipment department were two different work areas. In the transmission department. you had to be mindful that you were talking with the

Customer when you picked up the phone at the test board. I learned that their problem was to be treated as the "most important call" for the telephone company to take care of at that time. There were aspects of working in the transmission department. that I enjoyed as much as in the Equipment area but in a much different way. In the transmission area, you sometimes had the opportunity to work with other people from the Atlantic Coast to the Pacific coastal states. The different type of trouble reports you received while working on the test boards would always keep you on your toes. But I know most of this would not mean much to someone not knowledgeable in private line service in an AT&T plant office, so I'll move on.

After being qualified to do "acceptance testing" with Western Electric, I found I usually had the feeling of specific work activities I accomplished at the end of my workday. My coworkers were great, and their qualifications were the best. During my time in the test room, I passed my FCC second class radio license exam. However, I never worked in the Microwave relay group that maintained all our microwave equipment in our "radio towers" that, at that time, required a second class FCC license.

In the five years, I was in the central office test room in Wichita, Kansas. I met a lot of good men and women who were proud to be employees of "Ma Bell." I recall one man that retired while I was still there whose name was "Benny." He often shared stories with the new employees that took place during the depression years. He pointed out that AT&T was one of the few companies that paid dividends to its Stockholders throughout the depression. He told us that during the depression, two of his siblings lost their jobs, and both of them, with their families, lived with Benny and his family for quite some time. He would always add, "Working for AT&T was not just a job; it was a great job during the depression." You soon found out if you questioned the importance he placed on his job, he would let you know, "AT&T was still a great company to work for." At that time AT&T was the parent of all the Bell System companies from Pacific Tel. & Tel to Southwestern Bell, to New York Tell, plus all the other Bell Operating Companies, including Western Electric and Bell Labs. As I recall, twenty-three different companies made up the Bell

System organization called AT&T. I'm not sure, but I expect during that period was when the term *Ma Bell* was created, to recognize the respect and pride the employees had for their "parent" company, especially during the depression years.

There was always times of excitement or at least "out-of-the-ordinary" happening going on in the central office. I recall one such incident involving one of our older craftsmen. I'll call him Harold. Harold was the undisputed "top tester" on open-wire testing. All the open-wire linemen recognized Harold for his accuracy in using the Wheatstone Bridge test set, for locating, "right to the telephone pole," where the problem located.

In the wintertime, when the wind was blowing, and the snow was falling, the Linemen would often ask if Harold was there and if so, they would ask to talk with him. Harold had all the confidence in the world that he knew what he was doing when working on an open-wire outage.

Most of the troubles on open-wire outages were in the Western plains of Kansas, and most of them took place during the cold and windy winter months. Now, picture this: On one side of the picture you see a man standing in front of the test board, probably with his shirt sleeves rolled up, relaxed, maybe with a smile on his face, talking with a lineman and giving him the location of the open-wire problem.

His smile may be caused by his thinking as soon as the Lineman acknowledges the opening and starts climbing the pole (in the stormy weather), he (the man in the test room) could go for a second cup of coffee and wait for the Lineman to take care of the problem and call back for a continuity check. Now, on the other side of the picture, you see a man dressed in heavy winter clothing, his hood pulled tightly around his head, wearing heavy winter gloves, a pair of knee-high laced boots and slapping his hands together to keep the blood circulating. He is looking up at the cross-arms secured to the pole that held the telephone wires that were some twenty feet or more off the ground. It is clear; all the wires are in place—that is, the storm had not broken any of them. With a handphone next to his ear and mouth, the caption at the bottom of the picture (from his end) reads,

"I don't care what your D… test set is saying, I'm telling you there are no broken wires at this location, just like I told you about the other three poles you sent me, in this sub-freezing weather!" Now, that vision had been a reality more than once if you talked with any Lineman. That is also why, many times if the craftsman was talking with a lineman, shooting open-wire trouble, the craftsman, himself, would call for Harold to take over and if he didn't, the lineman would often ask for Harold.

The situation I recall, dealing with this type of activity happened in our test room shortly after I had started working for AT&T, and, it received a lot of attention from all the craftsmen working in the Transmission department. It was one day in midwinter when we had already experienced a couple of open-wire problems. We knew a new Lineman was now handling the "call-out" problems on open-wire lines going in and out of Dodge City, Kansas. His name was Eugene Kowalski (not real name). We had his phone number to contact when needed. At that time, because of the distance between Wichita and locations like Dodge City and farther west, making it difficult for the lineman to come into the Wichita test room and meet the craftsmen that worked with him on open-wire outages. At best the lineman might get into Wichita once a year.

As I recall, an open-wire problem existed during a cold winter day and was being worked on between Harold and our lineman Kowalski. Harold had, for a third time, dispatched lineman Kowalski to go to a different pole location and check for broken telephone lines. Each site called for Kowalski to drive in hazardous conditions, and on arriving at the new site, he would get out of his maintenance truck, and in the sub-freezing weather, check both directions from the telephone pole that Harold had sent him. After checking each location and finding no broken wires, Kowalski asked Harold, "Are you sure you know how to use that testing device?"

Now Harold, not only was good, he knew it and to indicate you didn't believe he was as good as he thought, was almost like insulting his mother. Harold stood about five feet four and probably weighed around 135 pounds. Not only was he a short man, but he also had a short temper when it came to doubt his knowledge of testing open-wire problems. When Kowalski, in subzero weather made his observation as to Harold's testing abilities, Harold proceeded to inform him there were many reasons a reading could be off, mostly due to the weather conditions at the site of the break. I understand Kowalski told Harold, after he had finished talking, "Look, I'm freezing out here, and you are not helping the situation by telling me how good you are. I'm going to go to one more location that you give me, and if I don't find a broken wire, I'm heading back home and notifying my supervisor that the Wichita test room isn't able to locate the opening and I am not able to take the blizzard we are having."

Before all those threats were carried out by Lineman Kowalski, Harold located the opening and Kowalski was able to fix the broken wire, and telephone service was restored.

The humorous part of that experience took place about two weeks later. Around 2:00 p.m. one afternoon, Harold was working on "circuit orders" at his desk when a man came in and asked one of the craftsmen that were standing about five feet from Harold, "Is Harold working today?"

The craftsman turned and said, "Harold, this guy wants to talk to you." As Harold turned, looking up at this six-foot-six, 285-pound man, and said, "I'm Harold, what do you need?"

"Hi, Harold, I wanted to come in and meet you and some of the other guys, my name is 'Eugene Kowalski, I'm the new lineman out of Dodge City." One of the craftsmen later told Harold, "You could have put a softball in your mouth, as far as your jaw dropped."

After gathering his composure, Harold stood up and said, "Hi, glad to meet you." As most big large men would do, Eugene replied, "When we were working on that open-wire problem a couple of weeks ago, I knew you were the top tester out of Wichita, and my supervisor confirmed what you said about various weather conditions that can make accurate measurements almost impossible. So I want to apologize for the remarks I made when I know you were doing your best, considering the weather."

Then Harold, like most "big" small men would do, said, "You don't owe me an apology, I was the one that wasn't getting the problem solved. I know it is much easier for those of us in the test room, in a nice warm environment, on a freezing day, too often forget the situation that exists outside, in the conditions our linemen are working. How about we go down to the 'break room' and get a cup of coffee and get acquainted?"

"Hey, that sounds good to me."

I understand Eugene and Harold parted company that day the best of friends and never had any problems during troubleshooting open-wire problems after that. It wasn't too long after that experience that all the open-wire facilities were removed from service. I never heard where Eugene Kowalski was assigned, but I know many of the linemen were brought inside and worked in the plant central office test rooms.

I have so many fond memories of the times I was working in the plant department. As I recall them from time to time, they bring a smile to my face. I remember another time when one of our craftsmen, after the latest issue of *Reader's Digest* came out; he would study one of the articles, I think it was titled "Word of the Day." Then he would come to work the next day and say something to one or more of the employees that included one of the *words* from the *Reader's Digest* article. Most of the time it was a word none of the craftsmen had ever heard and didn't know what it meant. The craftsman would use this word in talking with as many people (nonmanagement) that he could. After a while, when this happened, someone would often say, "Hey, if anyone is interested, Harry (not his real name) came in this morning with a new word, so that means the new *Reader's Digest* is out."

What made this an in-house joke was, Harry felt we were all amazed at his vocabulary; however, the comments more accurately were saying, "Get a life, is that the only thing you can find for entertainment?" However, I wouldn't be surprised if some of the craftsmen took that word home and tried it out on their wife or neighbor!

Another humorous event that got a lot of laughs in our office was the time a misdialed number came into our test board, and the "joker of all jokers" in our office answered the phone. I'd call him "Loy" for this story. Years earlier he had worked as an outside lineman. When

Loy answered the call, the voice on the calling end said, "Hello, this is Helen from the Wichita Arthur Murray Dance Studio."

"How would you like to have three free lessons for any dance of your choice and be able to dance like a pro by your third lesson?" Loy immediately replied, "Are you for real?"

"Yes, and I would like to allow you to join with one of our dance instructors and become one of the best dancers in Wichita of any dance you choose—guaranteed!"

"Oh, you have just made my day. You don't know how much I have always wanted to dance."

"Well, I'm so glad to hear that, because we can make your dream come true. When could you come for your first lesson?"

"Just as soon as my limbs come back?"

"Your limbs? What do you mean?"

"Oh, three years ago I was in an auto accident and lost both legs above the kneecaps and hearing your guarantee to enable me to dance in three free lessons, has made my day because the therapy group at the hospital has not been able to teach me to even walk, without crutches. And you are going to teach me how to dance in three lessons. How soon can I come to your Studio?"

By this time, the lady was probably pleading with Loy to not come down until after he could walk without any assistance. Finally, Loy told her that he would wait two weeks and if the hospital was not able to help him, he said, "I'm going to be on my way down to your studio and let you teach me how to dance. Then he said, "Thank you again, and I look forward to seeing you, Helen, in a couple of weeks," and he hung up. He felt the woman probably was on her way to turn in her resignation immediately and did not leave a forwarding address.

After a few minutes had passed, Loy called the studio and asked to speak to Helen. When she picked up the phone and said, "Hello," Loy said, "this is the man you just talked to and guaranteed me you could teach me to dance in three days. "The more I've thought about your offer, I've decided not to accept it after all."

He probably heard a sigh of relief when she asked why.

"I'm a former lineman for the telephone company, and if I never learn how to walk and the only thing I can do is dance, I'm afraid people may laugh at me when they see me dancing from my truck to the telephone pole and later dancing back to my truck."

"I'm so sorry to hear the situation it would put you in, and I understand the problems it could cause you. If your condition changes in the future, let us know and maybe we can work out a plan for you at that time."

"Thank you so much for calling back and have a nice day."

"I'll try."

There was never a dull moment around the test board when Loy was working. However, when a real problem arose, Loy was all business and one of the best testers in the group at the test board.

Becoming a more qualified craftsman

As I mentioned earlier, I was very impressed at the number of schools AT&T had for its central office craftsmen. These schools made the difference between giving our customers "quality service" versus "just service." All the schools were in Kansas City (KC), and I had the opportunity to help teach one of them while I was still a craftsman. I found the schools were valuable to the craft, and if given the opportunity, they were also a motivation to craft if we were asked to help teach a school.

As my experience level increased, I was sent to one of our offices in Northeast Oklahoma (Hugo) and did the acceptance testing with the Western Electric Installation group on a new system developed by Bell Labs. The work I did during the acceptance testing proved interesting as well as being helpful during my later assignments.

I was always proud to let my friends, neighbors, relatives, and even the "man on the street," know that I worked for "Ma Bell in its long lines department." And I felt this "prideful feeling" many times, during my assignment in the test room in Wichita, Kansas.

One that comes to mind was the time our district manager from Kansas City was visiting our office. It was Mr. Roy Middleton, the district manager that hired me over a year earlier.

The day Mr. Middleton visited our office, I was working on equipment troubles, and I had my schematic drawing spread out on the floor of the equipment room when he walked in and said with what sounded like a little surprise in his voice, "Lloyd? Well, how are things going? I see they have you already working on 'L' carrier equipment. Have you identified the problem?"

It had been quite some time since I had been in his office during my interview, and I'm sure he had interviewed many potential employees since I was there. I was as surprised as he seemed to be in our meeting that day, probably more so because he remembered my name.

Time to change jobs from plant to GCM

It was during the Cuban missile crisis when President Kennedy was our president. I was asked to come to Chief "Hutch's" office. When I arrived, he said, "I just received a call from the district office, and they told me there is an opening in our government communications management (GCM) office in Colorado Springs, Colorado. They wanted to know if I had anyone that might be a good candidate." Then he asked if I knew anyone in our office that I felt could handle the job. I was caught off guard since I didn't have any idea as to what GCM stood for or what it did, but I named two or three of my peers that had impressed me with their knowledge in the operation of our central office.

Hutch laughed and said, "You might be right, but what do you think about yourself for the job?"

"Well, I never want to turn down what sounds like a good opportunity, but I don't have any idea what GCM does."

Hutch said with a grin, "I don't either, but a couple of our district people seem to think you would fit in with this group, and they have recommended you." He didn't tell me who had recommended me, but it may have been our district manager, who hired me or possibly one of the supervisors that were instructors of the school I assisted teaching, in KC. "I told Hutch, if they feel I can, I'm willing to give it a shot."

"Okay, I'll call them and tell them it's a 'go' from you and to let you know when and what the next step is.

Within a week I was sitting in the division manager's office of GCM in Colorado Springs. We had a long discussion, and when he found out I was a Navy Vet (I found out later the division manager was a graduate from West Point Military Academy), he said, "Okay, you have been on that side of the fence—that is, the military—who will be your customer in GCM." I had no idea if that was good or bad, so I kept my mouth shut. He then had me talk with one of his district manager, who would soon be my boss. We also had a lengthy conversation about my background as far back as my being an eagle scout. At the end of my interview, the division manager said, "You've got the job, all we have to do now is to make sure we can get you a secret clearance. Once that is done, you are on our payroll. That will take about two or three weeks, and, by the first of next month, I expect you and your family to be here in Colorado Springs, and I'll sit down with you and layout what your assignment will be. I had to smile (to myself) in hearing his academy training in laying out my job description in a step by step scenario, almost in one breath. We became good friends over the next couple of years. I kidded him one time and asked him why he left the Army. His answer was, the pay was not that good, and you never knew when they were going to move you. You will see later, that part about moving a lot somewhat described the remainder of my career with AT&T.

On my way back to Wichita, I didn't know if I should be happy or not. What if they find something in my background that would get me fired from AT&T and sent to jail?

I did get a call the following week from my mother, telling me a couple of people in town had been contacted by some government people asking questions about me. I remember her asking, "You haven't done anything bad, have you? I told her what it was for, but I think she still wondered why the government was asking questions about "her son!" In less than three weeks, I received a call from the division manager I talked with earlier. He told me, "Your new job is in Colorado Springs in the GCM department, starting the first of the month, okay?"

"Okay!"

"Great, I'll have reservations made for you and your family at the hotel we use for our out-of-town personnel, we'll send you airline tickets, etc., and we'll be talking, but call me if you have questions. And as you Navy guys say, 'Welcome aboard!'"

GCM and new adventures

It was somewhat of a shock going to work in the central office test room in Wichita, Kansas, in a pair of jeans and sports T-shirt and now going to work in GCM in Colorado Springs, wearing a dress suit and hat. My big shocker was when I found our customer in GCM sales—none other than North American Air Defense (NORAD) command. I would be working with Air Force majors and as high as a "bird colonel." Out of respect for this very important customer, we were to wear a business suit and hat to work. We would also wear our dress hat anytime we were outside a building, during business hours. That almost sounded like my boot camp days. At that time, I had one suit and, as I recall, two-sport coats and several pairs of sport pants and no dress hats! Now, I find out, the only thing of value in my wardrobe was my one suit!

I remember thinking, I may have to take out a loan to buy at least two more suits and at least one dress hat that goes with black, blue or brown. I did not have to take out a loan because, I was able to use some of the money I had saved mowing lawns during my junior high school days along with some of the money I had sent Mom to put in my savings, while I was in the Navy. Things were not starting the way I had expected, but at least I didn't have to borrow money to take care of the dress code for my new job.

My first week was spent in the office getting oriented. Up to that point, to me, the telephone company was our plant central offices throughout the United States—period. GCM was nothing like a central office. At that time, I was having a hard time figuring out how this "ole" small-town boy from Kansas was going to fit in. Then the shock became worse the second week when my boss took me to the NORAD base. Being told our customer would be the Air

Force, I expected we would be going to someplace that had at least one airfield. Wrong, we went to a location at the edge of town that was only office buildings. On arriving, my boss introduced me to Bird Colonel Norm Bell.

I didn't know it at that time, but he would be my number 1 contact along with Major Lewis, who joined us later that morning. Being an enlisted man in the Navy, I had been trained to salute all military officers in uniform. However, before I met any of our customers, I was told that I should view my job as one that was not above or below that of our customer's representatives. Somewhat to my surprise, I never worked with any of our customers that indicated they felt a GCM sales rep was someone lower than them. Colonel Bell and I became very good friends and shared many stories about our backgrounds, our families, likes, and dislikes. He was a fighter pilot during the Korean campaign and saw a lot of action. More than once, he would give me a call and say, "If you can break away for lunch, how about coming out to the base, and it will be on me."

He would continue by saying something like, "I've had a bad morning, and I've got to get away from these Air Force clowns who don't know what direction they are flying. Can you make it?"

Our orders in GCM was, "If the customer calls you for anything, you can take care of, do it." So my answer was, "No problem; maybe we can discuss that order you gave us last week for your Omaha base

An example that comes to mind, that I had a hard time convincing myself it was my job to do, related to paying for everything. My number 1 project was to ensure the telephone company's needs in the Cheyenne Mountain project were identified and available when needed. I'll address this later, but at that time, I was learning the job and what the Cheyenne Mountain project involved and what AT&T required to satisfy the customers' needs with the rest of the world. This activity often called for joint meetings among different groups in the Air Force (US and Canadian) and groups in AT&T; primarily groups at Bell Labs back in New Jersey. Being the new man on the job, for the first five or six months, I was usually the junior AT&T representative in any meeting with our customer. I was somewhat shocked when told I was to pick up all the tabs for the GCM personnel and all the military guests. The military customers traveling with us would pay for their transportation and room, but I was to pick up the rest.

When I first started my job in GCM, it seemed I was always the junior AT&T Representative. "I understood picking up the meal tabs, but I found picking up the extra expenses a little hard to accept." One of my first trips out of town took place not too long after my assignment to the Cheyenne Mountain project. The meeting was back at our Labs in Holmdel, New Jersey. It included two US Air Force majors, two Canadian squadron leaders and an AT&T district manager from Kansas City, who joined us at the KC airport and continued with us on our flight to New Jersey.

On returning from our meeting with the Labs, I started filling out my expense voucher and was somewhat shocked. I had identified the group from NORAD, the AT&T district manager from GCM that joined us in Kansas City, and myself, on my voucher. I listed all our meals on my voucher and found the amount didn't even come close to what I spent! Why? Well, after we finished dinner everyone except me knew it was party time. That's why Mr. Moneybags had a problem filling out his voucher when he arrived back in his office. I knew we could not show certain expenses on our vouchers, but I sure wasn't planning on contributing my money to take care of those expenses. I called my district manager and asked if he had a minute. He said, "Come on in."

As I entered his office, I said, "We need to talk."

He said, "What's on your mind?"

"Well, you know, I've been on my first trip as a GCM representative, back to the Labs with a district manager from KC and two majors and two squadron leaders from NORAD and me."

"So what's the problem?"

"Well, I kept track of what I was paying for, and when I added it up this morning, I almost had a heart attack. I know we can't show certain things on our vouchers, so how am I going to get the money back for the meals I picked up including the refreshments?"

My boss laughed and said, "Welcome to GCM. Look, I don't care what you show for a meal for you and others, chop up the extras and add it to the meal costs."

As I picked up my voucher, I said, "Okay, but you are going to see we had some costly meals on that trip." He laughed and said, "I know what you mean, I've eaten some of those myself when I was the 'moneyman'!"

After a few similar types of trips, I fell in line with the procedures, and everything turned out okay. Later my boss said, "I know it looks like we are being taken advantage of, but if you knew the money we get from this customer for providing them the communications they need, you would see what it costs in maintaining 'good relationships and cooperation,' actually amounts to peanuts." After a while, I saw he was right, it was just part of the cost of doing business, and it was a common practice in both the military and commercial sales organizations.

Overall, I learned a lot during my tour with GCM. I made some good friends within the department as well as in the Air Force, especially when the excavation started inside the center of Cheyenne Mountain. When I was filled in on what the project was, I understood why I had to have a secret clearance. Looking back at that time and seeing some of the leaks of classified information problems we have today, in the twenty-first century, I feel sad, "When are we going to learn that, protecting America is more important than padding our pocketbook or getting reelected?"

The Cheyenne Mountain project was a real hush-hush activity. At that time the public was only told NORAD headquarters was going to move from Omaha to Colorado Springs; everything else was a secret. The closer they came to complete the Cheyenne Mountain project, the greater the activity was kept under wraps. Until, one day, after the project had completed and the facility was operational, as I recall, the Denver newspaper printed several pictures taken inside the mountain. I never heard if they found who took the photographs and who leaked them to the newspaper. I heard several years later that our telephone office inside the mountain was no longer maned and the service connection between the command center was by way of an interface with one of our remote central offices. Today I doubt if much of the communications equipment is still in service, that we installed. I don't even know for sure if NORAD is still using Cheyenne Mountain as its headquarters. But even though many aspects of the project are probably no longer classified, I feel it is not information that should be made public.

I still recall some of the activities I was involved with that were more humorous than classified, and many of these had a message of how some of the more important things in life center around people rather than the activities they are doing. One situation comes to mind that occurred while I was involved in an activity at the top of the mountain. It was not anything secret, but it was somewhat amusing and humorous as the problem continued, and no one seemed to know how it could be corrected. It involved a problem we were having at an opening for our waveguide "adits" to be installed from the top of the mountain and traveling down to the center area that had been hollowed out. That is a simplified explanation of what was much more complicated. However, the point of my story centered at the top of the mountain.

The more they drilled the opening, the more it would cave in. For some reason, this condition was not apparent in other places they were drilling. After several weeks of drilling, caving in, drilling again, and trying to shore up the cave in, Bell Labs was notified of the problem and asked if they had any ideas as to what was causing the problem.

About a week later I received a call from a man by the first name of "Gert." He informed me he was from the Labs and would be working on our problem at Cheyenne Mountain. He said he would like to come out and go to the site and see, firsthand, what existed.

He then stated, "I've never climbed a mountain before, is there anyone that could go with me and help me get to the location?"

I laughed to myself and said, "Yes, I will be able to go with you."

He then asked, "Would you be able to stay with me until I am ready to leave the site?"

Again, I said, "Yes, I'll do that."

He then informed me he would make airline reservations and let me know his arrival time at the Colorado Springs airport. I told him if he didn't want to rent a car, I could pick him up at the airport. He thanked me and restated as soon as he knew the flight number, time of arrival, etc., he would give me a call.

The next day Gert called and gave me the information on his flight. I told him that would not conflict with anything on my schedule. When I picked Gert up, and knowing where he would be staying, I told him I would drop him off at the hotel.

He then asked, "After we drop my bags off at the hotel, would it be possible to take me to the mountain so that I can check out the site?"

I thought it a little odd that he wanted to look at the area at that time since it was already late afternoon and he wouldn't be able to do anything except "look" at the opening.

I said, "Yes if you want to, but we won't have much time other than going to the site."

"Oh, that's okay. I only want to get a good idea as to what it looks like."

From Gert's first phone call until now, I had this feeling that we may not be on the same page as to what the situation at Cheyenne Mountain was. I was beginning to wonder if his conception of the problem was much different from what existed. Then, when I said, "While you change into something a little more suitable for our climb, I'll stop by my house and change clothes and then pick you up. Then we'll head for the mountain." My thoughts were becoming more confirmed as to what Gert knew about the Cheyenne Mountain project and the problems we were incurring.

Gert looked at me and asked, "Why do we need to change clothes?"

Now, as I mentioned earlier, I was required to wear a business suit and dress hat to work each day, and that was what I was wearing. I noticed Gert had a nice sports coat on and a pair of sports pants. So when I replied to his question, I said: "We've got about a ten- to fifteen-minute climb to the site, and you won't want to wear the nice clothes you have on." I noticed Gert's eyes open much wider than normal as he said, "You mean, we can't walk to the site but have to climb up the side of the mountain?"

"Well, not really, but it is a little steep, rocky and we'll be going through some brush-covered areas. Do you have some older clothes to wear?"

"Yes, but I thought we would be able to walk to the site and back without any danger."

"No, it isn't dangerous, and you will see that when we get there."

I drove home, changed clothes, and came back, picked Gert up and headed for Cheyenne Mtn. When we arrived, I parked in the parking lot that would be the best starting point for our climb. As we arrived, I pointed to the area of the site location, although you couldn't see too much because of the trees and brush.

As we started our climb, I told Gert, "Follow me, I'll go slow because the elevation here is between eight and nine thousand feet above sea level and if you are not used to it, you can get a little lite headed. He said, "Okay, I'll follow you."

As we started, I was convinced Gert was feeling we were climbing Mt. Everest. I took my time because I knew this was not what he had in mind when we were talking on the phone. We had ascended about thirty feet in distance and maybe five feet in elevation when I heard, "Oh my goodness!"

I turned around and saw Gert had his hands "choking" a little sapling tree. Gert had turned around to see what was behind us and realized we had gone *up* a noticeable amount. I told him not to look back but stay close to me, and we would be at the opening in just a little while. He said, with a little doubt in the sound of his voice, "Okay, I sure hope so!"

"Eureka, we made it!" I didn't feel Gert saw the humor in my comment. He sat down on a rock and said, "Man, I don't see how you can climb this every day." I told him I only climb it, maybe once a week, if that often, and once you get used to it, it is not a problem."

His reply was, "Maybe for you, but it sure would be for me!"

After we rested, and he regained his composure, he seemed to be okay. I pointed out the problem, and he could see how the sides of the hole were very "crumbly." He said he would like to take a few of the stones back with him so they could do some tests. When I pointed out we did not have anything to put them in, I suggested I could come up later with a container and get any amount he needed and send them to him.

He said, "I think that is a better idea."

As we were preparing to make our descent, I had no idea of the problem we were going to encounter. As we started down, I told Gert to only look at the ground in front of him, not farther down the path. With a weak, "Okay," we started down.

We had not gone more than ten yards when he said, "Can we go a little slower?"

I said, "Sure, we have plenty of time."

We might have continued another ten or twenty feet when I turned to see if everything was okay, and I had to bite my lip in what I saw. Try to picture this.

There was Gert, leaning backward, holding himself off the ground, as much as possible, with his two arms and hands extended behind him. His legs stretched out in front of his body, with his chest facing the sky, he was slowly walking on all fours, down the mountain. I didn't want to laugh because I could see he was almost petrified.

I said, "How about you hold on to my shoulders, and we will walk slow the rest of the way?"

"Man, I'm sorry, but this is the scariest situation I think I've ever experienced," I assured him I understood and told him he was not the only one that felt that way when they were coming down the path for the first time.

Step by step, foot by foot, we finally made it to the bottom. I tried to get him to relax and said, "Now when you get back to the Labs you can tell your friends that you are the only Bell Labs employee that has ever conquered Cheyenne Mountain in Colorado. He laughed and said, "You know what? I'm going to do that, and if they ask if I took any pictures, I'm going to tell them, it was too dangerous to climb and take pictures at the same time!"

As we were going back to the car, I noticed that with Gert sliding on his rear end, during much of the way down, he had worn a hole in the seat of his pants and stained them to a point the cleaners would not be able to clean them. When I pointed this out, he asked, "Is there someplace we could stop so I can buy a new pair?" I told him we would be passing a shopping center on the way back that had a SEARS store and we could stop there. "Good, let's do that."

Now, picture this. As I recall, Gert had two PhDs (not one but two). During the conversations we had later, I was amazed at his knowledge in so many areas, and yet he was one of the most down-to-earth men I had ever met. As we walked into the SEARS store, we are two men, one looking as if he had found his shirt at the Salvation Army and his pants he pulled out of the trash container outback of their store. I probably didn't look much better. One of the clerks asked if she could help us find something? She seemed to have an expression on her face that indicated, "Can I help you so that you can leave as soon as possible?" I

told her, "My friend is looking for a new pair of pants, maybe a pair of work pants?" While I was talking with the clerk, Gert had found a pair of work pants in his size.

He brought them to where the clerk and I were talking, and when she saw what he had, she looked at me and nodded her head, indicating, "Follow me." She took us back to the area Gert had found the pants he was holding. I'm not sure, but she may have felt Gert could not speak English when she said, "These were on sale last week, if he wants the pair he is holding, I'll sell them for the sale price and save him 20 percent, okay?"

For a moment I realized, Gert probably had more money in his checking account that she and I had, combined. And he had a far better formal education than either of us. If I ever experienced a real-life example of the old saying, "Never judge a book by its cover." I was looking at one that very minute, as I looked at Gert. I felt that afternoon; I had experienced a lesson in life that I will always remember. The Bible is right when it makes clear, time after time, "Man should never judge another person on anything," because we may have to eat our words and they won't taste too good. But more importantly, GOD Himself is the only one who can judge others.

When I dropped Gert off at the hotel, I told him if he didn't have any plans for dinner that evening. I would like to take him out to a very nice restaurant at the Broadmoor Hotel. He said he had heard of the Broadmoor Hotel and would like that very much.

I picked him up around 7:00 p.m., and we headed for the Broadmoor. While we were there, another surprise awaited me. As we were eating, I commented to him indicating I noticed he had an accent that sounded like he may be from Germany.

He said, "Yes, I was born in a small town near Berlin." Then he revealed one of the most interesting life history stories I have ever heard.

His father was a chemical engineer, and when He (Gert) was starting school, his father was selected to join the group of engineers who were working on the project to make an Atomic Bomb. This project was Top Secret, and all the people involved in the activity (including their families) were relocated from their homes to a housing area on the military base where the project was being conducted.

Gert said during the school year, he and his older sister would be picked up each morning and driven to school by military police (Gestapo) and returned that evening in the same manner. He said none of his family, including his father, could leave the base unless they had a pass signed by the base commander. From what his father told him later, the Germans felt they were ahead of the Americans in the development of the bomb, but as it turned out, they were wrong. He added, that his father felt, that was better for Germany, America and the rest of the world, because Hitler would have used the bomb on multiple countries throughout Europe, possibly even parts of Germany.

I never saw Gert after he returned to the Labs in New Jersey, but I did talk with him several times by phone. Before he left Colorado Springs, we met with the Civil Engineers that were involved in the problem area. I don't recall if the solution came from the Labs or not. However, the problem area was taken care of, and the project completed as planned. I'm sure Gert has since retired, but I will never forget seeing this man with two PhDs sliding down Cheyenne mountain on his backside! I admired his loyalty to his job and his ability in not "flaunting" his education (and wealth). He presented himself as a humble man that had lived a very eventful life and was now using his GOD-given talent to serve the "free" world.

Another event I felt was very interesting that I encountered during my time in GCM came from my good friend, Bird Colonel Norm Bell, that I mentioned earlier. He, like Gert, was a man that could have bragged about his exploits, but, in all our conversations, he said very little about any of his combat activities during the time he had served as a fighter pilot, throughout the Korean activity. We became very good friends, and he showed me his true friendship more than once.

One such event took place one day after a meeting discussing a project we had been working on for the past few months. The event I'm thinking of started after we had finished a group meeting and the only ones left were 'Norm" and me. We were kicking around some of our military experiences.

One thing led to another when Norm asked, "How do you like the telephone company, compared to the Navy?"

I told him I liked working in our 'plant' department of AT&T because each night I went home, I could recall the equipment and service problems I had worked on and cleared that day.

The problem working in GCM was I spend most of my time meeting with the Customer and discussing how we (AT&T) could provide more kinds of service than we currently were doing—that is, my job was all "talk" but not "doing" the work.

"I know the feeling; I feel the same way, setting behind a desk does not give me the thrill and satisfaction of setting in the cockpit of a fighter plane, engaged in a dogfight with the enemy."

I laughed and said, "I don't think my dissatisfaction example is quite as great as yours, but I guess we both have had more satisfying days." We both laughed.

Then Norm asked me, "Do you think you would be more satisfied with a government job, basically being on the other side of the table from where you set today in GCM? Before you answer, let me tell you that I am confident I can get you a job at a GS-8 pay grade." (At that time, a GS-8 paid $8,000 a year. That was a little more than

I was getting as a sales rep in GCM at that time. Remember, that was back in the late 1950s.)

He went on by saying, "However, I need to tell you first, what I feel is the downside of this kind of civil service job. First, in this job, you will probably be reporting to a career military officer. Some of them do not care for civil service employees, because they know it is difficult to fire them unless they commit a felony, or a detailed record on their poor performance is kept on them for an extensive period. And maybe more noticeable to you, it would be a job that would not afford you the freedoms to make decisions and the ability to meet at an outside location without obtaining permission from a higher level. Sometimes you would even have to obtain permission to meet at another location here on base, away from your office. You see all these restrictions as a GS-8 do not exist in your present job in GCM. You can decide, for the most part, when and where you need to meet, and you don't have to clear it with someone 'up the line' first. To me, it would be a job that is structured but not necessarily dependent on the quality of work you do. However, if money is your key concern, it could be a good job. And I may even be able to get you a higher-level position, but I would not have much control over that. What do you think?"

I thought about the amount of money I had spent on those first two new suits and the initial requirement for me to always pick up the tab for the customer (even though it wasn't my money, I felt it was more of a "hey boy" job.) However, that was no longer part of my "job description." The more I thought about what my civil service salary would be and thinking it would probably always be more than what I was getting with GCM, the more it seemed somewhat attractive.

"Do you want some time to think about it, maybe talk it over with the wife?"

"I appreciate what you are offering me, and I could use the extra money, but I don't see me being satisfied in that type of job structure. So thanks, but I'm going to have to pass."

Then Norm showed me he was a real friend when he said, "I was pretty sure that was what you would say, and I think I would have kicked your butt if you had accepted the offer. You have good work ethics, and that job would not call for you to use them—you made the right decision. Let's get a cup of coffee, and then I've got to get back to work."

When I left his office later, I turned and said, "Norm, now I know one reason you have that bird on your shoulder."

His response was, "Get out of here before I start believing that Cr—!" I know I would have been proud to work for Norm as an Air Force officer or as a manager in a civilian job. He was a good and honest man.

I must say that as much as I enjoyed working on the Cheyenne Mountain Project, what existed at the time it was turned up for service, I would probably not recognize over a few "things" inside the mountain today. With advancements in telecommunications as well as the customer's needs and requirements changing, it would be a new way of doing the job at NORAD. The support AT&T does in serving NORAD has also changed as the needs of our customer changes. I will always remember with pride, of being a part of the "team effort" that enabled our Military to provide additional protection for the United States of America via its activity in Cheyenne Mountain.

Back in plant operations

The GCM office and the district operations office were both located on the same floor in the bank building on the town square of Colorado Springs. I received a call one morning from Jim Palmer, Colorado Springs district manager in our operations department. He was also a lieutenant colonel in the Air Force Reserves. Jim asked me to drop by his office that morning if I had some time because he had a couple of things he wanted to kick around with me.

Even though our offices were on the same floor, I had only met Jim in a meeting a couple of times, but never talked with him at length. Jim was a "to the point" type of manager and wasn't known as someone who liked to "chit-chat" to pass the time of day.

Since he or I didn't have any meetings scheduled that morning, I went to his office and told his secretary why I was there. When she notified Jim, he came out, shook my hand, and said, "Mr. McJunkin, come on in." I was a little surprised at his formal type greeting as he invited me into his office.

As we sat down, he said "I've talked with Mr. Harris, your district manager in GCM and he tells me you are doing a very good job in connection with your work on the Cheyenne Mountain Complex (CMC). As you know, it looks like things are on schedule and some of the engineers have told me, our plant office will be ready, ahead of schedule. I know I don't have to tell you, but they had a lot of problems on the project, starting with the inside caving in before they completed the inside structure.

But the reason I wanted to talk with you is not the mountain, but about our underground office at Boone County that I'm sure you know about."

"Yes, I've never been there, but I do know of their connection with the CMC activity."

"You mentioned you have never been there. How would you like to go there?"

"It might be interesting, but I have a pretty good idea of all they do and what their maintenance areas consist of."

"That's why I would like to offer you the job of a first-line supervisor at Boone. Do you think you would be interested?"

"Well, you hit me on the blindside with that question."

"It sounds like an interesting and challenging opportunity. Since it would require moving to Pueblo, I'd like to kick it around with my wife, so I know she isn't going to leave me or anything like that."

"I would say you better check with her because if she is like my wife and I didn't check with her before I said *yes*, I would be preparing my meals for several weeks and maybe sleeping on the sofa."

When I told Sondra, who was about eight months pregnant with our third child (Grant Wade), that I had been offered a promotion that afternoon.

Her reply was, "Let's see, hasn't it only been about two years that you have been in GCM? Do you think this is going to happen again in two years?"

"No way, we'll be there, maybe when it's time to retire." (Famous last words!)

The next morning, I informed Jim, if the offer was still open, I would accept it. The move was not a problem since Pueblo was not that far from Colorado Springs and we were able to find a beautiful, newly built house, in a new development in the NW part of Pueblo. We moved in and settled before our son (Grant) was born at the Pueblo Hospital. Our Boone office was about eight or ten miles East of Pueblo.

After we moved to our new home and I met the plant manager, Glen Brooks, and all the crew. Glen started filling me in on what was going on in our maintenance area. It was much more than I had expected. I was not aware we were establishing a new microwave radio route between Denver and Albuquerque, New Mexico. Not only was Boone about the halfway point between the two cities, but we would also have about four microwave relay stations to maintain, some of which were involved with the Cheyenne Mountain Complex.

I want to point out one thing that GOD showed me at every new assignment I had. Much, if not all the functional responsibilities of each office I managed, were new to me, and I had never worked on or was I familiar with their day-to-day working capabilities and some of their responsibilities. In each new location, the Lord showed me, "When you have good people working for you—recognize their talent and give credit where credit is due." The craftsmen at Boone were no exception. I found two of the men, Frank Trujillo and John McKim, were the best. They knew their job, and they didn't have to be told how or when to do it. That was good because I never worked one day, in a radio relay group or office. The reason I mention that at this point is, I found the talent I had in my crew at Boon would be duplicated in all my future locations throughout the rest of my career. The only problem I had with Frank was I never could break him of the habit of calling me "boss." He called me that the first day I arrived and the last day I was there. Frank was one of a kind, aside from being a great technician, he was also very active in President Johnson's reelection as president of the United States. He even received an invitation to his swearing-in ceremonies, but he didn't attend.

As I look back on those days, I feel it was the good Lord, knowing I had people working for me who often knew more as to *how* to do the job than I did, and GOD was telling me, "Let them do it, and you (Lloyd), make sure the work is performed properly and safely."

Before I left Boone, I had that lesson down pat, and I remembered it when it came time for their "evaluation" reviews. When I left Boone, Frank was rated number 1 in our district, and John was number 2 or 3. They both ended up in management when openings presented the opportunity, and I knew both had earned the promotions they received.

Another exciting experience I found while working at Boone was the work we were doing with Western Electric, who did all the installing of our equipment. We would always have one of our men doing the final acceptance testing. I always felt there was not much I didn't know about what we called L carrier equipment when I was a craftsman in Wichita, Kansas, and in no time at all, I felt my two men knew at least that much or more about the new T-L carrier system equipment we were installing in all our relay stations. I was amazed at the times when issues presented themselves that Western was not familiar with, Frank or John seemed to figure out what was wrong, and the installation work was able to continue.

One example of this came when I had a call from John, who was covering Western Electric at one of our relay stations. His first words were, "It looks like we have a big problem that will need you and the Western supervisor to help decide what we can do."

"Okay, let me have it."

When they installed the C-1 alarm bay (this was equipment that monitored all of our radio channels coming into and out of our station), they installed the C-1 alarm bay 180 degrees backward. Now that we are installing new equipment bays, one of which is to be back-to-back with the C-1 bay. If we mount the new bay that way, not only will it also be installed wrong, but the bay next to it is to be mounted facing the same direction as the C-1 bay.

We had no justification for trying to work around the problem knowing it would end up with both new bays installed wrong. Since the Western supervisor was on site, I told John to tell him I was on my way to the station.

John and his counterpart with Western, along with their supervisor and I got our heads together and tried to think of any way we could get everything arranged the way it should have been in the first place—without causing a service outage! The Western supervisor made it clear; he could not approve the new bay to be facing in the wrong direction. I agreed because this could create even more problems in the future.

Long story short, after much discussion, John said, "It's too bad that there is not enough slack in the cables and wiring coming into the alarm bay that would enable us to turn the bay, very slowly a 180 degrees, without any of the cables breaking loose."

The Western installer said, "You may have a point, we always leave slack on the wire connections. We leave plenty of slack in case the engineers decide it has to be relocated." The Western supervisor asked me, "Do you think it would be worth trying?"

My answer was, "Let's first check the slack before we do any moving of the bay, if it looks like the slack is there, then, yes, I think it may be our answer."

John and the W. E. Installer checked the wiring and cables and felt there seemed to be plenty of slack in both. I told the Western supervisor I would need a detailed "method of procedure" (MOP) that is a routine procedure for any installation work.

He agreed and said, "If things look like we can proceed, I'll have the MOP on your desk by 8:00 a.m."

I don't know about the others, but I spent that night, carefully, inch by inch moving that alarm bay around 180 degrees (in my dreams). The next morning when the plant manager, Glen, came in, I filled him in on the situation. After he came down off the ceiling and finished his cup of coffee; and the Western supervisor dropped off the method of procedure. I checked it out with him, and everything looked okay. I advised Glen and explained the Western supervisor, and I agreed it was workable. Glen's reply was, "I guess we don't have any other choice. Let's do it."

That evening at 11:45 p.m., I pulled into the parking lot at our Cedarwood station. Western and John had already arrived and were preparing to start the move. Long story short, everything went as planned, and there were no service interruptions. We all agreed it was not an activity we wanted to encounter again! That was the tensest situation I encountered while at Boone, but many more events made me proud of the men we had at that time, doing the jobs they were trained to do and doing them in a quality manner. I was glad we had John covering the job, and that was noted on his next evaluation report. John's idea was not a surprise to me. I viewed both he and Frank as having that type of work ethic.

Near the end of my first year at Boone, I received word from the district office we would be getting a copier in our office. When the machine arrived, we powered it up for use, and I was not surprised when everyone wanted to make a copy of "something," even though all copies were black on white. As we watched the prints slide out and into the tray, we saw pictures of a driver's license, a handprint, and about everything else. One of the guys had a picture in a magazine of a beautiful young woman, sunbathing on the beach. When the rest of the guys saw it, they told him to make a copy of her. One of our men was an African American man and went by the name of "Izzy," short for Isadore. As the copy of the lady came out of the copier, the one that was printing it said, "Oh, she is much darker in the copy than in the magazine. To which "Izzy," stated, "I think she is more attractive in the copy than in the magazine." Everyone laughed, and the copying continued until everyone had a copy they had made to take home to show their families. Izzy was probably the most popular man at our station. He had a personality that you found yourself laughing with him on so many comments he would make. However, people respected him because they knew he would do anything for you that he could.

There was one gas station in Boone, and we used it to buy gas for our company car and van. It was convenient, and it allowed us the opportunity to do a little public relations work within the small community. Glen and I both started using it to fill our cars whenever we needed gas. The owner appreciated our business, and I expect we were his biggest customer, and we may have kept him in business. He was also a good mechanic, and often we let him service our cars and do minor repair work.

I encountered many exciting experiences while I was at Boone. I couldn't have asked for a better group of men for our maintenance area. Frank and John went out of their way, time after time, to help some of the newer craft to take care of their work. Even when they were in the middle of acceptance testing, and one of the newer men needed help, they were never too busy to help. I would sometimes comment to them about their helping the newer men, and I recall Frank saying, "I remember when I was in their position, and someone would help me, it sure made me feel good."

I told them, "What the two of you are doing will also be remembered by the ones you help, and that could be passed on for a long time."

They both said, "Let's hope so."

I knew, their quality of artistry (craft) work would continue after I left. I felt confident their outstanding talents would be positive factors for management openings when they became available I had them rated high enough they would continue to be rated high in the district. The last I heard, Frank was a supervisor in the Denver central office, and John was in the engineering department in our area office in San Francisco. I was sure they both would continue their work ethic in all their future assignments.

Two more years have passed

About two years after my promotion to a first-line supervisor in plant at our Boone, Colorado, office, I received a call from the district manager (Earl Auxberger) in the Denver District.

His first question was, "Are you aware of our radio relay office on top of Buckhorn Mountain?"

"I've heard of it, but I don't know much about its functions, other than it's a manned radio relay office."

He continued, "I feel it probably has the prettiest view of any manned office in the Bell System. On a clear day, you can look to the North and see the first radio relay tower out of our office in Cheyenne, Wyoming. Then, if you turn around 180 degrees and look south, you can see the top of Pikes Peak. If you look West, you can see the Rocky Mountains range. It's all very beautiful. How would you like starting each day with that view to get you going?" My response was, "It sounds like a beautiful place."

"Well, that is why I'm calling you this morning. The office is covered 24-7 with seven to eight artisans (craft) and managed by a central office supervisor. Out of this office, they maintain two radio relay repeater stations. It is on the transcontinental microwave route and carries the three major TV networks. It's a blast-proof station with two levels underground."

I said, "That sounds a lot like where I'm working, here at Boone."

He laughed and said, "Yes, but it is about three times larger than Boone, and although the type of service going through the offices, quality, and quantity are similar, Buckhorn has many government services and other transcontinental high priority services. Because of that, Buckhorn has an annual 'surprise inspection' conducted by a Federal inspector out of Kansas City, Missouri. So you can see it is more than just another 'pretty place.'

"In talking with your district manager in the Colorado Springs District, Emmitt McMann, he tells me you have a secret clearance, a good rating, and you have good work ethics. The craftsmen at Buckhorn are all well trained, and one is the highest-rated in my district. My question is, 'Do you think you would be interested in taking over that office as its new central office supervisor?'"

I was speechless, "Man, you caught me off guard, not only am I not familiar with Buckhorn, I had no idea I would be getting this call. It sounds like a challenge, and if I were single, I'd say yes. As you know, it would require a household move, and I have two children in school. So I would like to see if my wife would agree to move a second time in two years. Can I give you a call first thing in the morning with an answer?"

"Sure, I'm married also, and I know if Mommy isn't part of the decision-making, Daddy can have some real problems. Call me in the morning."

That evening Sondra and I discussed the job offer, and she said, "If this isn't going to be an ongoing two-year requirement, I have no problem in moving to Fort Collins, Colorado. And don't give me that story you told me when we moved to Pueblo about it probably will be the location where you retire!" I assured her the chances of my being offered a higher-level job again, in two years were very slim. (I thought that was a true statement unless I messed up and was reduced in level.)

The first thing the next morning, I called Earl and told him, "If the offer is still available, I'll take it."

He said, "Great and welcome to the Denver District. I'll get the paperwork started, and we'll be talking as things progress. If you have any questions, give me a call."

"Will do and thanks for the offer, I look forward to meeting the craftsmen at Buckhorn, they sound like a good bunch of men."

From the underground at Boone to the mountaintop at Buckhorn (also underground)

The paperwork was completed as was our move. My first drive up Poudre Canyon, on my way to our Buckhorn office, was beautiful. I couldn't believe the scenery. Even near the top when the road becomes a "switchback" road, and you are getting above "timberline" the long-distance view was so attractive.

Like all the places I'd worked, it was not the technical part of the job that was the most interesting thing to talk about; it was the people and the out-of-the-ordinary happenings that I recall most, even half a century later. These are the things I remember most. I soon found that Buckhorn was not going to change that part of my career.

My top two craftsmen at Buckhorn were Dicky and Paul, both outstanding technicians. Within, the first six months, I knew both had the potential for promotion into another plant office or even into our engineering department. Six months later, after testing their receptiveness, should such an opportunity arise, I was informed of their true feelings by both men. Paul said he wanted to retire at Buckhorn, known as, "The old man of the mountain." And Dicky said, "I don't want to work in an administrative office, even in our district office." When I left, I had not been able to change either of their minds. I did respect their desires (and admired their convictions). When I left Buckhorn, both were my two highest rated craftsmen, and as I recall, Dicky was rated the top craftsmen in our Denver district. As good as both were, they had very different personalities. Paul was the "Tell me what you want me to do, and then let me do it."

Dicky was very different, he was more the, "If you think I can do it, I'll sure do my best to accomplish it." Dicky was one of these guys that had more talent than he would admit. Not only was he our top craftsman when working on radio relay equipment, but he also had an ability in the mechanical field as well.

The one habit I never could break Dicky of was how he referred to me. He had the same habit that Frank Trujillo had at Boone, but more so. From day one, he called me "boss." I told all the men, the first day I arrived to call me Lloyd—not Mr. McJunkin or Mr. Lloyd, just Lloyd. No one had any problems with that except Dicky. Just like I came and left Boone, the same happened at Buckhorn, with Dicky I was "boss" the first day, and when I left, I was still "boss." Dicky was the type of person you couldn't get mad at because you knew he was always giving his "all." He was from Arkansas, and you didn't have to hear him say over five words before you knew he sure wasn't from New York.

Buckhorn, like Boone, also had two like type diesel engines for backup power, should the commercial power go out. Dicky either did all the mechanical plant routines or over-saw one of the newer craft, in doing the routines on the two Detroit diesels. One day after we had been having an intermittent starting problem with one of our diesel engines, I asked Dicky if he would like to go to Detroit to a maintenance school that the manufacturer was conducting.

He said, "Where is it being held?"

I said, "In Detroit." His reply was, "Where is that?"

By that time, I knew Dicky was a lot smarter than he let on, so I replied, "I think it is up North where they make a lot of cars." His reply, with a smile, "Oh, okay."

I sent Dicky to the school since it focused on the control panel functions and its electrical operation and maintenance requirements. When he came back, the first thing he said was, "Boss, the next time we have any problems with our two 500 KW power units, let me know, I'm sure I can fix them. I can take those 'puppies' apart and put them back together, and they will run like they did when first installed."

I told him, "I don't doubt that, and as far as working on the control panel problems, you've got the job if it's needed. However, as far as you or any telephone employee, if the problem requires tearing the diesel apart and putting it back together, I want a qualified Detroit Diesel repairman doing that and if it doesn't run, when it's put back together, then it's Detroit's problem, not Dicky's."

"Okay, boss, but remember, I offered."

Due to the type of work performed in testrooms like Buckhorn, our instructions were to never let anyone inside our building, regardless of who they were before we could identify them and know why they should be allowed entrance. We had two outside doors at Buckhorn, one was for emergency use, and the other was for day-to-day use by our employees and visitors. The "main door" had an outside buzzer and speaker. When the buzzer was pressed, someone from either the C-1 alarm bay or the circuit order desk would answer. If it was anyone other than one of our people coming to work, there was a series of questions asked, and if still more verification was required, additional procedures were followed.

Today with all the advancements in technology I'm not sure Buckhorn is still a covered office twenty-four hours a day. The annual inspection may no longer be required since AT&T has so many new ways of automatically rerouting services from one place to another should flooding, tornados, or natural causes make a station inoperable. Many stations like Buckhorn are no longer manned by twenty-four-hour coverage due to their capability—that is, they can be remotely operated from a distant office. New technology gives them many more options in protecting services than back in the fifties when I was in the plant operations department.

Time for inspection

Dicky kept us laughing at his approach to the job and life. One example of this came after I arrived. It was when we had our annual surprise inspection by the federal government inspector out of Kansas City. I'll call him "George" because I don't recall his name.

Our annual surprise guest arrived one morning around nine o'clock. When the door alarm sounded, I had one of the craft verify who it was. When he checked to see who was at the door, he found it was our annual government inspector. After he signed in, he was escorted to my office.

As he introduced himself, he asked, "You're not the same manager I spoke with last year, are you?"

I told him I had been there only a few months, and, I was aware we would be getting an inspection sometime during the year. I asked him if he would like a cup of coffee, or did he want to look around first.

"Coffee sounds good, and we can do a lot of what I want to check while drinking our coffee."

After we finished our coffee and answered his questions, he said, "I do have a few things I need to check visually and if you could have one of your men go with me, when I finish, I'll come back, and we can discuss how things look."

I agreed and called Dicky and asked him to take George where he needed to go. He did, and in about half an hour, when they came back, George said, "Everything looks good, and this young man was a great help." Then he said, "If you still have some coffee, I think I could handle another cup."

I told him the coffee pot was full, and I asked Dicky if he would join us in case George had any questions dealing with the areas they had inspected.

Dicky's reply was, "Okay, boss."

Our conversation turned from the "inspection" almost immediately and turned to every subject but the telephone company. While we were talking, "George' laughed and said (pointing to Dicky) this young man is a man of few words. I think about every question I asked he was able to answer it with a *yes* or *no*.

At that, he turned to Dicky and said, "I detect a little accent in your voice, where are you from originally?" Now by this time I knew Dicky liked to have a little fun if he was talking with a "Yankee." To George's question, he answered, "I'm from Beebranch."

With that, I knew the game had started, "Where is that?"

"Arkansas."

"No, what town is it close to?"

"Oh, Purgatory"

"Never heard of that either, how close to Little Rock is it?"

"Oh, that is a fur piece away, I've never been there, but I reckon it is less than half a day, even in a car." I noticed George was taking all of this in as factual information and in a sense, most of it was. Dicky did come from Beebranch, and he had informed me there is a town not too far from it by the name of Purgatory.

I told Dicky later, "You're going to get in trouble someday with that put-on accent."

He laughed and replied, "That is how I talk; it's when I get in Yankee land that I emphasize my talk a little more."

I said, "Okay if you say so."

However, I sensed it was time to change the subject, so I asked George, "Where are you from?"

Without any hesitation, he said, "I'm from Independence, Missouri, the home of the great Harry S. Truman." I felt I might have asked the wrong question. It was like I had lit a fire under George. He proceeded to tell us that his family was poor farmers when he was growing up and the closest farm to theirs, was Harry's dad and mom's farm. He told us how one of the Truman children would often bring food to them that their mother had canned the previous summer. He went on and said Mr. and Mrs. Truman knew his family often didn't have enough to feed all of us kids a good nourishing meal. That would be when Mrs. Truman would send one of their older children to George's home and drop off some food with the reason being, "We have more than we can eat and thought maybe you might be able to use it." He said they would also check on his family during the winter to make sure none of them were sick, needed medicine or a doctor.

I had the impression that Harry was one if not the oldest of his siblings and may have been the one that brought food to George's family. He wasn't clear about everything the Truman family did to help his family, but Harry's family did make a positive impression on George's family. While Harry was in the Army, they continued to follow his activities. After he left the military and became a successful businessman in Kansas City, Missouri, they kept track of his success. When he became involved in politics, they followed him. I had a feeling if I asked George if he was a Democrat, he would have responded, "I'm a Democrat, not so much for what the party stands for but because of what President Truman did for my family and our country."

Seeing George's admiration for President Truman, I recalled an event that took place while I was still in the test room in Wichita, Kansas, that I thought George might be interested in hearing. So to reinforce George's comments about Harry, I said, "Your words about Harry reminds me of a happening that took place with our radio relay supervisor in Wichita, Kansas, involving Harry and his family."

It happened after Harry had retired to Independence, Missouri, after serving as our president. One of the networks was going to have a live TV pickup program from Harry's home. AT&T would be handling the communications link from the president's house into the telephone office in Kansas City, and there the link would be connected to the network's TV channels. Before the day of the event, the radio relay supervisor in our KC office became sick, and their manager called our manager in Wichita and asked if he could send his radio relay supervisor to KC to take care of the "pickup."

A couple of days before the "pickup" was to take place our supervisor (Mel) went to KC, hooked up with the "TV pickup" crew, and went over the plans so everyone would be ready to go on the scheduled day.

The morning they were scheduled to go to the president's house, it was pouring down rain. The rain did not change the plans, and the crew left for Present Truman's home in Independence, well ahead of the time for the activity to start. The events that unfolded from that time on was as follows; according to how Mel and the craft told them on their return to the Kansas City office.

As they pulled into the president's driveway, they were met by a Secret Service agent who identified himself and asked to speak with the supervisor in charge. Mel showed him his company ID and told the agent he was in charge of the pickup activity. Now, from this point on you will have to take it for what it's worth, but the following is how Mel and his crew reported their events while they were taking care of the TV pickup program at former President Harry S. Truman's home.

Mel had checked with the crew and was satisfied; everything was ready for the program to start. Little did Mel or any of the crew know what was about to happen. The Secret Service agent Mel had talked with on their arrival came out again and informed Mel, "The president wants you and the crew to come in the house and have a cup of coffee before you go to work on the pickup."

Mel replied, "We can't do that, but tell the president we do appreciate his thoughtfulness."

The agent said, "Okay," and left.

While the crew was getting things in place for the feed to the KC office, the door to the house opened, and Harry, in a raincoat, came out to the truck and asked, "Who is Mel?"

The crew, in unison, pointed to Mel.

The president turned and said, "Now look, you guys aren't going to stand out here in the rain without a cup of hot coffee, now get in the house, get your coffee, and you will still have time to get things set up."

Mel and the crew followed the president into his house. Mel felt they did have plenty of time to finish the hookup, but he felt uneasy thinking about what Bess may say when she saw this group of strangers "clomping into" her home with rain dripping off their clothes and mud falling off their shoes on her nice clean floors.

As the story continued, everything went as the president had planned, the coffee was great, and they were able to return to their work, make the connection via their microwave channel back to the KC office and everything checked out "a-okay." And they did have time before the program was scheduled to go live on the network. Mel and one of the technicians remained inside the house during the program in case any technical problems arose, and the rest of the crew would be inside the "pickup" van where the transmission was being monitored and sent back to the KC office. Everything went as planned, no technical problems, and the network people were very satisfied as to how the program was handled. They thanked the AT&T crew for their role in making the pickup a success.

However, the rain never stopped throughout all the activity. Once the pickup was over, our crew again had to get out in the rain to secure the antenna and the equipment and make ready to return to the KC AT&T office. Mel and the technician that had been inside, came out to the van to make sure everything was ready to go. Just as they were preparing to leave, the same agent that had met them earlier returned and said, "The president wants everyone to come in, so he can say goodbye to you before you leave."

Mel remembered what happened earlier when he chose not to go in, so he turned to the crew and said, "Okay, guys, let's go in, but try to clean your shoes so we don't muddy the floors too much."

Harry met them at the door and said, "You guys did a great [a stronger word may have been said] job. Get in here and dry off, I don't want anyone coming down with a cold because you came out in this bad weather to do a TV program for an old retired president."

Everyone laughed, and Mel said, "Oh, we've been out in weather worse than this, don't worry about us, we will be okay."

As they entered the house, President Truman pointed down the hallway to the restroom. He then said, "After you get dried off the room next door to the restroom is a walk-in closet. It is full of clothes that were given to me by some of the best men's clothes manufacturers in the world. I want you to go in and pick yourself up some dry clothes that fit you, put them on, and then we can have some coffee, and you can get started back to your office dry and warm.

Again, Mel pointed out they would be okay, and they couldn't take any of his clothes. Then it seems the president made his point of "getting dried off" when he said, "No, I mean it. The clothes in the closet are full of all kinds and sizes of men's suits, sport coats, and slacks. Most of them I would never wear if you paid me. Some of them are too big, and some are too small. I want each of you to go down and pick something that will fit you, and you like and put them on. And if you see another suit or whatever, you like, take it also. I want to get rid of that stuff, and you guys earned a new set of clothes today. Now get down there and start changing into some dry clothes, and there are towels in the bathroom. Now go!"

Mel probably felt he would give a month's wages to be back in Wichita, thinking, "What am I going to do?" He turned to Harry and said, "Mr. President, we appreciate your offer, but we are not allowed to receive gifts in connection for what our job calls for us to do. We could even get fired if we accepted your very generous offer. We are thankful that you have been so thoughtful, thank you so much, but we will be okay, and we will never forget this day."

Harry replied, "I guarantee none of you will be fired, and if they try, I'll see that they understand they have made a mistake, and it will be corrected. Now, get down there and get some dry clothes on before I call Bess and tell her you are mudding up her house. And let me tell you, she is not someone you want to get upset!"

I never heard if any new clothes were worn back to their office that day, but knowing Harry's reputation, I can only assume the crew was dry and comfortable when they left Harry's home, and possibly one or more of them were wearing a new dress suit and maybe carrying a second one on their arms!

I shared the above story with George; he laughed for what seemed to be five minutes. Then he said, "That sounds like the Harry Truman I knew and admired. It was something I know he would do in that situation. As I said, we have never had a president like Harry S. Truman, and I doubt if we ever will."

By the time "George" left, Dicky and I both knew we sure didn't want to say anything negative about Harry or Bess or the Truman family. We both agreed, there wasn't anything we could think of that we could have said that was negative because he was a good president who knew the American people deserved better than what they had just gone through during World War II.

Let it snow, let it snow, let it snow

During the second of two winters I was at Buckhorn, we had record-breaking snow. All of us had regular two-wheel drive family cars. We kept a company vehicle, a four-wheel drive Chevrolet Carryall, in a garage in Fort Collins. The county road maintenance crew was good at keeping the roads clear of snow, especially during the school year. We had a contract with the county for them to blade our, less than a mile, "switchback" entry road into our station. The little extra snow clearing for us seemed to work quite well for the county since they would usually have their plows clearing the roads for the school buses to be able to pick up the children.

However, this year, it started early and lasted longer than normal. This one major storm started snowing heavy, midday on Sunday. Since there was no school on Sunday, the plows were not out. I had the 8:00 a.m. to 4:00 p.m. man, holds-over, telling him he would probably have to stay until 8:00 a.m. on Monday.

He said, "That's okay, I can use the overtime!"

But the snow didn't stop all night, and even though the next day was Monday, there was no school and no early morning plowing, on the road to our station. I called our man at Buckhorn and asked how he was doing. His reply was, in a very sleepy tone, "I can stay, but if we have a major problem, I'm not sure I will be able to work on it and may even cause an outage."

I told him, "I would see if I could find a way to get him relieved."

"I appreciate that, and if you do, they may have to let themselves in and then wake me up."

"Don't worry about that; we'll get to you as soon as possible."

I decided to take a chance with our four-wheel drive carryall to get us to the station. I checked with the county, and the supervisor told me they would be on the roads as soon as it stopped snowing and they would continue on our access road when they reached it at the end of their road. I knew that if we could drive our four-wheel drive carryall to the station, we could get our man out. I called three of our day crew and told them to meet me at the garage in Fort Collins, where we kept our four-wheel drive vehicle. I told the rest of the Day crew to stand by "on call." The four of us warmed the carryall up and headed up the road to our station. I think Dicky was driving and we already had the four-wheel drive engaged. We were making good time and even joked about how easy things were going.

When we came to the switchback portion into our station, we encountered a challenge. We all agreed that if we didn't get high-centered, we would make it. We made it by the first switchback curve, and one of the guys said, "The good news is, I don't think we are going to meet anyone coming down the road, so we won't have to worry about pulling over to the side to let them by."

We passed the second switchback and had one more to go. It was then we started feeling some vibration in the movement of the vehicle. At the time we noticed the vibration, it increased to the point our vehicle stopped.

I said, "If I had to guess, I would say we are high-centered."

One of the guys said, "You don't have to guess, we are high-centered."

We always carried what we called "winter gear" in all our vehicles that consisted, among other things, two "sharpshooter spades." These were small shovels that had a blade about half the size of a regular shovel, with about a two-foot handle. Without, waiting for me to select who was going to be given the honor to check the shovels out, two of the guys spread canvas on the snow, laid down on it, in front of the vehicle and started shoveling packed snow out from under the front axle. Long story short, we made it to the station. Praise GOD!

I asked the craftsman that had been on duty for twenty-four hours how he felt, and he said, "Great, now that you guys are here." He was confident he could make it down okay. I told him if he was sure he wouldn't fall asleep, he could take the four-wheeler and leave it in the garage and take a cab home if his wife was not able to pick him up. He said he felt he could make it and one of the other guys said if he left his car keys, he would drive it down when they were relieved, and the roads were clear.

I told the day crew, "We may have to stay until 8:00 a.m. tomorrow, so someone make the coffee, and the rest of you start our alarm checks and see if we have any significant problems. I then called the district office in Denver and found there were only two or three that were able to get to the office, at that time. Since the district manager was not one of them, I talked with one of the staff and gave him our status at Buckhorn and told him what we had encountered that morning and what I planned to do if the storm continued.

About midmorning, the snow let up, and by 2:00 p.m., it had stopped and the sun was out. I remember going out on the South parking lot and looking toward Pikes Peak. It was one of the few times you could see Pikes Peak, and the view was breathtaking, looking to the West you had a picture-perfect view of the Rocky Mountain Range. I thought, "GOD is great!"

Everything worked out okay that day. I had the other half of our day crew come up at noon and had one of them pick up the four-wheeler and bring it up, so we could get down when the 4:00 p.m. man showed up.

These kinds of events are the ones I remember, maybe not in exact detail, but I do remember the teamwork our people showed when needed. Also, I recall the positive attitude our men showed during situations when many would have given up or complained. These are the experiences that made me proud to have worked for a company that truly did take care of its people and its people, in turn, took care of the company, especially in the situation we had that day.

There were other events at Buckhorn, but the above reflects the closeness we had. The men had pride in *their* office and each other. We became a very close family during the time I was there, and overall, it was one of the best assignments I had throughout my career with AT&T. Even our wives became close friends, and our families and kids often visited with each other.

However, as my Uncle "Short" used to say, "Into each bowl of oatmeal and raisins, you often find a bug among the raisins."

There was one situation I experienced while working at Buckhorn that was not representative of our total crew. It took place one early morning, about 4:00 a.m. I recalled when the inspector (George) made our annual security visit; he mentioned to me that it might be a good idea if I made a surprise inspection about once a year. He added it probably would only be necessary on the midnight to 8:00 a.m. shift since we only had one man on duty during those hours and there was not a lot of activity going on during that time.

I told the crew what the inspector had suggested and indicated I probably would check them out, so "Don't be surprised if I show up some morning around 5:00 a.m. or earlier. Everyone laughed, and I thought to myself that, if I did inspect, probably the only thing it would accomplish would be, I missed out on getting a good night's sleep. The weeks passed, and one evening when I had dropped off for a nap that lasted longer than I intended, I told my wife I was going to get up early, around 4:00 a.m., and check on the office. I won't tell you what she had to say about that brilliant decision.

At 3:45 a.m., the alarm came on, and I immediately turned it off, got dressed, and took off for Buckhorn. Since I had a key to the outside door, and I knew the combination for the inside door. On arriving at the station, I let myself in and saw most of the lights were off in the equipment room. I walked toward the alarm bay that monitored all the remote stations and the service going through our office. I said in a normal voice, "Roger," (not his real name) no answer. I repeated, "Roger."

Still no reply. The reason I had chosen to check the office that night was the craftsman that was working that shift, at that time, was the only one in our group that seemed to spend more time trying to get out of doing his job, than it would take to do it. I felt if any of the guys slept during their shift, it would be him.

One more time in a little louder voice, "ROGER."

Still no answer. As I walked to the front of the alarm bay, I saw why I was not getting any responses to my calls.

You may remember the old Marlboro cigarette add, showing the cowboy laying on the ground with his head on the seat of his saddle and his ten-gallon hat over his face, fast asleep. When I came to the front side of the alarm bay, there was enough light coming from the little lamp bulbs from the various alarm positions that I could easily see the area. There, on the floor, lay the Marlboro man's brother, minus the saddle, laying on the floor with his ten-gallon hat over his face, fast asleep. I once again said, "Roger." No reply. I then leaned over and pressed the alarm test button that was loud enough to wake the dead. It worked, Roger jumped up and said, "Why are you here? Man, I must have dozed off!"

I said, "You sure did, and as of (I checked my watch) 4:55 a.m. this morning you are relieved from your job. You are responsible for checking back with me NLT 4:00 p.m. this afternoon to see if you still have a job. Is that clear?"

With a faint, "Yes," he left the building.

When the day crew showed up, I filled them in and was somewhat surprised when one of them said, "You should have fired him." And several others agreed. That showed me these guys had a lot of pride in their station, and they knew the quality of its people made all the difference in the world in having a quality workplace.

At 8:00 a.m. I called the district manager and told him what had happened.

He said, "Your inspection was what all the managers should do from time to time. I'll double-check with legal, but it sounds like you followed the right procedure in sending him home. I'll get back with you and tell you what they say our options are." I received a call back around 2:30 p.m. and the district manager said the legal department advised we fire him. A little before 4:00 p.m., Roger called, and I informed him he was no longer an employee of AT&T because he had violated our company practice that an employee could not sleep during the time they were, "on the clock" and *not* doing the job he was being paid to do. I informed him, if he had any questions, they should be directed to our district manager or our legal department.

That was the last we heard from Roger. Again, I was somewhat surprised over the next few weeks in seeing the morale among our office crew seem to improve, even though it was good before this incident happened. I think they knew what I would do if anyone violated the company's rules, and if they were doing a good job, they knew it would show up on their appraisal report.

Two more years had passed, and guess what?

I came in early one morning to discuss with our midnight to 8:00 a.m. craftsman, a couple of conditions that we had been monitoring over the past week. We had finished about the time our day crew arrived and checked in. The midnight to 8:00 a.m. man said, "I think I'll have a cup of coffee before I take off for home." I said, "If you don't mind, I'll join you before I see what's on my schedule for the day. We went to the break room, poured our coffee and thinking about our recent experience with "Roger," I started to ask, "Do you have any problem sleeping during the daytime? Before I was able to ask my question, one of the craftsmen had answered my phone and announced over the PA system, "Lloyd, you've got a call from Mr. Palmer."

The only Palmer I knew that had my office number was Jim Palmer, the district manager in Colorado Springs, who had offered me the job at Boone a couple of years earlier.

"What in the world would he be calling me for?"

I picked up the intercom and told the craft, "I'd be right there."

When I answered the phone, Jim said, "I know you are busy, but I think I have another opportunity for you, like the one at Boone, but much better." He mentioned a few areas concerning Cheyenne Mountain and changes that were going on there and then he asked, "I'm going to come right to the point, 'How would you like to have the plant manager's job at our Lamar underground office?' Before you answer, it has five first-line supervisors, and I think you know a couple of them, Jim Hildebrandt and Norm Larson.

"I know you are familiar with what a plant operations supervisor's basic responsibilities are. Your work at Boone as a first-line supervisor for a couple of years in my district showed me you did a good job there. During the past two years, you've had the Buckhorn office and have done a good job according to your district manager, Earl Auxberger. This job has all those plant challenges, but it also has a few more. And it's the 'more' I want to kick around with you today if you think you would be interested in taking the job."

"Jim, I would be interested in the job, but I'm anxious to hear about the extra 'challenges.'"

"I know your primary job with GCM was in connection with the communication requirements the telephone company would need to provide NORAD after they moved into Cheyenne Mountain, once the project completed. The job I have at Lamar is a second level (plant manager's job). Its maintenance area consists of seven L-1 cable power feed huts on the east side toward Kansas and an equal number south toward New Mexico. It has four Microwave repeater stations on the Denver–Albuquerque, New Mexico, TD-2 Radio route. Two of the remote stations currently are manned five days during the week. They are the Lamar South and Dalhart, TX stations. There are, on the average, about forty craftsmen in the Lamar office and two women secretaries plus a Test-Room supervisor and a craft at both the remote semimanned stations.

Other than that, it's a standard plant central office. Do you think you could handle that?"

"If the rest of the supervisors are as good as I feel Jim and Norm are, I think I can handle it. Since this will be my fourth move since leaving the test room in Wichita, so I feel I need to alert my wife, Sondra, and see if she will pack up the kids and go with me to Lamar!"

"I understand, and tell her Lamar is a nice quiet little town, they have good schools, and I would expect you won't have the 'opportunity' to move so often if you take this job."

"Okay, I'll get back with you tomorrow morning."

When I told Sondra that evening I had something to kick around with her, she said, "Don't tell me we are going to move again?" The only thing I could think to say was, "Wouldn't you like to know where our new home is going to be?" At the time we moved to Fort Collins, our girls were old enough to give their input, and they were all for the move. So we asked how they felt if we moved to Lamar. Again, they both were still in favor of moving. Then they both asked the same question, "Where is Lamar?" I think, by this time, Sondra had resigned herself to the fact that we were going to be a traveling family and we might as well enjoy the free ride, scenery, and all the other amenities!

From the top of the mountain to deep underground

I called Jim the next morning and told him Sondra said, she and the kids would go, but I have to take her out for dinner this evening.

Jim said, "Show it as a business meal and send me the voucher; it will be on me."

Our office complex was a few miles south of Lamar. From the highway, it looked like a concrete 'two-car' garage with a huge parking area and off to the left was a four-vehicle garage. This structure was next to one of the tallest microwave antenna towers in the State of Colorado.

When I arrived at the office, I rang the buzzer for someone to open the door, and I heard a woman's voice ask, "Who is there?"

I responded, "I'm Lloyd McJunkin, looking for a job." It was one of the secretaries who may not have heard I was coming, and she said, "Who?"

I responded, "If Norm Larson is there, he may vouch for me."

She said, "Just a minute, I'll get him." When she returned, she said, "Oh, I'm so sorry, Mr. McJunkin, I didn't know you were coming down today, I'm so sorry, and here is Mr. Larson."

Norm took the phone laughing and said, "Well, Lloyd, you can see we have tight security here at the Lamar underground station." He pressed the buzzer to open the door topside and then the blast door to gain entrance to the building, at its lower level. We all laughed when I entered the office area, except for the secretary and she apologized again.

Norm took me around and introduced me to the other supervisors, except Jim Hildebrandt, who was at one of the remote stations that morning. I met all the craftsmen that were working in the office that day and that included, "Craftsman Bob." I'll tell you about him a little later. Both secretaries were very polite, and as the days passed, I found they were also very proficient at their jobs.

It was about that time that I realized, of all the plant operation stations/offices I had worked in, after leaving the Wichita central office, all the plant offices were "underground." I don't know if there was a message in that or not?

Like my other assignments, I was about to find out; I was *not* going to experience any major disappointments in my new job. In a very short time, I found all my first-line supervisors were well qualified in microwave and cable supervision. Most of our craftsmen were well trained in both areas, and the rest were more experienced in one or the other carrier systems that we had. However, they too were being trained in both as time permitted.

I was to find out very soon that Sam Swadener was my "go-to" all-around supervisor. Sam was the oldest supervisor and had a personality that seemed to command respect from the other supervisors and the craftsmen. In a very short time, I pegged Sam as the one to call on if I needed an answer immediately and not get a lot of "maybe" or "I think" type answers. And there were times when that situation did arise.

However, over the first few months on the job, I knew we had a good office and a group of well-qualified supervisors and craftsmen.

I didn't know at the time I accepted the job, and I'm sure Jim didn't omit it on purpose when he was going over the various activities at Lamar, but we were scheduled to make the first "live cut" in the installation of the Bell System's new ESS switching machine. It was scheduled to take place within the next three months. Sam filled me in on the details about a week after I arrived.

A lot of details had to be worked out, but, soft-spoken Sam made them sound like, "a piece of cake to accomplish." I felt more at ease when I found Sam was the lead supervisor, and he assured me he had his best two men on the project.

I had a call from the district advising me that the week of the cut, Bell Labs would have one or two managers in our office, observing the activities. It was made clear that these men would be observers only and had no authority concerning changing the plans Western Electric and we had developed for the ESS cut. I was very impressed when I talked with the two craftsmen that Sam had assigned to the project. They both convinced me they knew what they were doing, and knew the importance of the cut being successful.

When the cut date was within a week of taking place, the two Bell Labs managers arrived and didn't make any suggestions but did ask many questions. They seemed satisfied with the answers we gave them. The cut was going to take place at 12:01 a.m. We had, in addition to the two Bell Labs people, a staff supervisor from both our district office and our division office. On the morning of the cut, I made it clear that I would appreciate it if all of our visitors would remain in the break room until after the cut was complete.

"Space is limited, and we don't want to interfere with our craftsmen and Western Electric Installers and supervisors involved in the activities."

I advised that, after the cut was completed and verified, my supervisor and I, along with our counterparts from Western Electric, would be available to answer any questions they might have. They all understood and enjoyed their coffee and donuts while the rest of us went to the work area. I don't recall how long it took, but I do recall when Sam and the Western supervisor shook hands, I knew that was a good sign that all went well since there were no alarms.

I never mentioned it at the time, but that cut was as nerve-racking for me as was the Alarm bay turn around activity we had at Cedarwood, several years earlier. Both could have resulted in significant service outages, and I think all who were involved and were "believers," knew GOD was the one who deserved the praise for the results. After everything was checked out, I thanked all the men who were involved in the cut, as well as those who came from the Labs, division and our district for being on-site and observing the first "hot cut" of an ESS switcher in the Bell System. (Praise GOD!)

The Lamar newspaper had a write-up in the paper, but if you didn't know the technical aspects of the event and what the consequences could have been if the cut had failed, you probably were not too impressed in reading the article. But it was the thought that counted.

The ESS activity was the highlight of my tour at Lamar as far as what could have happened. But I recall there was the floodwaters that almost washed out our underground cable one year and several similar situations dealing with our microwave systems, all in all we came through with flying colors. That was because we had well-qualified supervisors and a great bunch of qualified craftsmen.

Now, let me tell you a little about "Craftsman Bob." Bob was another guy that I couldn't break from calling me "boss." He was about six-foot-one tall with a medium build. Bob had more self-confidence than any two men I ever met. For example, one of the impressions I had that first day I entered our office and noticed our equipment room walls were unattractive concrete. Little did I know, but Bob was waiting for me to get settled so he could offer me a solution.

When that day arrived, Bob asked me, "Boss, what would you say if I told you 'my boys' and I would paint the walls of *our* office, and all you have to do is buy the paint?"

I laughed and said, "I might take you up on that offer, but I can't let you do it on company time, we didn't hire you to be painters but as craftsmen. "No problem, we'll even do it on the weekend."

"Let me think it over while you make sure you have the labor force to do the job," I called Sam and two of the other supervisors that spent most of their time in the building to meet with me in one of our training rooms. I told them what Bob had offered and what I had told him. I also told them that, although I felt I would not get approval to have painters come out and paint the walls, I agreed it would sure make the place look a lot better painted.

They all agreed, and Sam said, "I'll bet Bob will be back within a day and tell you he and 'his boys' are ready to paint."

Sam was right. Bob saw me the next day and asked, "When can we start, I've got 'my men' ready."

I said, "There is one more person we need to discuss this with, and that is your union steward." (Since I had been a union stewards when I was a craftsman in Wichita, I knew if management started doing things with the craft that were not in the union contract, they would get very upset.)

Bob said, "That's no problem, I'll take care of that."

I said, "No, let's both sit down with your union steward and make sure we are all in agreement."

I asked the union steward to meet me in the "training room." He, Bob, and I went over Bob's proposal. I explained that I might be receptive to buy the paint if the work was done in off-hours and not during any of their assigned work schedule times. After some discussion, we all agreed it would make our office look so much better than it was at that time. I laid out what Bob and some of the other craftsmen had offered to do and asked what the union steward thought about it. "I think it is a good idea, as long as it is not on company time. If they want to come out and do it on their own time and do work that is not part of their job description, I don't see any problem."

Long story short, I made it clear what the conditions were, and they knew the importance of *not* getting any equipment splattered with paint. They all agreed, and there were a few other craftsmen that joined Bob and his crew. The walls were about ten or twelve feet high, and the upper portions could only be reached using ladders. I observed the first Saturday's operation, and it looked like they were going to do a good job. I think it took them three weekends to complete the job and clean up. I must say I was very pleasantly surprised when I saw the result.

During that time, we had a new district manager take over our district (I'll call him Dan). He was quite a man. He was a lot like Dicky French from Buckhorn, and they both could use that Southern accent. Dan could turn it on in a split second. One day, shortly after the painting project had completed and everyone in the office seemed to feel it made our work area look so much better, I laughed when I heard Bob had told some of the craft.

"Of course it does. I knew it would improve the appearance, and that is why I talked Lloyd into letting us do it!" That did not surprise anyone in hearing Bob saying what he did. That seemed to be how Bob got his satisfaction, and he usually was able to make good on what he said he was going to do.

Not only did we have a new district manager, but we also had a new division manager out of Denver office (whose first name was Jim).

One day Dan called and said, "I'm bringing our new division manager down to Lamar tomorrow to show him our number 1 office in the district."

I said, "Okay, we'll be looking for you."

I alerted the supervisors and told them to make sure everyone knew who was coming down. It never dawned on me that neither our district manager nor the division manager had seen our new paint job.

Tomorrow came, and so did our visitors.

I had told Sam, "Bashful Bob's supervisor, to tell Bob not to do anything he shouldn't.

Sam laughed and said, "I'll do that, but you know Bob!"

When the district (Dan) and division (Jim) managers arrived in our office, and Dan had introduced the division manager, Jim, to me, I never noticed it, but Jim was standing next to one of the three-by-three-foot columns that we had recently painted. I'm sure he didn't realize what he did when he leaned back on the column and bent his left leg, placing the sole of his shoe against the column.

Now picture this. We, three managers, are standing, talking away. Dan had turned on his Southern drawl in telling Jim what a great office Lamar was and how dedicated all the people were, when "Craftsman Bob" walks by close to where we were standing. The thought flashed through my mind to introduce Bob to Jim, but then I said, "No, Bob will never leave."

That thought no more than disappeared when Bob stopped, turned to Jim (our division manager), and said, "Excuse me, but we take a lot of pride in our office, and you have your foot on one of the columns that were recently painted, and it will probably leave a print of your shoe if you keep it there." If I could have disappeared, I would have been "long gone."

I looked at Dan, and he was as speechless as I was. However, he recovered and said to Jim, "See, that's what I was telling you, these guys are unbelievable, they are all well-qualified technicians, and they look at their office as their home away from home. I even kid them about being the "Banana Belt" of the Colorado Springs District. You won't find another field office anywhere in the division that takes more pride in doing quality work and showing quality pride, than the crew from Lamar." And then to add the frosting to the cake, Bob said, "That's right, Dan."

Jim immediately dropped his foot and said, "Oh, I'm sorry, I don't know what I was thinking. Did I leave a mark on the column?"

Bob bent over as if he was going to pull out a magnifying glass and look, and said, "No, it doesn't look like it."

I told the supervisors later how Bob made the day. Dan saved the day and our division manager will never forget the day he visited Lamar, and it may be his last visit. I figured Dan would tell me later the next time he brought someone to Lamar to be sure Bob was out of the office. But he didn't.

He did ask me, when he called the next day, "How long have your walls been painted? That makes a dull-looking test room look like a professional building!" I told him they were painted soon after I came to the station. I didn't add any more, and Dan didn't ask for any more details.

It was not too long after the above visit had taken place that I knew Bob felt he was on a roll and the game was not over. Our driveway from the highway was about fifty yards to the parking lot in front of our above-ground structure. Bob came into the office area one day and said, "Boss, what would you say if my boys and I would plant some poplar trees on both sides of the entryway drive at about ten feet apart?"

"All you would have to do is buy the trees, and we'll plant them." He went on and informed me that he had checked with the local nursery, and they had given him a reasonable price. I don't recall what it was, but I know it did seem reasonable. I thought a little while and said, "Tell you what, Bob, if I can get approval from the district to buy them with no labor costs, I'll take you up on your offer *if* you again, do it on your own time."

Bob replied, "You've got a deal."

"No, I haven't, not until I get the approval to buy the trees. You need to see how many trees you'll need, what the cost will be and let me know your plan in how you will plant them."

"No problem, I'll have that probably tomorrow." I talked with the union steward about Bob's new suggestion, and he laughed and said, "If he and some of the others want to spend their weekends doing it outside their assigned working hours, I don't see any problem with it."

I think it was a couple of days later when Bob came back with what I needed to go to the district. I called Dan and told him what "Bashful Bob" had offered to do and what the cost of the trees would be.

I said, "It will add a lot to the attractiveness to our outside appearance to anyone driving down the highway."

There seemed to be a pause, and then Dan said, "You know you may be right, if the entire job, cost, and labor, can be done for what the trees will cost, it sounds like a real bargain, do it and let me know when you are finished. I want to come down and see what it looks like."

"Okay, and I'll keep you informed of the progress."

Bob had the trees delivered after they borrowed a trencher and dug a ditch on both sides of the drive. Once completed, they followed the directions of the nursery owner; by filling the trenches with water and then placed the ten-foot-tall trees about ten feet apart. Next, they filled the trenches with dirt and soaked the soil for over a week. They continued this until the trees looked recovered from the shock of being planted.

Again, we had coverage by the local newspaper, including a picture on the front page. I thought I was going to have to tie Bob down; he was walking on "cloud nine." Bob was rated as an average craftsman for his technical ability and seemed to be satisfied with that view of his job performance. The supervisors and I looked at the craftsman who was viewed by Bob as "my boys." My supervisors and I viewed these men as craftsmen who knew their "telco" job descriptions and knew they were expected to perform at a high performance. Some of them ranked in the upper quarter of our craft at Lamar. However, these same men did not seem to have any desire to offer suggestions as to how a work function could be improved and done better, faster, or safer. They were viewed by their supervisors, as not wanting to be given any responsibility, in case a problem arose. These same men would, however, join others of a similar mindset, if for no other reason than to be part of a group and in this situation, Bob's, "My boys" was their group and Bob was their spokesman.

A few years ago, Sondra and I took a vacation and drove back to Colorado and visited the places we had lived. We drove out to the Lamar station and saw they had put a ten-foot-high wire fence all around the parking lot. The weeds had grown up on the outside of the fence, and even though it brought back a lot of great memories, it made me feel sad to see how the Banana Belt of the Colorado Springs District had changed. I don't know when all that took place, but it was quite sometime after I had left and I'm thankful I was not there when the decision was made to maintain the station remotely. The Lamar office had become remotely managed, and the trees have all died since their life expectancy was about fifteen years.

This visit to the underground office at Lamar, Colorado, reminded me that the changes I saw at Lamar were somewhat typical of what had happened at Buckhorn, Boone, and Cheyenne Mountain, and even at my starting place in Wichita, Kansas. With new technology advancements, changes in business operational procedures have also changed. Over fifteen years, specific areas and activities that were "secret," no longer have that requirement. Like life itself, "Time does change everything." The need to have a forty-some craft, five supervisors, two secretaries, and a manager in an office has changed, and today, some of these offices no longer are staffed with people. Many top priority services to customers' data can now be transmitted in an unintelligible data stream among offices. So many of the operational procedures of yesterday are not required today. These changes are good for AT&T and its customers. But as I've mentioned several times in the previous chapters, it was not the technical functions of the offices I was responsible for that I remember and miss, it was the people that worked in those offices that I recall with many fond memories. Those were the type of people that made AT&T the top telecommunications company in the world, at that time. I have thanked GOD many times since I left the plant department when I recall all the things that took place among those people who always took pride in their job and in the locations they worked.

When I left Lamar to spend the remainder of my career in AT&T headquarters in New York City (NYC), I quickly became aware of the importance of never forgetting the people who made my job easier and our company greater. It would be nice if I could thank each one of them for showing me the essential things in our job are its people. They showed me they had pride in telling their friends and family they worked for a company that cared for its employees. They showed me they had respect for their supervisors who expected loyalty from them. Their pride in their job was evident when they told others, "I work for the great Ma Bell."

I found life continued when I left Lamar for NYC. But I also found when my job with AT&T was now located in NYC, there was a noticeable difference, and the difference was in the people themselves. I noticed many of the AT&T managers had titles that were higher on AT&T's organization chart than what I had seen in the field offices. I knew this because NYC was where our corporate headquarters located. At first, I noticed I didn't hear many employees who were then working in headquarters, voice their "pride in Ma Bell." But as time passed, I found many of my new coworkers were those "great people" I knew and worked with while I was in the Western Area, during previous assignments. I soon realized when working in NYC; we didn't have time to talk about those types of feelings, at least until we were seated on the commuter train taking us home that evening. However, I found that at the beginning of each new day, the sun still came up in the east, and life continued. It took some time to accept the fact, our jobs were okay, but our location was very different from any we had in the area, division, district, and central offices throughout the Bell System. And we realized we would soon make our own decision as to how we were going to “fit in” our new location! I must add, today the AT&T headquarters is no longer in New York City, but it is in Dallas, Texas. Since I retired, I haven’t talked with any of the people about their views of AT&T, now they are out of NYC, but I expect it has changed!

Chapter 9

The Second Half of Thirty Years with AT&T

Half of my AT&T career was in the New York City and New Jersey areas!

The first few months after arriving in NYC and getting to understand my job responsibilities; I started noticing some of the comments from my coworkers. They seem to not have many good words for working in "the Big Apple" (a synonym for Lower Manhattan.) My first thought was, "Why is everyone looking at everything negatively?" I decided my motto was going to be: "No matter what things look like or how you feel, get up, dress up and show up."

But I'm getting ahead of myself. While I was still at Lamar, I recall the day I had a call from Emmitt McMann, my former district manager in Colorado Springs that I worked for during most of the time I was at Lamar. Of all the district managers I reported to in the operations department, Emmitt was the most impressive. I recall the first managers' meeting he held. He said, "This is the first plant assignment I've had. I know very little about the plant operations department, but that's why I have 'plant managers' like you guys. You will find me very supportive as long as you do your job and keep me out of trouble." And that is how he operated.

While I was still at Lamar, Emmitt was offered a job in headquarters back in NYC. He called me one day, shortly after he was settled in his new job and told me he knew of an opening in headquarters in the engineering department that I might be interested in if it was offered to people outside of headquarters. It involved developing a new electronic language that would speed up the processing of data throughout the Bell System's electronic data processing (EDP) systems. He said, "I think you would like the job because it involves working with Bell Labs as well as all the operating companies. It's a light district job, but as the project grows, I expect it will develop into a full district, and I'm sure you can handle it. But I wanted to check with you before I put your name in the pot as a candidate."

As we talked, Emmitt told me about the shock; I would experience when I first come to headquarters and how you get used to it as time passes. I knew he was telling me how he viewed New York City and working in Lower Manhattan. The more we talked about the job, I was grateful for Emmitt's interest in taking the time to consider me as a candidate. I was somewhat surprised he was willing to sponsor me for the position. He also pointed out this move, if I were asked and accepted, would be under the company's "buy-back" program. This was a program that was established a year or so earlier stating if you transfer into headquarters on a lateral management level, you will return to your original department and area with a promotion in two years. Or if you are promoted in, you would lateral back to your home department and area at the end of two years.

After some thought, I said, "I expect the chances of me getting an offer to take the job is not very high, but it sounds like a challenge and a job unlike any I've had up to this point in my career; if you want to, toss my name in, and we'll see what happens." I thanked Emmitt for considering me and feeling I could do the job.

That evening I told Sondra about the possibility, and she asked, "Would that mean we would have to move to New York City?" I told her Emmitt said most people live in New Jersey and commute into New York City.

"Well, that sounds better than having to live in New York City, I don't think that would be worth it."

I agreed and told her the chances that anything will come from Emmitt's call is probably "slim." About three days later, I had a call from Jim Greek, a division manager in headquarters engineering department. He indicated he had talked with Emmitt who told him about our conversation. Jim said, "It's my division that has the opening, and from what Emmitt tells me about you and your qualifications in working in his district, I think you would be a good man for the job, and I'd like to offer it to you, if you think it is something you would be interested in."

I told Jim that I had discussed the possibility, with my wife, that I might have an opportunity to take a job in headquarters. I mentioned what she said if we didn't have to move into the city. Jim laughed and said, "Your wife sounds like mine did when we moved here from Kansas City about five years ago. So does that mean you would be interested? "Yes, I think I would, it sounds interesting."

"Great, I'll get the paperwork started and get back to you with the details as soon as I can."

On the road again, going to the Big Apple

Jim called back two days later and told me he would handle the airline tickets, send me the expense money and make reservations at the Grand Central "Y" for me to stay while I was getting settled in my new job and finding a house in New Jersey so my family could move from Lamar.

School was still in session in Lamar when I first went back to NYC to meet my boss, Jim Greek, and the rest of his managers. On my cab ride from LaGuardia Airport, I encountered my first "welcome" and an opportunity to save money.

Before we pulled away from the curb, the driver turned to me and said, "You're new to the city, right?"

"Pretty much so."

"Okay, this is what I can do, I'll take you to your destination for $10. That is about half the fare if I flip the flag down."

Before I thought about his offer, I said, "Nah, I don't want you to get in trouble and besides my company is picking up the fare so flip the flag and let's go."

"Okay, I was just offering you a bargain." When we pulled up in front of the office building at 220 Church Street, where my new office located. The meter said $4.75! I gave him $5.25 and said, "Keep the change." Remember this was back in the early 1970s.

As I exited the cab, I was thinking, maybe all the stories I've heard about NYC are true. Here I am, my first cab ride into downtown, and I've already experienced a "con" job.

Now in all fairness, I found all the people in NYC are not as bad as many portray them. I'll give you an example that shows why I feel most of the commuters into NYC give an impression that is unique while they are in the city. However, once the workday is over and they return to the commuter train that takes them back home, they become the friendly people who grew up in a distant city, town, or state; like many of us! At the time I came to NYC, it was said to be around eight thousand people. When I left Lamar, it had a population of approximately eight thousand people! Those three extra "zeros" in the NYC population represented the difference between my commuting into NYC and working near the city of Lamar. As the plant manager in Lamar, Colorado, I recall the fifteen-minute drive home at the end of a challenging and fulfilling day at the office. I would often turn in our driveway to our home, and sometimes I would pause for a moment and thank GOD for all the blessings He had given my family and me in that little town named Lamar.

Now, as I exited the cab that took me from LaGuardia Airport and let out at 220 Church Street, where my new office located, I felt I might be entering a different world. As I took the elevator to the third floor, I found myself thinking, "I sure hope I haven't made a mistake." After meeting Jim and the other men in his group, I felt a little better. At that time five of Jim's "lite district messengers, including me," started with AT&T in the Kansas City District. That made me feel a little more at home.

Our personnel department had arranged for me to have a room at the Grand Central YMCA, a short ride on the subway from our office. The Y had most of the third floor reserved for incoming people who would be working for AT&T or at the New York Stock Exchange, two blocks away from our office. As I was checking in, a man (Andy) from Georgia, was also checking in. Andy would be in training at the "stock exchange." Over the next few days, we became good friends, along with the "Y" manager (Herald). Herald was a native of Kansas and had graduated from Wichita College. During the time I was living at the "Y," Herald insisted on being Andy and my "guide" each evening. He wouldn't let us pay for his meals when he was taking us to places like Coney Island or in one of the other Boroughs. We couldn't have found a more knowledgeable person to show us the "excellent sites" in NYC. We tried to pay for his meal each evening, and he would not allow it. He told us it was so nice to have someone to spend the evenings with that was not from the northeast, especially NYC. I know now that Herald was not making a "statement" against people in NYC as much as he was showing a "longing" to hear those Midwestern and Southern "accents" and talk about things that most people don't understand, or care about, who are native-born and raised in our Northeastern states.

While I was still living at the "Y," Andy and I both felt very fortunate to have someone like Herald to take us to places like the World Trade Center, Empire State Building, The Bowery, the Brooklyn Bridge, Grand Central Park, Times Square and so many places that most people only read about or view on TV. When I think of those places today, I think of the exciting experiences we had as we visited each one. Herald also took us to a couple of "off-Broadway" stage shows and explained how they were the best way to see Broadway-type shows for a fraction of the cost, and many of them would eventually make it to Broadway. The list of sites Herald took us to, seemed endless. It was too bad we didn't have cell phones with camera features like we have today. But I still recall and visualize in my mind many of the events and sites we visited.

Being away from my family and living in the "Y" started to get to me around the third week. I had been spending the weekends in New Jersey looking for a place to buy and being disappointed in what I was finding. One day at work, I ran into my old district manager, Jim Palmer who lived in Middletown, New Jersey. When I told him what I had been finding, he called his wife, and they insisted I come and stay with them, for at least a week. Jim said, "I'm sure you can find something in that time frame, and my wife knows the area and can take you around and tell you all about the neighborhoods, etc." I didn't want to impose on their kind offer, but I needed help.

On my third day in Middletown, I found a new Cape Cod house that just went on the market. I felt this was the best location, etc. of any house I had looked at and I bought it after doing some bargaining. Jim's wife said she felt I made a good buy for what I ended up paying for the house. I flew back to Lamar, had the moving van load our furniture, got their estimated time of arrival in Middletown that was about a day after we would be there. And we all headed East to New Jersey.

Moving to Middletown, New Jersey, is not like moving to Lamar, Colorado

The moving van arrived as planned. It had unloaded and was pulling out of the driveway, in the dark. It was getting late, and the kids were tired. I laid a couple of mattresses on the floor in one of the bedrooms and told the kids to go to bed, and we would start unpacking in the morning. Sondra and I sat down in the front room, exhausted, when, in the darkness of night, the doorbell rang. Now, back in New Jersey, and I expect in many East Coast communities, most homes have a storm door on all the outside doors, due to the cold winters. As the doorbell rang a second time, I opened the inside door and before I could say anything, in walks this woman followed by her "burly" husband. As they entered, I noticed the woman was carrying something in her hands. I glanced at her husband and immediately remembered what one of the men from our district office in Colorado Springs told me at our going away party. He said, "Whatever you do, do *not* get too friendly with those Italians because they are all tied in with the Mafia!" Looking at the man that was now standing inside our home, I recalled the "words of wisdom" given to me at our going away party about Italians and for a moment I wondered if this guy might be one of the "bosses"? He was big, dark complexion and had a stern expression that could turn into a mean expression if you said the wrong thing to him. (Another lesson

GOD's Word teaches and we need to heed—that is, "Don't judge others, especially by their looks, because GOD made all of us. Jesus told the disciples that only GOD has the authority to judge us.") You will see later how I found this to be true, concerning this stranger standing in the middle of our living room that evening.

As I was about ready to say something, the woman said, "We know you have just moved in, you are tired, and probably haven't eaten, and we are not going to stay." As she set down a pot of coffee and some cookies on our coffee table, she said. "We are your next-door neighbors, Vince, and Kathryn Bonavita." We later found that both Kathryn and her husband Vince were second-generation Italians. To my surprise, in a very short time, Kathryn and Vince became one of the best neighbors we ever had. They and their two children were one of the most beautiful families you would ever want to live next door to."

The above was an excellent example of why we should know other people's hearts and never form opinions based on their nationalities or looks. The danger of forming early opinions was made very clear in my next encounter with Vince. I was mowing my yard one afternoon, several days after moving in when my mower broke down.

As I was standing looking at the mower and thinking what I was going to do, Vince came walking over and said (remember, we had only known each other about a week), "What's wrong with that piece of junk, did it break down?"

"Yes, it's old, and I should have tossed it in the trash in Lamar and bought a new one when we moved here."

"You're right, so, since you didn't, go over in my garage and get my mower and finish mowing your yard."

"No, I don't like borrowing mechanical things that could break down, then I'd feel I needed to replace them."

Vince, in a serious tone, replied, "Look, everyone on both sides of the block knows me, no one knows you. If you don't get my mower and finish mowing your yard, I'm going to get my mower and mow your yard. Since no one knows you and everyone knows me, when they see me mowing your yard, they are going to say. "Look at that, the new family that just moved in has poor ole Vince out mowing their yard. How awful!"

I finished mowing my yard that day with Vince's mower, and in a short time, I felt if the reverse happened, Vince would come over and even if I was not home, but my garage door was open, he would take my mower and finish mowing his yard. His wife and Sondra also became very good friends, and Kathryn, who was a nurse, was the one who talked Sondra into going to college and getting her degree in nursing. When our youngest child started kindergarten, Sondra started her degree work at Monmouth College, to be a nurse. Kathryn was always available to help her when needed since she had been an RN for several years.

After I found out how to talk to Vince, and how to take his words, we were talking about how the Italians were very family-oriented and "Momma" made most of the interfamily decisions. Vince was telling me when he and Kathryn started their family; they felt they needed to get a little more distance between them and all the brothers and sisters and in-laws who lived within a few blocks of each other in Brooklyn. When Vince and Kathryn found the house in New Jersey that they bought (the one they were living in at that time), they decided to fill everyone in on all the details. Well, according to Vince, he thought his mother-in-law was going to put a "contract out on him" for stealing their little daughter and (soon-to-be) grandchildren and taking them to New Jersey, on the other side of the Hudson River.

He went on to say, "My family is no different, when Mom and Dad come to spend the weekend with us, they pack enough clothes you would think they were going on a trip to California."

And all the time they are here, Dad keeps asking, "Don't you have a long way to drive to and from work?"

Vince was a salesman for an insurance company and traveled all over New Jersey and upstate New York, but his dad always felt if they were living in Brooklyn, where they grew up, it would be so much easier for him to travel to his customers, especially those in New Jersey.

Another humorous Italian and (Polish) story I was made aware of some years later, but it shows the closeness and pride within nationalities, and it seems to fit in nicely, but with a little different slant so I'll share it now.

With the breakup of AT&T that took place in 1984, the department I was in, moved to New Jersey. The company offered to buy our existing house and move us to a closer location. Sondra and I both had wanted to get farther inland and away from the cold ocean winds in the winter months.

We ended up buying a new, colonial-style house with about three acres of land located in Hillsborough Township, just north of Princeton University. It had an old barn that, with a few repairs over the years, still had the original wood siding and inside beams. It was listed in the State Historical Society archives as being over 180 years old. At one time, it had caught on fire, and you could still see charred places on some of the beams. The hand hewed beams ranged in size from four by four, four by six, four by eight, four by twelve, and twelve by twelve inches, and many were fifteen to twenty feet long. Over the years the beams had become petrified. I was never able to drive a spike nail into any of the beams. The smaller beams had initially been nailed together with handmade iron spikes.

The more massive beams were anchored together by burning a hole near the ends of two beams. Then they would line up the holes and drive a slightly beveled peg through the holes. On the smaller end of the beveled peg and next to the beam, they would burn a hole in the peg and drive a smaller peg through the larger peg, thus keeping both beams secured together. I was impressed when I thought of how people, "back then" had the determination, imagination, and patience to do what they did. With one exception, the barn became an interesting conversation piece when talking to people about our home. The one exception was, our barn stood within twenty feet from the road that ran in front of our new house. Our house was somewhat located about fifty yards back from the road and to the left side of the barn, as viewed from the road. Until I painted the barn and repaired the roof, ignoring its age, it was still an eyesore. I fixed the inside so our daughter, who had a horse, would have a stable to keep it in at night and during inclement weather. It also offered me a lot of storage room for items that were not used too often but needed to be kept inside out of the rain and snow.

We received several compliments from our neighbors after I completed all the repairs and painted the barn. I guess during all my "restoration and painting," word got back to the New Jersey State Historical Society (NJSHS). One day I received a call from them asking if I was planning to tear the barn down. I assured them I wasn't, at that time. They informed me that since it was registered as a New Jersey State Historic Structure, it could not be torn down or removed without concurrence from the (NJSHS) office. They indicated, if it was a safety hazard or causing a problem within the area, they might relocate it, at the state's expense, to a more suitable location. I informed them I would keep them advised. I'm not sure, but I seem to recall one of the later owners did have it removed.

However, our next-door neighbor, whose names were Salvador and Irene Richie (sound a little Italian?), bought their oldest daughter a pony and then realized they didn't have a place to keep it, during bad weather. So I built the second stall in our "historical barn" for them to use. We still had plenty of spare room for all my "stuff."

Since our son was a good friend with their son and our middle child (daughter) who had a horse was friends with their oldest daughter who was in our son's class, and she had the pony. Then to top it off, our oldest daughter babysat with their youngest daughter. With that combination, you could see why we became good friends with the Richie family.

The father, Sal (short for Salvador—yes, he was an Italian), was a salesman for an insurance company in Newark, NJ and proved to be another good neighbor. He was always willing to help me if he could. You would have no problem, after meeting Sal, to know his ancestors came from Italy. Irene, however, was a very nice and attractive lady whom we found traced her ancestors back to Poland.

When I think of the above ancestry combination, I recall the following story. One day, Sal, seeing me working in the back-pasture, came over laughing all the way. When he got within hearing distance, he said, "Sal Jr. [that was what he called his son, whose first name was also Salvador] just came home from school and told his mother and me about getting an A on an English paper the class had to write, concerning their family ancestry." He said the students had to read their paper before the class and then the class voted on who wrote the best paper after all the papers had been read. I knew their son was very smart and was an A student, so I wasn't surprised he shared the following with me. Being proud parents, Sal said they asked Sal Jr. to read his paper to them that he had read to the class.

When he finished, he said, "The class voted my ancestry story, as the best written and presented in class."

Then Sal (Dad) said, Irene blew her lid and asked, "Sal Jr., why didn't you tell them about your Polish ancestry?"

Sal Jr. replied, "Because the Polish people are not as well-known as Italian people!"

What a way to lose points with Mom!

At the time Sal was telling me about Sal Jr.'s accomplishment, he said, "Now Irene is not talking to Sal Jr. or me, but she'll get over it."

Irene did survive, and we never brought the subject up in front of her, and she never mentioned it either. I was tempted to ask Sal if sleeping on the couch was as nice as sleeping in bed, but I didn't.

This incident didn't take place until we had moved from Middletown and lived in our new home in Hillsborough for at least a year and during that time we had become good friends with Sal and Irene. We found our nicest neighbor in that area, again, turned out to be an Italian family (at least 50 percent), the Richie family.

But now, back to finding out life in New York City is not the same as life in New Jersey

Let me get back to before our move from Middletown to Hillsborough took place, and I was still commuting into NYC. During this period, many things happened that only the good Lord could have orchestrated. Some of the events would prove very beneficial in the future years of my life. As you read the following events, think how some of the events came about at just the right time, especially those that took place just before my group moved from NYC to New Jersey.

One would think the short drive to the train station from our house, boarding a commuter train, relaxing and talking with a friend you had previously met on the morning run, would be the ultimate in going to work. Well, that is what I thought for the first six months while commuting from Middletown to Newark, then boarding the *path*, going under the Hudson River to Lower Manhattan, and walking a couple of blocks to my office, that altogether it took about two hours to do.

However, you can only take so much of that kind of pleasantness before it turns into "Oh no, not another day of being bounced around in your seat while riding in coaches that looked like they had dents in the side where the Indian arrows had hit during an attempted raid a hundred years ago."

When you looked out one of the cracked windows while traveling through some of the less attractive cities on the New Jersey coast, I would often glance skyward and ask, "GOD, what did I do to deserve this?"

It was at that time I would soon encounter "the plan of GOD" I mentioned in chapter 2. It was something I had almost convinced myself; I was incapable of doing.

My next two-plus year assignment was the biggest change between any two locations I had worked throughout my Bell System career. In my new job in NYC, I often thought of the short drive from my home to the train station. Then between a one-and-a-half to two-hour commuter train ride between our home in Middletown, New Jersey, into Newark, New Jersey. There I boarded the *path* that took me *under* the Hudson River to lower Manhattan, NY, followed by another ten-minute walk to my office. This sequence was reversed at the end of the day and totaled to about four hours commuting to and from work. At the end of my going home commute, I often felt it had been another "hectic' day of meetings and phone calls at my office in NYC.

Going home on the Jersey Coast commuter from Newark to my stop at Middletown

I was talking with a man I had met some time earlier. As quite often happens, people tend to stand in the "same" place in the Newark terminal at the "same" time each day waiting for their train to arrive. In following this routine, you end up in the "same" car and sitting in the "same" seat, next to the "same" person, day after day. On one such day, I sat down alongside the man who had become my "commuter friend." A few minutes after the train left the Newark terminal, I was telling him some of my frustrations in wasting so much time (two hours) going home and (two hours) coming to work (four hours on the commuter each day). His response sounded rather strange when he asked me if I had a college degree.

I said, "No."

Then my friend said, "You sound a lot like I felt a few years ago."

"One day I was talking with a friend and telling him how I felt, having to spend so much time riding up and down the Jersey Coast RR line five days a week. As we talked he asked me the same question I asked you, and I gave him about the same answer you just gave me—that is, "No, I don't have a college degree."

"My friend went on to tell me about Brookdale College, that was only a short drive from where I got off the commuter train each day."

As I was listening to my friend talk, I realized I, was not the only one dissatisfied with their daily commute into NYC. Suddenly I became a little more interested in what my friend was sharing with me. He continued; "When I found Brookdale Junior College was only a short distance from where I lived, I checked into what they had to offer." He then proudly announced that "A few years later I had earned an AA degree, and now I'm thinking about continuing my college studies at one of the four-year colleges."

I started thinking about what my friend was saying and what he did, and I asked myself if that was something that maybe I should try.

As we arrived at the Middletown stop and as I stood up to leave, my friend said, "You might want to consider Brookdale, I enjoyed going there, and it sure made a difference in my attitude toward 'wasting so much time' on this train."

I told him I would think about it, but at that moment I thought to myself, "I don't think college is what I need."

After the discussion with my "commuter friend," I would often ask myself, "I wonder what kind of a program Brookdale has that might be of interest to me?" I knew where the campus was, and it was only a short distance from where I got off the commuter train. Then, less than a month later, after arriving one afternoon at the Middletown station, and leaving the parking lot to drive home, I turned the other way and headed toward Brookdale Junior College.

I went into what looked like an office building, and just inside the door was a sign pointing to the office across the hall that said, "Admissions."

I walked in and at her desk was the admissions director, who immediately asked, "May I help you?"

My reply went something like, "I've been thinking I might be interested in taking a course at the college level, and I was wondering if you had any information along the lines of, courses taught, times, costs, etc.?" Well, I think this lady may have been a car salesman prior to her present job because she immediately started telling me about Brookdale, its programs and before I knew it she was saying, "If you signed up for a couple of courses today, we could get you started this next semester that starts in about a week. How about English 101 and Business Math?"

Before I could think of a *no* type answer, I heard myself saying, "Well, I might be interested in the English 101 now and see how that turns out."

"Fine, let me get some information from you, and we can get the paperwork moving immediately."

On my way home, I kept asking myself, "What have I done?"

A couple of days after enrolling at Brookdale College, I received a folder in the mail that had my acceptance in taking English 101, and a letter with a note attached that said I needed to sign the letter and give it to the teacher who would be teaching English 101 that semester. It had her name, classroom number, along with the date and time of the first class. It stated that since they did not have time to process my enrollment through the normal channels, I could give it to the teacher who would handle it through the next step in the processing cycle and this would allow me to start the following week! Should I back out? No, I've come this far, I might as well see how far I can go." I think the start date was on a Monday and the time was around forty-five minutes after my train was scheduled to stop at Middletown, and it all seemed workable. Then Monday arrived, and as I was coming home that day, I remember thinking, "What would my classmates think if they knew this old man (thirty-two at that time) was starting college today?" As I am typing this in early 2019, and will be eighty-five in October, I am tempted to omit the words *old man*, but since that is how I saw myself at that time, I'll leave them in.

The train was on time that evening, I disembarked and headed for Brookdale College with my admission sheet in hand. Upon arriving in the college parking lot, I noticed many of the students were already going in, and they all looked young enough to be my children! I took off my suit coat and tie and left them in the car, but I still thought I looked like and felt like an "old man" compared to those "youngsters" who would be my classmates.

As I walked into the classroom, the teacher was sitting at her desk reading a letter. When I approached her desk, she looked up and smiled and asked, "May I help you?" I handed her the envelope with the papers and said, "I was told to give this to you since I'm enrolled in your class." She looked at the documents and said, "Yes, you are. However, I am already filled up with the maximum number of students I can accept in a class. You can leave the admissions sheet and be one of the first accepted next semester."

Then she said, "I am sorry, but I have to follow the rules given to the teachers." I told her I understood, and I think I even had a smile on my face, thinking, "Well, I tried, and it was not what GOD wanted me to do." We need to be careful making statements that suggest what has happened is what GOD wants versus what we are willing to accept.

As I started to go to my car, I reached to open the door to exit the building, just as a man on the outside began to enter. He looked a little older than me and opened the door before I could. As he began to enter, he held the door open for me and said, "Hello, are you going to be one of our students this semester?" To this day, I can't think why he would ask that question, I'm sure I looked older than a typical college student. I would think he might feel I was someone who was selling something or checking on certain activities at the school, but a potential student? I don't think so.

My answer seemed to confirm this man knew what he was talking about when I replied, "I was, but now I'm told English 101 is full, and that is the only class I signed up to take."

He replied, "English 101? Follow me, I think we can do something about that."

The next thing I knew, we were headed toward the room that I had just been told was at the maximum number of students it could admit. As we walked in, I could see there were only a couple of seats empty. Approaching the teacher's desk, she looked up and said, "Well, hello, Mr. Mills, is there something I can do for you?"

"Yes, I would like to enroll Mr. McJunkin in your English 101 class this semester."

"Well, as I told him just a few minutes ago, we are at the maximum limit already."

"Yes, I know, but you can still take another student, and I'm sure it will not be a problem."

"Okay, if you say so." Then she looked at me and said, "Mr. McJunkin, you can sit in any of the empty seats." I had already noticed the only empty seats were on the front row, and as I thanked her, I took a front-row seat.

The following week I saw Mr. Mills again, as I was going to my second class in English 101. I spoke to him, and he responded, and then I said, "I appreciate your helping me get enrolled in English 101 class last week, but how did you do it?" He laughed and said, "It was nothing, because the number that enrolled for the class, I expect at least five or more will not show up tonight and close to a quarter of those that started last week will not be in the class at the end of the semester. And that is too bad because most of them will never come back and receive a degree."

I said, "Is that right? I would think a young person, like most of them, seemed to be, would want to get a degree, if given a chance."

When I thought of the above experience, I couldn't believe it had happened. What I experienced from the time I felt led to stop at Brookdale (only for information) but ended up enrolling in a class, then being turned down due to too many students were signed up for the class I was scheduled to take and told I would have to wait for the next semester. Then, as I was leaving the building, I ran into a man who, after he found out I had been denied attending the class I had enrolled in, said he could probably help me. He took me back to the classroom I had just come from, and there proved what he said he could do. Then after all these things had transpired, I asked him how he was able to get me enrolled for that first class, and he told me, it was no big deal because "I am the president of Brookdale College."

Now, to me, all of those "happenings" were way beyond being "coincidental." I find it much easier to believe it was a "GOD thing" to put me on a path He wanted me to pursue. As the weeks passed, I found I was enjoying college, and quite often I would use the time on my commute home as a last-minute "study hall" in going over a paper I had written earlier and touched up during my lunch period at work that day. Around two years later, I received my AA degree in business administration and graduated with a credit high honors (CHH) grade or "A."

There is no doubt in my mind from the day I drove to the campus and enrolled in English 101 to the day I received my AA degree, too many things fell in place for me to believe they were "just coincidental." What makes more sense is to think they could only have happened, "By the grace of GOD." (Period!)

Three situations seemed to enable me to do what I did. I could not accept what had happened as being "just coincidental."

I knew GOD loves us because of WHO He is, not because of anything we do or didn't do!

First situation—I felt it was part of GOD's plan to show me how I could use my commute time better as a "study time" if I had something to study. After He arranged for me to hear what a friend had done that helped him take his mind off his long commute and use it to study, GOD asked me, "Why don't you show yourself you can do the same thing?"

I felt I had to give it a try. I filled out an application form, and three days later, in the mail, I received my acceptance letter from the college advising me I had been accepted as a student.

I never told anyone, but over the next few days, I felt great, being a college student!

Second situation—however, on the first evening of classes, the teacher told me the class was filled, but I could leave my papers and be at the top of the list for next semester. (Could this have happened by GOD allowing it, to show me how much was I willing to do?)

Third situation—just as I was walking out the front door after being rejected, I met a man coming in who spoke to me and asked if I was going to be a student that semester. On finding out the class was at the allowed number of students, this stranger said, "Follow me, I think I can help you." Little did I know, I was talking with the president of the college. (Those two words, "Follow me," were words Jesus Christ often used in communicating with His followers.) In less than ten minutes, this stranger I had met in leaving college for good, had informed the teacher to add me to her class and assured her there would be no problem in doing so. Without any argument, she did what this stranger "suggested" she should do.

I am thinking, "Why is this man doing this? Is the teacher going to tell him she is only following orders? Why is he not accepting what the teacher is telling him? I still can't understand why this stranger felt I was interested in being a student since I was thirty-two at that time." Little did I know, I was talking with the president of the college.

One other thing that seems beyond the norm was, "What were the odds that I would run into a person that was willing to help me get enrolled in the class from which I had just been rejected?" At that time, I was willing to accept the fact, "I gave it a try, but it was not meant to be."

"What were the odds that the man I met leaving that evening would be the most powerful man on campus, the president of the college?"

"What were the odds that we would meet me at that critical time and place?" If either of us had arrived at the door a couple of minutes earlier, we would not have seen each other, and I would have returned to my car feeling, "I tried, but it was not meant to be."

I can't believe all these things falling in order were coincidental! To this day, I believe the only explanation for all of that to have taken place in one word: *GOD*! I felt it then, and I still feel it more so today.

Now I ask you, do you think those three situations mentioned above, especially the casual meeting the president of Brookdale College, as I was leaving after being turned down from taking the class I had signed up to take, was 'just a coincidence'? Or do you think it may have been the beginning of the plan GOD had for me to continue my education? I chose to think of the latter. (See Appendix F numbers 9, 11.)

I still remember when I started that first class (English 101) with much apprehension. I would never have guessed when the semester ended, I would feel much more confident, and I would complete with a grade of CHH (credit high honors equals to an A!). At that time, I would not have told people I was going to complete my program in business administration at Brookdale with a CHH 3.9 GPA, A average. Long story short, in checking the college out and enrolling in that one English class, I never thought at that time, in just a little over two years I would have earned my AA degree in business." After it happened, I knew who to thank for making it possible.

On completing my associate in arts in business at Brookdale Community College, I wondered if GOD had more in mind for me than earning an AA degree in business. I'll explain this later.

But one question kept coming to mind: "How did it happen? Of all the rational reasons I could come up with, none seem to be convincing. Today I feel the real reason I was able to attain an AA level of education was that GOD wanted to show me if I was willing to do my part. He would do the rest. Up to that point in my life, I had convinced myself I was not capable of earning even an AA degree at the college level. I feel the Holy Spirit may have turned from me because I had turned away from Jesus Christ's teachings. I seemed to have decided I was going to do things my way. I cannot emphasize enough the danger in even thinking that way. Doing so could result in the rest of one's life could be one disappointment after another. Also, though we may not be aware of it, we will be missing out of so many blessings that GOD wants to give all His children. Before we can address that point, we must be sure we have already accepted His Son, Jesus Christ, as our Lord and Savior. If we haven't, we need to start doing some deep thinking and praying. When we close the door of communications with GOD, we are placing all the cares and worries of the world on our shoulders, and I have never met a person that can handle that big a load!

I accepted Jesus Christ as my Lord and Savior at eleven years old, and there was no doubt in my mind He heard and accepted my request. GOD had already shown He created me to live longer than three months. He knew I needed help, and He knew I had to convince myself that I needed help. He seemed to be saying, "Now that you are thirty-two I'm going to show you I have given you the ability to continue your education. To convince me of that need, He decided He would place me in positions that would convince me I knew I had to go to Him for help. He would put me in the position I would feel He was the only one that understood what I needed and the only one that had the power to enable me to do what He wanted for me.

Today I believe the college and universities He led me too was proof of what GOD wanted and expected from me. Although many would say, "GOD had nothing to do with it." I have no problem in believing that His Word tells me He is involved in *all* things, through His Son, Jesus Christ, and His Holy Spirit. (See Appendix F, numbers 1, 3, 6, 12, 16.)

In all three institutions I attended, my degrees were earned "with honors." At Brookdale College, I received my AA degree in business administration and graduated with a CHH or "A." While attending

Rutgers University, I was a member of the Honor Society, "Alpha Sigma Lambda—Beta Zeta Chapter." These accomplishments were made possible only by the "Grace of God," who gave me the desire and willingness to spend the time, to further my education at a level that would help enable me to provide a nice home and a good standard of living for my family. It also helped me and their mother to be able to make it possible for our children to go to college if they wanted to go for education versus "fun and games." I had no hobbies at that time because I enjoyed going to school and sporting events in which our children participated. During their high school years, their events took up most of my spare time.

I would not have been able to do this if it hadn't been for GOD and my wife, Sondra. Who, at that same time, was furthering her career by earning her nursing degree, working at the hospital AND was the primary caregiver of our children when I was traveling on business, out of town.

Good or bad, it was while I was working at the AT&T headquarters, in NYC (the one city location I enjoyed less than any other area I had worked), that I felt led to start college, again. Throughout about ten years, I found going to college was a form of "therapy" from the pressure of my job. I discovered that I liked going to college, and during those ten years, I earned three college degrees, and I give GOD all the credit for making that possible. One of the regrets throughout those ten years was the feeling I may have put my church, job, and college ahead of my family.

However, at the end of my college years, I found my obtaining these degrees had an impact on my promotion to a full district. It enabled me to support the church better, to enjoy my new job more, and to provide for my family in ways that I would not have been able to do, had I been content with the status quo. I doubt if all of our children viewed it that way, but as they grew up and had their own families, I think they realized there is a cost in providing for your family.

During the time, between finishing my degree work at Brookdale and transferring to Rutgers, we moved from Middletown to Hillsborough. Our move made going to and from Rutgers possible, and it was much closer to my job. Since I was now driving to work, everything was working out great in the evenings I had classes. If we had not moved when we did, I would not have been able to drive from Middletown to the Rutgers campus in time to attend evening classes. Some would say, "That was just a coincidence." Possibly, but I will always believe GOD was guiding each step of the way from the moment I set foot on the Brookdale campus to the end of graduation on the campus at Fairleigh Dickinson University. The changes that came about ln my group moving from NYC to New Jersey made it possible for me to attend Rutgers University and earn my BS in business administration.

I know GOD's hand was the catalysis in our move out of NYC over to Bedminster, New Jersey, at a time that I could enroll at Rutgers University, the following semester after I had finished my studies at Brookdale Community College. This move made it possible for me to drive from work to Rutgers in time to attend my classes. It also meant *no more* riding the Jersey Coast RR commuter, for about four hours each day. All that was now "history."

With my transferred credits and my taking a rather heavy load of courses, I finished my BA in Business Administration in 1977, some five years after leaving Brookdale. I graduated from Rutgers with honors and was a member of the honor society, Alpha Sigma Lambda / Beta Zeta chapter. My GPA was 3.9 out of a 4.0 maximum. Who did I thank for helping me get to this point in college? First, I thanked GOD, and second, I thanked my wife, Sondra, for all the help and understanding she gave me. If someone were to tell me, "I would like to get a degree but, I'm too old or not smart enough, etc. I would stop them and say, "I know what you mean, and I know who can make it possible if you are willing to do your part, His name is Jesus Christ."

In chapter 4, I said I would explain later how I came out of my "shell" (in one area) while I was going to college. It started when I felt sorry for the teacher in one of my required "business" classes. She was Chinese and had a very soft voice. Often she would turn and face the blackboard and write one or two words that addressed the question she was about to ask. By turning her back toward the students made her question harder to understand. It seemed most of the students didn't understand what the teacher was asking, and they used this as justification to not say anything. When the students remained quiet, it made the teacher more uneasy. The silence of the students not responding to the professor's questions accounts for why today I usually don't hesitate to give my opinion when someone asks for it. I was not always that "bold." I would not answer or reply to a question unless it was addressed to me. Feeling uneasy and not volunteering answers in a college classroom continued during my studies at Brookdale Junior College and carried over into the early part of my time at Rutgers University.

The Chinese teacher of this particular class had developed a habit of turning to the blackboard and writing words that she wanted to emphasize, as she was speaking or asking a question, and possibly was not aware her back was facing the class. To make matters worse, she would then turn and face the class when she asked the question. Since the class was an evening class, some of the students were in their late thirties or forties, but most of them were students who had graduated from high school a year or two earlier.

When the teacher asked her question, I would slide down in my seat and say nothing, as did many of the other students. I found this response had not changed with the younger students in my college classes. To my surprise, many of the older students also seemed to resist giving their views relating to the teacher's questions. When the teacher would ask her question, it felt minutes would go by with no one volunteering an answer. The silence from the students seemed to make the teacher more nervous, and I even felt a little embarrassed. Before I realized it when the teacher would pose a question and ask if anyone had a thought, I would start counting slowly to ten. If no one had given their view, I would give mine. As the semester continued I noticed the class was more than happy to let, me answer, knowing that if it was wrong, I would be the one corrected by the teacher, in front of the class. I also noted that when the teacher would ask a question that had more than one correct answer, and I had given my view, the teacher would wait and then say, "Does anyone else have an idea?" She would pause and then say something like, "Mr. McJunkin has given one answer, but there are other responses that we should also identify as being valid for the question I posed." In a short time, an additional one or two students would give their views. At the end of the semester, several younger students were also "willing" to give their opinion.

Over the years, I noticed this same characteristic was seen not only in the classrooms but also in Corporate business meetings. While I was still working at AT&T in a management position, I found I would do the same thing—that is, If a question was asked in a meeting and I had an answer I felt, or I knew it was valid, I would count to ten and if no one had spoken, I would present my view. Now that I have retired, I've tried to break that habit a little, but it still pops up occasionally, especially if it relates to what I feel is an important point.

When the final semester for my Bachelor of Science degree in business was coming to an end, I still had the urge to continue my college studies. Before the following semester started, I felt a Master's degree in business would not help me much in my job. The main reason was, I knew AT&T was receiving applications from places like MIT, Harvard, Princeton, Columbia, etc. and these were graduated students much younger than me, and they all had at least an MBA and many had PhDs, mostly, in the engineering fields.

Accepting these facts, I felt I should study in a field that had always interested me. It was the study of "why do we humans do some of the things we do"—that is, psychology. I have always wondered why we humans do some of the things we do when we know it will be hurtful to others and even to ourselves. I was aware of a University not too far from where our new office located in New Jersey, but I had no idea how their school of psychology' was rated. I applied for admission in their Master's program, in its school of psychology and was accepted. I found out later the School of Psychology at Fairleigh Dickinson University, was rated number 1 among all major colleges on the East Coast. This rating also included the ivy league schools. I soon found out why this may be true after taking a few core classes and seeing the proficiency of their professors. They were all outstanding.

Once I started in this new field of study, I continued enjoying college life. I was fortunate to have the Dean of their psychology department as my professor in several of my classes. His name was Dr. Cell (spelled Chel). He and I seem to connect in the first class I took that he taught. His talent to teach was so impacting, so clear, and he was always able to explain his position when a student would challenge his view. He was not influenced by a common belief among student body groups, as we see on many college campuses today. He explained things in a way you found yourself, saying, "I never thought of that." He was a PhD graduate from Columbia University. Near the end of my master's program, he almost convinced me to apply for entrance into the Doctoral program at Columbia University. Dr. Chel said he had enough contacts in their school of psychology that he felt he could arrange for me to be accepted. However, I would have had to commute into NYC at night, and there was no way I was going to do that, even for a PhD! The real reason I didn't give it much thought was, I knew I would be retiring before too long, and we would be moving back "out West" to be closer to at least one of our children.

After I received my MA in personnel psychology, I feel I have used it more than I expected. In my work, in my social activities and even in the Sunday school classes I taught. It helped me to understand better, some of the characteristics among people I worked with, in and outside of my job. It gave me a broader understanding of why we humans act the way we do, under different circumstances. Without a doubt, it was the most interesting study that GOD directed me to take at the college level. Like Brookdale and Rutgers, I also graduated with honors from Fairleigh Dickinson. Again, I know it was only by the grace of GOD. Its teachings have helped me in working with people, before and after retirement and even in and outside the church. I have come to understand more clearly why we humans are some of the most unpredictable creations in some areas and yet, some of the most predictable creations in other areas. GOD has placed us at the top of his creations, and He observes our actions each moment of the day. He has given us the ability to do or not to do what He wants. He tells us we will have "eternal life" in one of two places! However, the human species often try to do it their way, only to find GOD will not change His plan to agree with our desires!

Now that I've finished explaining how I feel GOD led me through my college studies, let's jump back to where we started chapter 9—that is, The last half of my career with AT&T, when I was still commuting in and out of NYC.

As I think back to those days when I was one of "those commuters," that daily encountered and endured commuting to/from NYC. We seem to understand we had, knowingly or unknowingly, developed a common attitude toward this situation that stated:

"Don't laugh or cry; continue to go where you need to go. Remember, you are in NYC, and there is no other place in the world, quite like the Big Apple!"

From that first day, I arrived in NYC; I became aware that it was different. My initial reaction was one of "judgment, of the city and the people that worked there." It was so different from any place I had lived, worked, or visited in my adult life.

As I look back, I see I started forming an opinion about NYC based on what I saw. Using what I observed each day led me to "judge NYC and all the people I saw as natives versus commutating workers into the city. Judging by what we see is not only doing what Paul tells us in 1 Corinthians 4:3–4, and it is what we should *not* do because GOD is the only one that can judge other people and He goes beyond what He sees.

As I reflect on the time I was working in NYC five days a week for a couple of years, it was a new experience. Being born and raised in a small Midwestern town in Kansas (Toronto), having a population under a thousand and serving time in the Navy and living in several places that were much larger than Toronto, NYC was different from all the other places I worked and lived.

During the time, I commuted into and out of NYC. I experienced so many different views and feelings that I felt I didn't know how I was going to endure the challenges. I could go in detail telling about all the strange and different encounters I experienced during my time working in NYC, but I would instead like to tell you WHY I had the view I had of the Big Apple (NYC).

First, I was comparing every day I was in NYC with either my life growing up in Toronto, Kansas, or the time I was in the US Navy. The difference between NYC and either of the other two places I had lived was miles apart. I did not recognize this at the time, and because of that, I viewed NYC as being a terrible place to work, five days a week. The more I used this comparison; the more NYC became a place that was one step above being in "hell," especially on those hot summer days when the air conditioning was not working in the commuter train.

As I think back, that part of my life is behind me, and now I believe it was only as bad as I conceived it was. If I had taken a different view and looked at my time in NYC was going to be a temporary one and as they say in the military, "Suck it up and move on," I would have been better off. Well, that is easy to say now, but I'm not sure that would have been something I would have been able to do at the time I was there. Fortunately, GOD only left me in NYC for a short period, but long enough to teach me many lessons about how weak humanity is and how powerful He is.

Today as I think back to that time in my life I see how GOD enabled me to endure this unattractive place for a period, so I would later see the love He has for all His children and shows them He can do all things IF we go to Him in our time of need. I will show how, at a point, I felt I couldn't take much more of the pressure my job was causing me. I recall I was asking myself if I was willing to give up on my job, my family, and myself. It was at that time GOD's Holy Spirit within me, seemed to be saying, "I have a plan for you, and now I'm going to lead you to do the things I want you to do, *but* you are going to have to follow me versus trying to do it yourself, your way."

I believed GOD was telling me He was in control, but I didn't see any immediate changes in my life. I know now it was not because of GOD not doing what His Holy Spirit told me He would do; it was because I was still focusing on my life as I had been. The following shows how my time in NYC didn't seem to change my views too much. But today, I see that GOD was testing me, not to show others, but to show me what I was willing to do to follow His plan.

Take a cab, take a cab!

GOD was now going to show me how powerful He is and what He and only He can do to help take care of our needs. He only asked that I believe (have *faith*) and follow (have *hope*).

I soon realized that things could change fast and often, in NYC. I recall experiencing a not-so-enjoyable change when using the subway to the airport, on my way to an out-of-town meeting. During the first year in the "Big Apple,' if I had to attend a meeting in another city, the procedure was straightforward. I would catch the subway at the basement level of Thirty-Second Avenue of the Americus building and with my suitcase in hand (a flag showing I am traveling and may have a lot of money on me). I would take the subway to the LaGuardia Airport and never give a second thought to its safety factor.

Before we moved to New Jersey, the method of traveling from our office in lower Manhattan to the airport changed from taking the subway to "taking a cab"! This change came about when several people were attacked, and some had been assaulted when taking the subway that traveled through the northern part of Manhattan. I had never experienced this problem, nor did I know of any telephone employees being robbed or assaulted. I had read of these events happening in the city from reading the *Daily News*. Because of the news of assaults in the city, AT&T was willing to pay the cab fare, which was considerably more expensive than a twenty-five-cent subway token. Taking a cab became the new mode of transportation to LaGuardia or Kennedy airports.

Although NYC had so many exciting events and places of interest that no other city in America had, they also seemed to have more crime-related situations that, if you were not well versed in areas that were not safe, you could end up in some very dangerous situations and locations.

As I recall, it was in the second year I started working in NYC when the CWA union had gone on strike against AT&T. The company was asking for people that had experience in plant offices to volunteer to work in one of the central office locations within the city. By that time, I had more years in a plant office than I had in any other department, both as a craftsman and in management, so I volunteered. My assignment was in the central office on Ninth or Tenth Street. (Too many years have passed to remember the exact street!) When I left in the evening, I walked a couple of blocks east, from the telephone building and then south a few more blocks and caught the subway down to the *path* train that took me to Newark.

One day, during my second week on assignment, I was comparing notes with the office manager in whose central office I was working.

"We were discussing the job of being a manager in a central office like the one we were in, that he was the manager of versus my job as manager of the Lamar, Colorado, central office. There was no doubt in either of our minds, he had the more demanding job, as far as work location safety—that is, ease in getting to and from work and safety conditions in and outside the office area.

As we talked, he asked me how I went home each evening. I told him the route I took each day (as I described above).

He said, "Man, don't do that anymore, that is no area to walk by yourself after the stores close."

"Why is that?"

"Haven't you noticed men laying in the recessed areas going into the stores?"

"Yes, but they were asleep or looked like they would be asleep in the next couple of minutes."

"Looks can be deceiving. A lot those guys, seeing someone like you, walking by yourself, as 'fair game.' They could pull a knife or a gun on you and demand your billfold. If you refused, they would use whatever they had, and you could end up losing your life. When you leave today, take a cab!" He pointed out, "There is often one parked in front of our building, knowing people get off at different hours starting at 5:00 p.m." Then he said, "This past week, on the street you have been turning South on; a man was killed by two guys that sleep in the doorways at night. After killing him, they took his billfold, watch and even stole some of his clothes.

"You do need to take a cab when you leave today!" That evening when I left to go home, I caught a cab to the *path* terminal. As we were traveling to the *path* terminal, I believe I was thanking GOD for sending a guardian angel to protect me on those days I didn't know I was walking down some dangerous streets.

As I look back to those days, I realized I was going through a cycle that probably all out-of-state commuters to NYC go through. At first, everything looks and acts differently from where we grew up. The attitude of the people also seems different. It seemed to me this was more noticeable to those of us who were from the Southern or the Midwestern states.

The second phase you experience is when you no longer see any beauty or humor in any of these sights or encounters. Then stage number 3 is when you make the all-important decision—that is, "Am I going to let this get to me or am I going to ignore the negatives and convince myself, 'If others have survived this environmental change, then I can too'?" If that is your choice, you've made the right decision to survive in NYC. I eventually made that decision, even though there were days I had to force myself to cycle quickly through the first three stages to keep my wits about me, but I was able to do it, even though it was challenging at times. It was at that same time I felt GOD, might have caused me to realize I had just experienced His involvement, as He had said He would do in protecting me, starting with my taking a cab to the path terminal versus walking down those dangerous streets. At that moment, I realized if it were not for GOD's intervention, I might have been that man who was murdered on the street I walked on each evening after work. Today I feel the Holy Spirit was reminding me how GOD had impressed on me to take a cab to the path terminal.

I somewhat doubted the story of the man being killed, but I knew it could have happened. It made me realize; without Jesus Christ as our Lord and Savior, and we don't show the *faith* and *hope* in GOD's Word, and even doubt its validity. We are *not* following

His commands. Without Jesus, as our Savior, we will not have the fulfilling life GOD has planned for us, all because we rejected His plan or because we wanted to interpret GOD's plan to match our lifestyle.

It was at that point I felt the Holy Spirit was telling me what GOD said He was going to do in my life, did take place. Today I still have a chill run down my spine when I realize what could have happened to me when I didn't see it was GOD's intervention that could have been the difference between being alive today or possibly being killed in the prime of life. GOD has a way to get our attention. But we must realize He has given us the freedom to follow or reject His plan for our eternal life. If we accept His plan, we will try our best to follow it, and GOD will carry through His promise, and our eternal life will be with Him in His heavenly kingdom. If we reject His plan, WE will be deciding as to where we will spend eternity, but it won't be in agreement with GOD's Word (Bible), and it won't be with Him. GOD's Word tells us there are only two eternal places of life after death, one with Him in heaven and the other with Satan in Hell. Humanity determines its own eternal destination each day we remain here on earth. I have come to realize our eternal life is nothing we should take lightly.

Having shared the above, let me go back to the time I was working in NYC, and find coming to work was a major change from any job I previously had. I recall one such experience that took place each morning on the way to work. The train cars we rode were not like the ones that the railroads use for long-distance, high speed runs. At first, you don't notice some of the differences, like many of the windows in the trains were cracked, the seats were not at all comfortable, because of the many years of usage. To me, even the noise level between stops seemed louder than regular passenger trains. GOD was showing me life can be anything but a bed of roses if we don't have Jesus Christ as our Lord and Savior. When we arrived in the Newark terminal, many people did not casually walk to the *path* terminal, some almost ran to get on one of the cars and get a seat, so they wouldn't have to stand during the short distance to the World Trade Center terminal on the other side of the Hudson River. (GOD was showing me when we try to do things our way He will let us, but the results are usually not what we want.)

I recall the times when I arrived in NYC and walked the short distance to my office and often found the elevators were not working in our building. As I walked up the stairs to the third floor, I would think, "I hope this is only a temporary location." The inside area was dark, and the windows looked like they had never been cleaned on the outside. What a way to start a workday! I felt Satan knew that GOD was in control, but Satan was going to try and get me upset any way he could, even at little things like making the elevators not work when I arrived in the morning. He hoped by the time I arrived in the office my day would already be going "downhill." However, all of that was to become history when, in a little over a year later, we would move across the Hudson River into New Jersey. I joked with some of my coworkers saying, "I think that move to New Jersey made me as happy as any promotion I received."

My trip home, after a workday in NYC, would often pose even more disappointments than coming to work in the morning. One example that often occurred about halfway to Middletown, where I would be getting off. It was most impacting in the Summer when the temperature was close to one hundred degrees, and the humidity seemed about the same. If the air conditioning on the train was not working as it should, I knew the trip was going to be very uncomfortable.

Even with all these little "roadblocks," GOD helped me adjust, and life went on. I will say if you came to New York City from one of the Southern or Midwestern states, you probably never became completely oblivious to these little irritants. You might recall before coming to NYC; you would read about them when you were back home in places like Atlanta or Dallas and thought, "How funny." Now that you were in the "Big Apple" you didn't see anything amusing when you experienced these events each day, going and coming to and from work. But by the grace of GOD, I and most of my other "commuter friends" were able to "adjust" one day at a time. If nothing else, in the hope these experiences would show us that wherever we are and whatever we are doing, life is not always going to be a bed of roses. Many of us found we needed the help and guidance of GOD to be able to do our jobs in the location we were working and not dwell on what may happen in the future or how it might affect us individually. I don't think many people wanted to give up when things didn't go as they wanted, but they knew there was a limit they could endure.

At the time I became a full district manager, I had twenty-plus people located throughout our offices in Chicago, Cincinnati, Atlanta, White Plains, New York, as well as a group in headquarters in Bedminster, New Jersey. Each of these groups had a Second level supervisor with three or four First-line supervisors reporting to the second level. My people worked at the same location as our field design engineering districts were located, in the above cities and was located in the same buildings. The cost of moving data from one Bell Operating Company (BOC) EDP system into another BOC's EDP system or to a different EDP system in our headquarters design group; was becoming a factor in the costs of transmitting data between two or more EDP computers. Moving data among the various EDP systems was most noticeable in the design engineering districts that were responsible for designing and transferring data in EDP systems accurately, and speedily to all involved groups. It was becoming more noticeable in the costs and implementation time was becoming a growing problem and could no longer be ignored as a problem that had to be addressed.

My district was assigned to work with Bell Labs and the district design engineers throughout all the BOCs and headquarters design engineering departments. These groups were all within the Bell System, whose parent company was known as AT&T. I shared this additional responsibility with another district level from the headquarters engineering department. We were charged, as cochairmen, in supervising the development and implementation of a new inter-EDP computer language throughout all the Bell Operating Companies (BOCs) that made up the Bell System before "divestiture" in 1984. The other district manager was selected for his engineering background, and I was selected for my many years in the plant operations departments. The project was called "common language." Before "common language" became a reality—each of the existing electronic data processing (EDP) systems throughout the Bell System had to design a translation process called a "Black Box" that would take incoming data from one BOC and translate it into the EDP language within the receiving BOC's computers language.

I could go on, but to the average reader, this page in my thirty-plus years' experience with AT&T would not mean much. So I'll move on by saying the Common Language project was by far the most difficult project I was associated with because it required convincing the developer (Bell Labs) and the user (the BOCs and various headquarters EDP systems used by headquarters engineering group) that common language had merit. Today after the "divestiture" of AT&T in 1984, I would not be surprised if common language is still being used among those companies that are not part of today's AT&T.

At the time I retired, common language seemed to be moving forward; within the Labs and those operating companies that remained with the current AT&T data systems. However, with the breakup of the Bell System, I have no idea if the words. "Common language" is still used throughout what was the former Bell System. My announcement to retire was at least six months before the time; the issues that arose between the labs and the various BOCs were discussed. I have no regrets of leaving on a good note. I will long remember the quality work my people provided to our design engineers. I will recall the memories of people I met and worked with, worked for, and who worked for me. I truly believe it was the people that made AT&T one, if not the most, popular worldwide corporate name involving "telecommunications"!

PART 4

Chapter 10

AT&T Retirement (March 3, 1987)

What awaits me in my retirement years? Is this all there is to life?

One of my great-grandsons informed me recently that he could now count to one hundred, and I listened as he slowly proved it.

On my birthday he asked how old I was. I told him eighty-five.

There was silence, and then he asked, "Did you start at one like I did?"

At this writing, I look back in time and thank GOD for sending me to Fort Madison, Iowa, in the mid 1950s, not for a job as I thought, but it was so He could give me my wonderful wife, Sondra, and then He provided us a job with AT&T that lasted for thirty-plus years.

During that time, we were blessed with three wonderful children, and each had a unique personality. GOD blessed us financially to provide them with the things all parents want to do for their children that will enable them to obtain their goals in life. Like many young children, I'm not sure that truth registered with them at that time and maybe I was at fault by not pointing out this truth better than I did. I'm not sure they understood that GOD expects each of us to obey His commands and accept His Son, Jesus Christ, as our Lord and Savior first and be willing to work for the things they want to do, especially in their post-high school years. When we don't, Satan is always ready to tell us we can blame everyone and everything else, but when we ignore GOD's commands, we are in for a challenging and sometimes hurtful future.

All three of our children have done a good job of taking care of what they have, some probably more than others. As parents, we are proud of what our children have today. We often recall what their teachers told us concerning their potential, but, only GOD knows if they lived and obtained what He enabled them to have. In the end, we will all be judged by how we followed His commands. We can judge others, but our views are of no value to GOD. We can interrupt His law of life, but the law is already explained and available for all to read in GOD's Word, the Bible. At this writing, one of our children lives on the West coast and another lives on the East coast, both near their children. Our third child lives about twenty minutes away from us as do their children. Only GOD knows how close each of our children and their families is living according to His commands.

Their mother (Grandma) and I go to GOD each evening and lift all of our children and their families to Him. We ask forgiveness for our sins and theirs and pray they also ask for His guidance each day. GOD's Word tells us we have all sinned and fallen short of His commands. We take comfort knowing this is true, and we believe GOD forgiveness our sins IF we ask.

We must try our best to follow GODs commands versus our interruptions of His law. He will forgive and guide us, but the results in each of our lives will depend on us, not GOD. His rules were written in blood that day His Son, Jesus Christ, was crucified on the cross for our sins, and we will reject it or accept it as fact, but the choice is ours alone.

All of our children grew up in the Christian church and that was where they were led to accept Jesus Christ as their Lord and Savior. I sometimes felt that I might have looked for the church to do all the teaching what being a child of GOD was. During the high school years of our girls, their mother (Sondra) earned her degree in nursing. She made many sacrifices during the time she was going to school. However, she was always there when the children needed her. My job with AT&T, after my first promotion, required me to dedicate more time on and off my job to maintain good evaluations that resulted in more promotions and increased my ability to provide our children with more opportunities. These included having nice clothes, going to summer camps, going to events their friends were attending that were suitable for children their age. With each promotion, I found we were also able to give more to our church.

After finishing high school, our children each made decisions as what pathway they wanted to follow. The girls both found jobs that enabled them to take care of most of their needs. Our son went to college and played football until his collarbone was broken and ended his football career. Later he joined the Marines during the war in Iraq and was awarded the Bronze Star for bravery in combat. Our children are all married now, and as of this writing, our two girls are grandparents, and one is a great grandparent. Our son and his wife have two boys and two girls. He also has a daughter in Texas and a granddaughter and grandson.

While our children were still going to school and living at home, GOD enabled us to live in parts of this great nation we call America and live in different cities and states that many only read about. I thanked GOD for all He did for my family and me, and when it came time to end my active career with AT&T, GOD confirmed it was time to *retire*! I believe GOD has always been the source of everything good in my life, and He will continue to be until He brings me to my home He promised me on July 14, 1946, when I invited His Son, Jesus Christ into my life as my Lord and Savior.

As I think of all that GOD has done for me, I truly believe, "If GOD was willing to take someone like me, who many felt I was destined to follow in the footsteps of my father who some felt was an "alcoholic," He would surely take those who believes in His Word and asked for His help.

If He was willing to give me the wonderful woman he had for my wife, and give me the friends, jobs, education, and family members that have and still do mean so much to me, why wouldn't GOD do the same for you? All He asks is for us to believe in Him by faith and hope, for our salvation. He asks that we believe in His Son, Jesus Christ, as His only begotten Son, and confess our sins and then invite Him into our life as our Lord and Savior."

"I challenge you or anyone to find a better guarantee for eternal life in heaven with GOD, His Son, Jesus Christ, and all the saints and believers that have preceded you and are now waiting for your arrival when GOD calls you home! The cost for all of this is zero because Jesus Christ paid for your salvation as well as mine, and He did it with His life. Do you truly believe you can find a better offer for eternal life in heaven? I pray that as you read about the blessings GOD has given me as well as my family, you will see He will, or He has done the same for you and your family."

GOD guided and enabled me to graduate from high school, spend four years in the US Navy, one semester at Kansas University, one year with Santa Fe RR in its communications department. Today I realize these were things I learned from in my learning years. GOD was now going to turn my focus to the future and it started when He enabled me to meet a beautiful young lady by the name of Sondra. After many weeks and months of our dating He joined us together as husband and wife. Within a few months He next led me to the job with AT&T, knowing I would realize years later it was the job I had dreamed of but never could find. Then GOD enabled us to start and raise our family.

Throughout the next thirty-plus years, GOD enabled our family to move multiple times to parts of the United States of America and spend a minimum of two years in each location. Our children saw there is beauty everywhere and when they were friendly, they met friendly people. They saw there are GOD loving people living in all parts of our nation. In my midthirties, while working in NYC, GOD enabled me to return to college, and over the following ten years, He enabled me to obtain three college degrees. Two were in business plus a (master of arts) degree in psychology. During this same time, Sondra enrolled in college and earned her nursing degree. I found my college degrees had a positive impact on my final promotion to full district with AT&T. Sondra is still utilizing her nursing knowledge, especially within our family and friends

"What is left?" When I ask that question, I feel GOD is reminding me, my accomplishments were all enabled by Him, as was the many opportunities I was able to take advantage of and pursue. Today I feel He often asks me, "Are you still using those opportunities (blessings) to glorify My name?" I pray this book will show others how great and powerful GOD is and how He wants to help all humanity to reach the potential He has given them.

Have you ever thought how easy it is to recognize faults and shortcomings in others, but we have a hard time thinking about how we are serving and following what GOD wants us to do?

"We don't want to admit our shortcomings and faults?" It seems to be human nature and so easy to talk about the sins and faults of others. Do you think we may all be a little guilty of doing that? It reminds me of the old saying, "Any fool can criticize, condemn or complain, and most fools do!"

In my retirement years, GOD often reminds me how "imperfect" my life has been when looking at the times I didn't use the talents He gave me to glorify His name. He seems to be asking, "Don't you know I brought you (and all mankind) into the world to glorify My *name*?"

I believe GOD is asking us, "Don't you see many of the abilities and talents I have given humanity are being used to bring attention to humanity, not Me? Humanity has used My gifts to gain recognition for him or her. I often see they have done very little to glorify Me!" These words are hard for us to hear, read, or believe. Right? But we know they are often true in our own life. Right?

GOD knows the abilities and talents He has given us that we aren't using as He intended, even in our retirement years. I think He is also telling us that, if we did what He wants us to do, we might find we won't have to ask Him for help to get out of the "messes" we often find ourselves in!

After I retired, Sondra reminded me I could not lay around the house and bother her every day. So in my immediate post-retirement years, I tried a few jobs that checked my selling ability, and two areas mentioned in number 3 and 4 below, I used some of my experience from my former occupation—that is, developing and then managing the implementation of a new concept within an established company.

1. For a little more than one year, I sold new cars for Mazda.
2. For the next three years, I sold men's suits for JC Penney.

3. For the next seven years, I developed and managed a quality control dept. for Sears in Garland, Texas. Once this was in service, it enabled SEARS to inspect clothing merchandise received from vendors in the United States and various foreign countries.
4. Due to the success of our group in Garland in finding and returning a high percentage of defective clothing apparel and returned them to the vendors, I then helped establish like type groups in California, Maryland and Illinois.

In each of these ventures, I noted common factors existed that brought about success, not only to my satisfaction but also to the organization for which I was working. As I reviewed these common factors, I concluded the following:

1. When we give GOD the praise and glory for guiding our work, success will be the result.
2. If *we* take all the credit, we will probably not enjoy the successes that we receive.
3. We must acknowledge that GOD is the source of our real success.
4. When we forget the important "fact" of acknowledging GOD, and we understand "we" are only His "instruments"; we may be successful in the eyes of man, but our conscience reminds us it was *because* of GOD, our efforts brought about successful results. GOD shows us how great He is, and we know the truth. If we believe what others tell us, we can become "prideful," and this could be the cause of future failures and disappointments in our lives and the lives of future generations.

For us to enjoy our retirement years the way we "hope" we can, I've found the more we talk with GOD and give Him praise for everything good in our lives, the more He takes care of our needs. GOD shows us it is very important we don't try to be the person we were when we were between twenty and forty years old if we are now between sixty and over eighty. We need to spend our time being the person GOD made us, at the age we are today.

Living the truth stated in the above paragraphs will leave more fond memories with our friends and family by their remembering us as a person that truly loved Jesus Christ and tried to do what we could, to glorify His name, right to the very end.

At the end of the above ventures, I often found myself asking that age-old question, "Is this all there is to life?" I may have misinterpreted GOD's blessings because He was quick to point out, "*No*, now you can devote more time for ME, your family, your church, and to My people."

Today I still shake my head in disbelief when I realize GOD was about to give me exactly what I was missing. I was searching so hard to find something that I felt was needing attention, and something that I felt I could do, to serve GOD. My entire pre-retirement years was based on, "Am I making enough money to take care of my family and our financial obligations?"

"Now, how could I change this feeling and start enjoying serving GOD as He wants?" (Notice the number of times the word *I* is used in the above two paragraphs, eleven times. Now count the number of time I used *GOD*, four times. Maybe there is a message here, you think?)

It was at that point; GOD took over. Two of my friends in our church (Troy and Bob) had invited me to join them on an "outing" one weekend. I felt I couldn't be bothered with an activity that a couple of my friends in the church were involved with because I was looking for something to do that gave me an awareness of serving GOD. I'm not sure I even showed them the courtesy the first time they asked, to let them finish telling where they were going. I remember telling them, "Thanks, but I don't have the time." After all, I was busy looking for an activity that would give me a feeling of doing something of value for GOD.

Fortunately, my two friends proved they were not only friends, but they showed me *they* were doing what GOD wanted them to do—that is, telling others how they could serve the Lord by witnessing to those who did not have Jesus as their Savior. Who better to witness to than those who had turned away from GOD and lived a life outside of His Word? Who were these people who, when they came to the fork in the road of life, chose the wrong one?

After several weeks of Troy and Bob asking me to join them on their next visit to one of the prisons throughout northern and northeastern Texas, my reply was, "Are you kidding? You want me to go inside a prison and talk with men who have committed all types of crimes?"

I think it was Bob who answered my question with, "It's not us, it's GOD who wants you to do it!"

I finally agreed to go if they would back off after I went and verified I was *not* called to visit and talk with people in prison. As I recall, they both agreed, and Troy said something like, "Okay, but you'll be asking us when the next visit will be with the Bill Glass Prison Ministry and where will we be going?"

As I recall, it was on September 18, 1999, when I joined the Bill Glass Prison Ministries, day or weekend of champions. I joined Troy, Bob, and a large group of Christian brothers on a visit to the Billy M. Moore Correction Center near Overton, Texas. Starting in the year 2000, I think all the prison visits I was able to go on were in Northern Texas. A few units we visited after the one to Overton was Venus (close to our hometown in Red Oak, Texas), Colorado City, Texas (the farthest away), Tarrant County Jail in Fort Worth, Texas, 2000. Then we went to Huntsville, Texas, on a Weekend of Champions; we visited two days on the weekend. Over the following four or five years, I went with my two friends and many other "brothers in Christ" on one or two-day weekend visits throughout the Northern part of Texas. We didn't go every weekend, but after the first few visits, "I missed not being in prison over the weekend!"

Prison ministry with the Bill Glass Prison Ministries continued to be a blessing that I enjoyed very much. It allowed me to witness to men of all ages who had made mistakes, and many felt society had written them off. I found Christian groups like the Bill Glass Prison Ministries showed these men that GOD still loved them, and His Son, Jesus Christ, gave His life that they might have eternal life with Him and all who accepted Jesus as their Lord and Savior. Many of these men who society had written off as having "no value," during our visits, came to accept Jesus Christ as their Lord and Savior. GOD enabled me to stay involved in the prison ministry, but I lost some of my records during our move to Granbury, Texas in 2010, but I think I was with the Bill Glass Prison Ministry around six-plus years.

During the last couple of years, my wife, Sondra, joined me. As far as I know, Bill Glass ministry still has a tradition that when one of his "champions" make five visits to prisons, they received a gold-colored iron cross, made from a former prison (or jail) cell. I had already earned mine when Sondra joined, and when we visited a Juvenile Unit, we would go together. It was not too long before Sondra earned her iron cross. She and I both have our "crosses" in our living room as bookends, and when asked, we are proud to tell how we received them.

I found many of the youths and even older inmates had made friends with the wrong people who convinced them to do the wrong things. They were caught, tried, and sent to prison. The thing that might surprise some people is, very few prisoners, especially the juveniles, told us they were "not guilty" of the crime they committed. Almost every one of the juveniles told us, "I made a bad mistake, I know it, and I'm paying for it now, and when my time is up, I'm going to try and help other young boys and girls not to do what I did."

It was so noticeable when we would go into a juvenile unit, and Sondra was with me, there would always be two or three boys come up to her and talk to her as if she was their mother or grandmother. Often, we found it was their mother or grandmother that raised them and had taught them the right things to do, like going to church and staying in school. They showed they were sorry for what they did that hurt their "mom" or "grandma" and being able to talk with another mother and grandmother, "confessing" they knew they did wrong and wanted to tell someone that would understand, how sorry they were. Sondra and I always felt they were saying what their hearts felt at the time; only GOD knew if they would stay true to that feeling after they left prison.

Many of the boys would show Sondra pictures of their family and tell her about each one of them. She always drew a gathering of young boys that wanted to talk about their families and how sorry they were that they had been a disappointment to those they loved.

My experience with the juvenile boys was quite different. Usually, if they even mentioned their father, it was not with words of admiration. I remember one of the more extreme dislikes came from a young boy, around sixteen years old. He said his father never said anything good about him. His father never encouraged him, never complimented him when he did something that others had congratulated him on doing. His Dad never said anything about him that was the least bit good, in front of other adults. When the two of them were alone, his father would belittle him and tell him he would never amount to anything. Then he paused and said, "I guess maybe he was right." By this time, I could sense the level of dislike for his father was becoming more intense as he continued talking. Then, as if he had been waiting to tell someone how he felt, he said, "I will get out within a couple of years and when I do, if my father ever contacts me and starts belittling me again, "I'm going to kill him!"

I was speechless, but after neither of us said anything, I finally said, "Well, I hope it doesn't come to that, after all, you are still young, you have a long life ahead of you. If you did what today you feel you would, your father might end up dead, but you will have just thrown your entire life away. You will have let him prove to you, he was right. Don't you think you would have much more satisfaction if, when you get out, you start making a life for yourself and not listen to those who are trying to make you feel you are a failure? It won't be easy, but if you have Jesus as your Lord and Savior, you will have someone to talk with, seek guidance from, and He will always be there to listen to your prayers."

"Remember, GOD made you, and GOD never makes mistakes. There are many successful men in the world today that have made big mistakes in their lives, and many have had to pay for them like you are today. But they came to a point in their life when they said, "I'm going to change, and I know it is going to be hard, but I can do it, with the help and guidance of Jesus Christ." At this point, the young boy's voice changed from one of hatred to one of hurt, sorrow, the voice of a young boy who was pleading for help. We prayed, and then he said to me, "I hope you are right, and I am going to try hard to do it." He told me he had accepted Jesus as his Lord and Savior several years earlier but had drifted away because of his relationship with his father. I told him to share his story with the prison chaplain. I encouraged him to start attending Sunday church services regularly and ask the chaplain if he could help him in setting things up for their Sunday service or something during the week. I pointed out those kinds of activities would keep him mindful of the importance of serving GOD.

There was another experience I will always remember, and how it showed me the value of prison ministry. It also took place early in my involvement in the Bill Glass Prison Ministry, and it seemed to repeat itself in a little different way in each subsequent visit I made that first year.

It took place in an adult prison unit near Colorado City in West Texas. I was still a little uneasy in sitting down, within arm's length of a "convicted criminal." I had not yet had that conversation with myself that I think most people have, shortly after joining the prison ministry, when we ask, "Do I have the faith that GOD is in control of all things, including my protection while I'm witnessing to prisoners face to face?" Later, after talking to two different prisoners, GOD gave me the answer to my question.

On one of our visits to the prison in East Texas, I decided to set down at one of the round steel tables bolted to the floor in the center of an "open" area. Each table had four round, twelve-inch diameter seats attached to the steel table. As you might imagine, this was not the most desirable place to have a conversation with someone about Jesus Christ. I saw a man sitting at one of the tables, and I decided to join him. As I sat down, I said, "How are things going today? My name is Lloyd." Somewhat to my surprise, the man responded, "Hi, I'm Ted" (not real name). For a reason I'll show later, I chose one of the steel seats that would be ninety degrees to Ted's right side. "I'm with the Bill Glass Prison Ministry, have you heard that name before?"

"Not before yesterday when they announced you would be here this weekend."

In the time, I had been with the prison ministry. I found a good way to help the person I was talking with feel at ease was to tell them a little about our ministry.

"Have you ever heard the name Bill Glass?"

"Not before yesterday."

Ted's comment seemed to give me the "green light" to share a few words about Bill Glass that included him being a former NFL, all-pro, lineman for the Cleveland Browns during the 1960s. Sports talk usually perked up the prisoner's attention. Then I shared a few words as to how Bill decided to start his "prison ministry." I told him how Billy Graham (Ted had heard the name, Billy Graham, but not who he was.) I told Ted a little about Brother Graham, including his asking Bill Glass to be one of the platform speakers at the upcoming revival in Cleveland. Pastor Billy Graham's crusade was going to be in the Cleveland area during the next couple of weeks. Dr. Graham later encouraged Bill to think about becoming an evangelist. Bill had proven his talent as a professional football player in the NFL and many that had known him for several years knew him also as a strong Christian. With that combination, it looked as if GOD was saying, "I have given you multiple talents that you can now use to reach unsaved people, easier than many evangelists can.

I found as I visited more prison units, two areas will get the attention of the prisoner's faster than about anything, and they are well-known sports figures and motorcycles. I don't know if Bill can ride a motorcycle. However, the fact that he was one of the best known NFL football players during his career, that and being a Christian offset the motorcycle popularity many times over.

As I continued talking with the inmate Ted, about Bill Glass, I shared how, at the end of his professional career, with the Cleveland Browns, he was encouraged by Billy Graham, to start a "street ministry" type of evangelism. Bill followed Mr. Graham's suggestion and not too long after that; he started the Bill Glass Prison Ministry. I pointed out that at the time Ted and I were talking, I had heard the

Bill Glass Prison Ministry was one, if not the largest "prison ministry" organization in America, if not the world. Ted seemed to be impressed. His reaction seemed to open the door to tell him about the booklet that Bill Bright wrote to use in his ministry, "Campus Crusade for Christ," starting back in the mid 1960s and is titled, *Have You Heard of the Four Spiritual Laws?* Bill Glass was very impressed with the booklet and is now using it in his "prison ministry" by his "champions" when witnessing in prisons. It has been a great help for the inmates to better understand what God has done for mankind through His Son, Jesus Christ and continues to do for all humanity.

The four spiritual laws explain how GOD loves us, regardless of who we are or what we have or haven't done, or regardless of where we are today. I then asked, "Ted, I'd like to show you what this little booklet tells a person, hearing it for the first time."

(Authorization to use the booklet titled, *Have You Heard of the Four Spiritual Laws*, written by Bill Bright, copyrighted 1965–2019 The Bright Media Foundation and Campus Crusade for Christ, Inc. All rights reserved. Permission to use in prison ministry.)

(Note: The following highlighted words are quotes from the above mention booklet, *Have You Heard of the Four Spiritual Laws*? The example was from an inmate I witnessed to a few years ago when I was part of the Bill Glass Prison Ministry, and the inmate's name Ted was not his real name.)

As I opened the booklet, I read,

> Just as there are physical laws that govern the physical universe, so are there spiritual laws that govern your relationship with God.

Law 1 tells us,

> God loves you and offers a wonderful plan for your life.

This is explained WHY in John 3:16, I then quoted this verse and I explained how this Law also points to the words in John 10:10 (Christ speaking),

> I came that they might have life and might have it abundantly.

I then asked, Ted,

> Why is it that most people are not experiencing the abundant life?

"Maybe no one has told us about it."

"I think you hit the nail right on the head. So many people today have never heard or read the message that God wants all humanity to know. And that is the main reason Bill Glass Ministries exists. We want to share the "Good News" with those who may have never heard or heard bits and pieces but never the story of forgiveness and Salvation."

And this brings us to law 2:

> Man is sinful and separated from God. Therefore, he cannot know and experience God's love and plan for his life.

In Romans in 3:23, we see,

> All have sinned and fall short of the glory of God.
>
> Man was created to have fellowship with God; but, because of his own stubborn self-will, he chose to go his own independent way and fellowship with God is broken. This self-will, characterized by an attitude of active rebellion or passive indifference; is an evidence of what the Bible calls sin."

Romans 6:23,

> The wages of sin is death.

This illustrates that God is holy, and man is sinful.
The third law explains the only way to bridge this gulf...
Law 3 goes,

> Jesus Christ is God's only provision for man's sin. Through Him, you can know and experience God's love and plan for your life.
> He died in our place. (Romans 5:8)
>
> He rose from the dead. (1 Corinthians 15:3–6)
>
> He is the only way to God. (John 14:6)

Think of that Ted, five hundred people saw Jesus alive *after* they had seen him killed just a few days earlier." The Law goes on showing how Jesus stated that *he* is the only way a man can obtain Salvation. Jesus Himself said,

> I am the way, the truth, and the life; no one comes to the Father except through Me. (John 14:6)

If we think of God being in heaven and man being here on earth, it is easy to see that man can't reach, fly, or use any tool man has made, even the most advanced rocket of the day; he will never be able to reach God doing it man's way. Now, if we imagine a huge cross with the name Jesus on it and it extends from heaven to earth, we see that He, Jesus is the only way we can reach God, it's the only way He will accept us.

Law 4,

> We must individually receive Jesus Christ as Savior and Lord; then we can know and experience GOD's love and plan for our lives.

In John 1:12, we are told we must receive Christ in Ephesians 2:8, 9. It tells us we receive Christ through faith. John 3:1–8 tells us when we receive Christ, We Experience a New Birth. Now, up to this point, we have only been told how and why we have GOD as our Lord and Savior through His Son, Jesus Christ. But what must we do to complete that all-important connection?

It's very easy: We have been shown we must individually receive Jesus Christ as our Lord and Savior; then we can know and experience GOD's love and plan for our lives. No one can do this for us, you and I both must ask Jesus to be our Lord and Savior and acknowledge that we are sinners.

Receiving Christ is much more than having Him as an acquaintance. He will be our one and only Lord and Savior, the only pathway to GOD the Father. Again, John tells us in 1:12,

> As many as received Him, to them He gave
> the right to become children of GOD.

At this point, I looked at Ted and asked, "Do you know Jesus as your Lord and Savior?"

"No, I don't think I do."

"Do you understand what I've discussed with you as to what we all have to do to receive Him as our Lord and Savior?"

"Yes."

"Are you ready to ask Him to come into your life and be your Lord and Savior from this moment on?"

"Yes, but I'm not sure I know how."

"That is not a problem because GOD is not as concerned with the exact words we say as He is with the sincerity of our heart. If you are ready to take that all-important step, I will say some words that address your view, you can repeat them *if* you agree in your heart they say what you believe, okay?"

"Okay."

As I say the following words, if they express the desire of your heart, I invite you to repeat them, but only if they are what you feel in your heart. "Lord Jesus, I need you." (Pause for Ted to repeat.) "I confess that I am a sinner, and I thank You for dying on the cross for my sins." (Pause for Ted.) "I open the door of my life and receive You as my Lord and Savior." (Pause for Ted.) Thank You for forgiving my sins and giving me eternal life." (Pause for Ted.) "Take control of my life." (Pause for Ted.) "Make me the kind of person You want me to be." (Pause.)

I then asked Ted, "Do you feel those words you just said to GOD, express your true feelings?"

"Yes, I do."

"Then I want to shake your hand as my brother in Christ. One more thing I want you to remember. You have just ticked Satan off, and he knows he has lost you, but now he is going to try and make you as ineffective a Christian as he can."

"Each day until it is your natural reaction, go to GOD's Word and use it to show Satan, you have GOD's word and His authority. As a Christian, you will live by "faith" (in GOD and His Word) from this day forward."

If a nonbelieving friend should challenge your newfound Savior, use GOD's Word to respond. In Paul's letter to the Ephesians, he addresses this issue by telling them, "By grace you have been saved through faith; and that not of yourselves, it is the gift of GOD, not because of (your) works that no one should boast."

At that point, I handed the booklet to Ted and told him I had written his name on the back, and I added, today's date followed by the words (date of being born *again*).

The above words were shared with Ted and other prisoners by members of the Bill Glass Prison Ministry. Then a copy of the booklet *Have You Heard of the Four Spiritual Laws*? is given to those who listen and accept Jesus Christ. The words shown above during my conversation with Ted were as near as possible being a way of verbal witnessing. The booklet helps prisoners understand why GOD and Jesus Christ must be a part of their lives if they want Salvation.

As Ted and I continued our discussion, I noticed out of the corner of my eye; someone was standing at our table, directly across from me. As I turned and looked, I noticed a man standing, looking at me with both of his arms were crossed in front of his chest and both covered with what I call "prison tattoos." Almost without thinking, I asked him, "How about you, do you know Jesus Christ as your Lord and Savior?"

His reply, with somewhat of a smirk, was, "I don't believe in that stuff."

"Oh, have you ever heard of the four spiritual laws."

"No."

"Would you like to hear them?"

He paused for a moment and then, as if he didn't have anything better to do, said, "I might as well, I'm not going to be going anywhere for several years."

At that point, Ted thanked me again and excused himself. I asked the man that GOD sent to check me out, "What is your name?"

"Bob." (Not real name.)

"Glad to meet you, Bob. My name is Lloyd, come over and sit down where Ted was sitting so you can see better, what I was telling Ted." I asked Bob if he had heard of the Four Spiritual Laws, and he said he hadn't. I then asked him if he would like to hear about them, and his reply was, "I guess so since I don't have any place to go for a few years."

As I went through the four laws and asked after each one, if he understood it, Bob would nod or make a faint "grunt." I explained each law, and then I asked Bob if he understood it, and as soon as he acknowledged my words, I moved on to the next law.

At the end of explaining the four laws, I asked Bob if he understood them. He said, for the first time in a clear voice, "Yes."

I then asked if he was ready to accept Jesus as his Lord and Savior and invite Him into his life. There was no answer. Since I had been pointing to the different figures in the booklet while I was talking, I was not looking at Bob. When I did not hear an answer, I looked up and saw this man, arms covered with tattoos, a man that had a rather mean expression on his face, and, whose name was Bob. The man who, a few minutes earlier, had, with some hesitation, agreed to listen to what I had to say. As I looked up, I now saw the same man sitting at the table with his chin on his chest and tears running down his cheeks.

"Bob, do you feel it is time for you to get your life in order and accept Jesus Christ as your Savior?"

Sobbing, Bob looked up and said, "Yes, but I don't know how."

I told him the same as I had told Ted. I then said the prayer, and at each pause, he repeated the words. As we finish, the tears were still falling, but for the first time, Bob had a smile on his face. I gave him the booklet, and he thanked me for spending time with him, and then he got up and left.

For a few moments, while I was sitting at the table alone, it seemed I heard the answer to the question I asked myself earlier—that is, "Do I have the faith that GOD is in control of all things, including my protection while I'm witnessing to prisoners?"

At that moment, I seemed to hear the words, "See, I am with you, even when you're inside the walls of the prison. My Holy Spirit is still within you!" I didn't realize it then, but later I was telling one the other men that Bob was one the meanest looking prisoners I had ever talked to and one of the few who broke down and cried when the Holy Spirit touched him. "Thank You, Father!"

Even though I was only in my midseventies and enjoyed witnessing and talking to the inmates (at this writing I am eighty-five). I felt the strain on my legs and heart were taking its toll. It was at that time I knew this would be my "final days" in prison ministry. It was then that I realized GOD always has something we can do to glorify His name if we are open to doing it. Sondra and I both had asked GOD to give us another ministry that we could do together, without the interference of feeling the hard stools and cement floors. We were about to see what GOD had next, not just for me but Sondra and me.

I felt GOD was telling me He had a ministry He wanted Sondra and me to do to glorify His name. A ministry that would not require the physical endurance that prison ministry requires, but rather the desire to witness to another unique group of GOD's children that often have special needs and some may not know Jesus Christ as their Savior. This new ministry is covered in detail in Appendix D. We call it our "R" ministry ("R" standing for *restaurant*).

On January 12, 2015, we feel GOD showed Sondra and me that He wanted us to view our "R" ministry as a ministry to glorify His name. This ministry has given both of us some of the most blessed moments of joy and a feeling of GOD's approval. Appendix D shows we officially started this ministry in Granbury, Texas, and when we moved back to Waxahachie, Texas, we continued our ministry. At this writing, most of our witness has been in the two cities of Granbury and Waxahachie, Texas, however, we have witnessed in Mesquite and Red Oak, Texas multiple times, and other cities throughout the area when stopping for something to eat. The numbers have grown considerably at the time of this writing, and we plan to continue it until GOD asks us to do something else, such as "bringing us home." The figures at the end of Appendix D gives a hint of the success GOD has enabled us to experience in this ministry, to glorify His holy name. As you read this book today, know the figures in Appendix D have increased considerably—all by the power of GOD's will. He has blessed Sondra and me by letting us be His "instruments" to show others how GOD the Father, through Jesus Christ His Son and His Holy Spirit who dwells within each believer is the *message* of salvation for all humanity. If you could hear some of the "prayer requests" waiters have given us, you would understand why we feel so blessed in being GOD's instruments. Appendix D shows how GOD seems to send the right person to our table who needs to know GOD as their Savior or to have the *faith* that He will take care of their need, if they remain faithful to His commands. The numbers shown on Appendix D have not only increased but, they continue to prove GOD is truly good—all the time. He is the only one that can take care of our needs. Sondra and I always make sure the waiters understand our prayers are, in no way to replace their prayers, but they are to show the waiter, that even strangers who are children of GOD want to join the waiter in prayer, in lifting their needs to Him.

I want to now touch on some other important events in my life that have had a major impact on Sondra and me serving GOD. I mentioned some of them when talking about an earlier time in my Christian life. I continue to repent of my sins each day, but with more conviction, because GOD has shown me time after time that, not only is He the creator of all things, His love is a never-dying love.

Without one bit of pride, I admit I have been "a sinner among sinners," in my younger years. I have seen and done many things of which I am not proud. As I've said before, I find no comfort in saying, "Yes, but I can name a lot of people that have done much worse than me." GOD's Word makes it very clear that He does not judge us by one another. Satan is the one who tries to get us to compare our sins against those of others that our society might say is much worse than ours, but society is not our judge. When we let Satan influence us in this way, we have set the stage whereby we will never feel the true love and forgiveness of GOD.

I have come to believe that it is so important to know and understand the facts—that is, the causes surrounding the actions of others. If we don't know the cause for their actions, we tend to "judge" them by what we "see" and that will often lead to losing friends and family because it is not our "right" to judge others. That is GOD's and GOD's alone.

If we are not conditioned to have faith in Him and believe He will see us through even the worst of experiences, we will never be conditioned to roll with the punches that await us in adult life. What gives me peace of mind today is thinking of the fun times and the hurtful times in my early preteen years. I always felt my parents loved me, and so did GOD and His Son, Jesus Christ, and once I asked Jesus to be my Lord and Savior, I knew GOD's Holy Spirit was within me.

On November 24, 2019, Sondra and I celebrated our sixty-third anniversary. Only GOD could have arranged the series of events between a boy from Kansas and a girl from Missouri to meet in a town in Iowa, fall in love, get married and within a few months' interview for a job with AT&T in Kansas City, Missouri, and then move to Wichita, Kansas. to start a family and have a thirty-plus year successful career with AT&T that ended in NYC and then retired to the State of Texas. The only one I know who could arrange that scenario is GOD!

Sondra and I both agree if someone had told us when we were married, we would enjoy sixty-three years together; we would have responded by saying, "The odds are slim that we would both live sixty years, let alone be married that long. For that to happen, it would take a "power" far greater than any human possesses. It would take GOD Himself, and why would He pick two insignificant people like us to give such a "blessing"?

However, since it did happen, and it happened to Sondra and me, there is no doubt it was GOD that orchestrated the entire series of events that neither of us was aware of until that day we met in Mamie's home in Fort Madison, Iowa. We have figured every angle we could think of as to how all those things could happen, without GOD directing them, and we determined it was impossible. So regardless of what others may say, we're sticking with, "GOD did it because He not only had a plan for each of us, but He also had a plan for both of us as a couple." It is hard to believe how anyone could doubt the existence, the power, the love, the forgiveness of the one that Christians and Jews alike call, "GOD"!

During those thirty-plus years with AT&T, we moved twelve times throughout Kansas, Colorado, and New Jersey. After retiring, we moved to Texas and moved four more times in that state, after retiring, over the next thirty years. Many have asked how our children survived during those early years of moving. My answer is, "Great," by the time they started school in a different location than they attended the previous year they felt at home in the new school and town, because of the friends they had made. In our girl's high school years, we only moved once, and that seemed to have some impact on our oldest (Vicki). She had become very close friends with a girl in her class, and they had many plans for their remaining years in high school. But after our move and school started, she became friends with another girl in our new location that rode the same school bus with our daughter, and the previous location and friend became history in a very short time.

Today our children are all grown, married, and have children and our two girls are Grandmas. At this writing, our oldest daughter (Vicki) lives in the State of Oregon, not too far from their kids who live in Washington State. Our middle child (Stephanie) lives in Texas, close to all her kids plus Sondra and me. We all live in Waxahachie, Texas. Our son (Grant) and his wife live in Florida with their two boys and two girls. He also has a daughter, a granddaughter, and grandson who live in Texas.

As I reflect on all our moving, I see how GOD enabled our children to see the world in a much broader spectrum than if we had remained in the small suburb of Wichita, Kansas, by the name of Haysville. Haysville was a nice town, and we had some wonderful friends, neighbors, and a church family there, but we would not have seen the places GOD led us to live. Our children would not have met the wonderful people that are the spouses of our children today who, by the way, none of our in-laws are from Kansas or Missouri! There is no doubt in my mind that, "I now believe GOD sent me to Iowa, not for a job with the Santa Fe RR but, to meet a girl from Missouri, to be my wife."

We have lived in different parts of our great country like New Jersey where our children realized most people of Italian descent are just as nice and friendly as people from Kansas and Texas whose ancestors may have come from Ireland, Germany or Norway. They saw, in person, the Pocono Mountains in Pennsylvania are just as beautiful as the Rocky Mountains in Colorado, and the difference is only their height, not their scenery. They found, when you get to know them, the people in Colorado, Kansas, and Missouri are as proud of their states as the people in Texas are of theirs. As I reflect on all the places we lived, I feel GOD gave Sondra and me and our children, an education in seeing what a beautiful place America is and how much more we all have in common than what the politicians, fake news, and TV often suggests. Hopefully, our children will pass on these truths to their children and realize all they encountered at a very young age gave them a free education in geography, psychology, and religion, arranged and provided by our heavenly Father. Hopefully, they give GOD the praise and glory that only He deserves.

During my forties and fifties I often asked myself two questions:

1. How could an only child from a small town in Kansas, whose father was considered an "alcoholic" by some, who

didn't know for many years "why" or "the cause" of his father's drinking. How could he ever amount to anything when his mother had to take in ironing clothes for people to make extra money so they would have food when her husband wasn't working?"

2. I have often asked myself, "Why was it that I didn't follow the lifestyle of my father and accept it as my destiny?"

The answers to these questions were always the same "because GOD had a plan for me, and He has for everyone who is reading this book. We each travel on the road of life, and we each will come to that portion when the road splits into two directions. We and we alone must choose which one we will take. If we have Jesus Christ as our Lord and Savior and try to follow His commands, we will take the "right" road. We reach that point at different times in life. I realize I needed to follow GOD's plan and not yield to Satan's lies at the age of eleven. That realization started to unfold shortly before that day in 1946 when I went forward and gave my life to GOD by repenting of my sins and asking His Son, Jesus Christ to come into my life and be my Lord and Savior. However, I did not realize, at that early age, all that GOD would do for me *if* I were willing to follow His Son, Jesus Christ and obey His commands versus interrupting them to what I wanted them to be. Even during the times in my teenage years and my time in the military when I turned from what I knew was GOD's will, He never turned from me. But praise GOD, I soon found I not only owe my life on earth to GOD, but I also know GOD owns my eternal soul, and He will soon call me home to be with Him in His heavenly kingdom.

I have shared some of my life experiences with people in prisons, gyms, restaurants, and even in the church. If even one person came to accept Jesus Christ in hearing some of my life's experiences and encounters with Satan and turned from his temptations on their lives, I praise GOD. I would pray that regardless of their age or how hurtful their early life may have been, hopefully, they would come to know, "With GOD, all things are possible!" Hopefully, we can all understand when we try to serve GOD through His Son, Jesus

Christ, we will be with Him in His heavenly kingdom where there is no sin, no pain, no suffering. I believe it is only by the grace and mercy of GOD, that I am where I am and who I am today. I have tried to show from my preteen years, through high school, a tour in the military, a career with AT&T and various diverse jobs in post-retirement; I believe it was GOD who led me to my one and only wife, who has been my pride and my bride for sixty-three years on November 24, 2019. I praise GOD for the life He has given Sondra and me and our children. Has it been perfect?

"No, but I know that Sondra and I, and hopefully all of our family, will experience that perfect life when we move into our mansion in heaven and kneel at the throne of GOD, giving Him praise and glory.

We will never be able to repay GOD, Jesus Christ, or the Holy Spirit for what they have done for my family and me. I believe GOD has forgiven my sins, and when I stand before His throne, I and all the others with me will be sin-free, never to sin again. GOD still loves me and has forgiven me. I pray you also believe that He has or will do the same for you IF you only accept His Son, Jesus Christ, as your Lord and Savior and do your best to follow His commands. It is not easy at times, but we never want to lose *faith* and *hope* when we consider the alternatives.

I pray some of the experiences I encountered throughout my early preteens will give faith and hope to those readers that had similar childhoods. As I share these hurtful times in my life, I pray the reader will see my faith in GOD's Word and my belief (*hope*), He always took care of my hurt and pain, even when I didn't know *why* the pain and hurt were happening. If we have faith in GOD, I hope we will understand; WE are not alone. I pray we will believe on faith that GOD wants to show us the same grace and mercy He has shown others. He only asks that we believe in Him, repent of our sins and invite His Son, Jesus Christ into our hearts, as our Lord and Savior. Jesus himself tells us in John 14:6,

> I am the way and the truth and the life. No one comes to the Father except through me.

I pray for those who have not accepted these words of Jesus Christ as "truth," will do so now and not waste time listing to Satan's lies that will lead them away from the many blessings GOD gives His children while we are still here on earth. I pray the nonbelievers will understand GOD's Word tells us those who refuse to accept His Word on faith and hope; they, not GOD, will be determining their eternal destination.

As I have grown older, it has always amazed me why the nonbeliever will scoff at the faith and hope of the believer. The nonbeliever seems to have no problem in thinking the sins Satan leads them to do each day will not bring consequences of pain and suffering in the end. Logic shows neither the believer or the nonbeliever of life after death can be proven. However, doesn't it make more sense to believe the one that promises us an eternal life with GOD than with Satan? When we die and find out which one was telling us the truth, it will be too late to change our mind! And none of us know when our life will end, here on earth. At that moment of death, our soul will be in one of two places. Why take a chance of being in the wrong one? John 14:6 tells us there is one and only one way to GOD, and it is through Jesus Christ. We will all come to that fork in the road of life, and *we* must choose one or the other. Why wouldn't we eagerly choose to follow our creator whose Son gave His life so that we might have eternal life with Him, throughout *all* eternity?

Once we make that decision, Satan will try to make us feel like, "We are nothing, we have no value." He will try to make us feel we are so bad that even GOD won't do anything for us. Now is the time when we need to remind ourselves of what GOD did with the people society looked down on during the Old Testament era. We need to remember how the people probably felt they were worthless. These were people like those listed on Appendix G, and there is a much larger list of those same kinds of people that live in our neighborhood, city, and yes some may even be in our family. Regardless of where we are, we are GOD's creations, and He loves each of us and wants to help us, but He won't force His blessings on us if we turn our back on Him.

Remember, Abraham was too old, Leah was ugly, Joseph was abused, Moses stuttered, Rahab was a prostitute, and we read what GOD did with these believers. GOD will do the same for you, me, and all believers in His Son, Jesus Crist.

It's one thing to gamble your wealth on tomorrow, but it is quite different if we gamble our eternal life on today. That is what the nonbeliever is doing. If he/she does not wake up tomorrow morning and find they were wrong, it will be too late to change their mind. If you have not accepted Jesus as your Lord and Savior, think about the gamble you are taking when you go to bed tonight!

Chapter 11

Final Retirement

Growing old sure beats the alternative of dying young.
So HAVE a plan for the first Monday after retiring!

In March of 1987, near the time of my retirement from AT&T, I attended a "pre-retirement" seminar AT&T made available to management personnel in headquarters. It included a lawyer, a psychologist, and one or two other professional people to speak to the managers who were planning to retire within the next quarter. The lawyer talked about the importance of having an up-to-date will or a trust. He cautioned not to make the mistake of thinking, "I have the rest of my life to do that." He pointed out that we might be right in that view. However, we don't know if we are going to be alive to see the first day of our second year of retirement.

The psychologist made several recommendations that I thought were very good. He made one statement that has come to mind more than once since I retired. He said studies show that it is very important, before your retirement, you should commit to doing something on the first day after you retire that you have postponed while still, working. It can be anything as insignificant as painting one of the chairs from your patio furniture. Let's say you retire on Friday. On the following Monday, start what you committed to doing and DON'T COME UP WITH ANY EXCUSES. IT'S MONDAY, SO DO IT! If you say to yourself and your spouse, "We've got plenty of time for that later, I'm going to lay back, unwind and enjoy life." The problem with that is, the longer you postpone that "first Monday project," the easier it will be for you to start postponing other activities that require you to get out of your house and move around. In the meantime, you are probably developing the habit of taking a midmorning nap, shortly after finishing breakfast, and then you find you need a midafternoon nap so you will be wide awake for the 6:00 p.m. news. That becomes very important because you are usually in bed and asleep when the 10:00 p.m. news comes on. (Get the picture?)

Studies show over 50 percent of the retirees asked, spent their first Monday in a lounge chair in the back yard trying to get a suntan or some like type activity. They never took care of their commitment and then found it was so easy to postpone other activities, *why*? Because they felt they had the rest of their life to fulfill their commitment!

He went on to say this pattern will continue unless your doctor starts questioning what you are doing in the way of exercising. Your response might be something like, "Exercising? I didn't retire to train for the 'Mr. America' title." The psychologist went on by saying, "If you have a good doctor he will probably respond with, "You could be right, but following your current schedule, you are conditioning yourself for early death."

He made another point that my wife and I had already started making plans to do. The psychologist pointed out that too many retirees had become a slave to their job's during their working career. After retirement, they did not realize their job was still controlling their lifestyle.

Their life's routine boiled down to their thinking, "We just don't have the money now." or "This is not the time to take that cruise we both want to take, but we will someday, but not now."

Unfortunately, they didn't take that cruise, even after retirement because they were still using the same excuse. The husband and possibly his wife if she worked, both spent their entire lives continuing to follow their pre-retirement routine that did not allow time for a "getaway vacation."

Hearing the importance of *not* "following the structure, their jobs required them to follow," before retirement reminded me of an experience I had a few weeks before attending this seminar.

At the time I was planning to retire, AT&T had a program that enabled a management employee to visit an AT&T stockholder who had responded to a letter from headquarters public relations office. The letter acknowledged he/she was a registered owner of AT&T stock. It continued by asking if the owner would be interested in having a manager from corporate headquarters come to their home and answer any questions they might have, concerning their AT&T stock. At that time, the stock owner would have the opportunity to ask about anything concerning AT&T. The manager that would be visiting the stock owner had no knowledge of the number of shares the stock owner had and would not ask during their visit.

The purpose of the visit was to see if the AT&T stockholder had any questions or comments about our stock, business, in the future or other concerns. Often, the AT&T manager might not be aware of one or more of the areas the stock holder had a question on, in which case he/she was instructed to make a note of the question(s), the Stock owner's name and their telephone number and ensure them a follow-up call would be made to them within the following week.

I had volunteered for this program a few months before and received a name and telephone number of a shareowner who had indicated an interest in having a representative visit him. The shareowner lived just a mile or so from our home.

My visit was with Mr. Jones.

Upon my arrival at Mr. Jones (not real name) home, I was greeted by a gentleman who looked to be in his mid to late sixties. As we started our discussion, I sensed he might be more interested in just talking to me about anything, and if it were only about AT&T, that would be okay as well.

As our conversation started, he informed me his first name was Thomas, and he was a retired New Jersey highway patrolman who, at the time he retired was three years before the meeting with me. He told me his wife of thirty-seven years had passed away a year before our meeting. And with that, he began telling me how his retirement had become nothing like he and his wife had expected. He admitted his job had been his life. He loved being out on the highways of New Jersey. He took pride in wearing his uniform. Their friends were mostly people that worked within the state highway department. They did not belong to any outside club or organization, including church and they never felt an interest in getting involved in other activities, even after he retired—that is, they had earned the right to relax and take it easy.

Then Thomas told me when he retired; he soon realized he had nothing to do, no one to talk with, not even his friends in the department. He felt they would only want to discuss the events of the day, the experiences they had recently encountered, especially those out-of-the-ordinary events they had incurred for the first time. He continued by saying, he was not interested in talking about their recent involvements and, "I felt they really wouldn't care about going over the past happenings when I was still working."

Thomas said after his wife died, he found himself not leaving the house for days at a time. He knew this was not good for him, and eventually, it would affect his health. He said when he was going out in the backyard to do something and seeing his neighbor in his backyard; he would return to his armchair in the living room. He knew that if he went outside, his neighbor would holler at him and say something like, "How's retirement?" Or "What are you doing with all your free time?"

After his wife passed away, he said he would often recall the times when he and his wife would talk for hours about all the things they would do when he retired. There would be a cruise to Hawaii, a trip to England and so many different places in the United States that neither had seen. Now, Thomas knew none of those dreams would ever take place. His wife was gone, his one son and family lived in Florida, and both he and his wife were still working. Any spare time they had was spent attending their son's school and sporting events. Thomas was all alone with nothing but dreams he knew would never be fulfilled.

Then Thomas made an unexpected statement. He said, "I knew that if I didn't start doing something and doing it soon, I might be dead within a few months." He continued, "It was then that I realized I had never been interested in any activity outside of my job. Now that I am retired, I know no one wants to discuss my job as a Patrolman, and I don't care to talk about those events either, because it reminds me they are no longer my life, they are my history."

Thomas then said something I was not expecting to hear. "But you know what? I was sitting in this chair one day feeling down and out. I felt no one cared if I was alive or dead, and just then the phone rang. For a moment, I considered not answering it because I didn't want to hear someone talking about their active life, but I picked up the phone and said, "Hello," and something unbelievable happened.

When the voice on the other end said, "Thomas Jones, you old rascal, what are you doing to stay out of trouble?" I immediately recognized the voice of Captain Pearson from my old station. "I'm not having too much trouble staying out of trouble, because I'm not getting out too much these days."

"I hope you're not ill?"

"No, I just don't get out like I used to."

"Well, maybe I can help you take care of that. I'm calling because a friend of mine has a successful photography business, but he is having some problems. I thought of you, thinking if you had some spare time you might be interested in helping him out."

"I doubt if I could help anyone, but what is his problem?"

"I remembered you were our 'backup' man in taking accident pictures when there were two accidents, and Jerry wasn't able to cover more than one at a time. Even though it was not part of your job description, you would always volunteer to cover one of the accidents. I don't know if you are aware of it, but there were several of us that felt your pictures were as good as Jerry's, but don't tell him I said that."

"Now the problem my friend has is he mistakenly scheduled a wedding and a Bar mitzvah on the same day. They are both large events, and there is no way he can cover more than one. I told him that you know how to use a camera quite well and I even showed him some of the pictures you took. He was very impressed and said if there is any way you could do one the events he would give you all the money the party has agreed to pay. He also said the Bar mitzvah would be the easier of the two events since it only requires taking pictures of the boy, his family and then walk around after the celebration starts and take random pictures. He said he would explain what would be required if you could find the time to help him."

I couldn't speak for, what seemed like several minutes, and then I said, "I don't think I could do that. The only pictures I've taken were of accidents and not of anything as important as a Bar mitzvah."

"Well, I understand, but would you mind if I gave my friend your number, maybe he could explain the problem better than I have."

"Okay, you can give him my name and number, but I sure wouldn't want to do something that would ruin his reputation."

"Thanks, Pal, I know you are probably busy with a lot of things, but I know my friend would sure appreciate it if you could find the time to help him out of this crisis. His name is Peter. Take care and when are you going to drop by the station and say hello?"

"We miss you and your coffee. You were the only one who knew how to make a good pot of coffee. Do stop by and we'll let you make a fresh pot, and we'll kick around the good old days, okay?"

"I'll try to work it into my busy schedule."

By this time, I noticed Thomas was talking with more enthusiasm. I felt he just needed someone that would listen to him. However, he was not through with his story. He then said, "I received a call from Capt. Pearson's friend the next day. He again explained the situation and said he was sure I could do the job, especially the bar mitzvah. Then he told me how much it would be helping him." By now Thomas was sitting up in his chair, and the expression on his face made me think he was not through telling me about this "opportunity" he was given by someone he had never met.

Thomas continued by saying, "Peter told me he knew I was retired and may have a lot of activities going on and because of that he said he would not even consider asking for my help if he was not in a critical situation." When he seemed to almost plead for my help and said if I could help him, I'll be forever grateful, what else could I do? I thought for a moment and then said, "How about me coming down to your studio this afternoon, and you go over what I would have to do, and then I'll decide?"

"Name the time, and I'll be here, and thank you so much."

I noticed for the first time since we started talking, Thomas had a smile on his face. I couldn't help but ask the sixty-four-dollar question, "Did you take the pictures, and was it for the bar mitzvah?"

"Yes to both," he replied.

He then continued, "I've never been a 'churchgoer,' but what some of my Christian friends tell me, all that I've told you was a "GOD thing," coming at a time I needed *his* help." Before I could say anything, Thomas let me know he was still not through with his story.

"Let me tell you what happened. The bar mitzvah went off without a hitch. I had the feeling the family thought I had done bar mitzvahs many times." Thomas then told me after the wedding, and the Bar mitzvah had both been taken care of, Peter and he were having a cup of coffee in Peter's office. And again Peter told him how much his taking the pictures meant to him. "I told him he might not feel that way after he saw them. I left the film with him since he told the family they would be ready in a couple of days."

Two days later, Peter called me, "Can you come down to the office this afternoon, I'd like to talk to you about your pictures?"

Thomas said, "My heart sank to the floor. Not so much because my pictures were not of good quality, after all, I told him I was not a professional, but apparently, the Jewish family was very upset with them."

I told him I would be there at one o'clock, and when I arrived, Peter was sitting at his desk. As I entered, he stood up and shook my hand and said, "Man, you will never know how you saved my rear end." He went on to say, "I've talked with the family and gave them their copies of your pictures. In looking at them, they couldn't say enough about how great they were. They told me to be sure and let you know if they ever have another event, they would insist that you take the pictures."

Thomas then said, "I know you probably aren't interested in all of my stories, but I just had to share them with someone."

"I feel I found a new life at a time I was ready to call the undertaker; I had to tell someone what happened. Now, maybe you can share my experience with someone you know who is feeling they don't have any reason to live. By the way, I am now working for Peter almost every week. He told me if I would be "on-call," he would give me enough work that I would feel I had a new full-time job again. And that is pretty much how I feel, but more than that, I feel I do have value and a new life."

Then with a wink, he said, "Since you were kind enough to come and listen to my story, I want to tell you that I feel AT&T stock is great and tell your president to keep those good dividends coming. Maybe with the money, I'm making from my new job, I'll be buying some more AT&T shares."

Thomas was still not through, "You know something? If I had it all to do over again, I would do one thing differently. The day after I retired, instead of sitting around in my armchair just passing the time, I would get my camera and take pictures of all my neighbors' pets and print them on "thank-you" cards and give them to the owners with a note saying, "Thanks for being a good neighbor!"

Hearing Thomas's words, I thought, "What a coincidence!" Thomas's postretirement experience seemed to validate the point the psychologist made in our retirement seminar—that is, "Have a plan for the first Monday after retiring." Then make sure you do it and not say, "I don't have to do it now."

Thomas and his wife never took that vacation they probably talked about dozens of times before his retirement. From what he told me, they probably never even enjoyed any mini vacations to Pennsylvania to see the Pocono Mountains or down to Washington, DC, to see the sights there.

It almost seems like he didn't even have a "bucket list" to work on, but instead he spent countless hours sitting in his armchair thinking about all the things he and his wife talked about but would never do. He probably did sleep late in the morning and had an extra cup of coffee at breakfast, still in his PJs.

I wasn't sure if he had made friends with all his neighbors, but if he hadn't, with his new view on life, I expect he feels, "It's not too late to do it now." Hopefully, he will do what he shared with me and took pictures of his neighbor's pets and printed them on cards that said something like, "Thank You for being such a nice neighbor!"

I hope he has contacted his son and told him, "When it's okay with you, I'd like to come down for a few days visit and spoil my grandchildren a little."

After hearing Thomas's experiences and thinking about some of the things I heard when I attended the AT&T pre-retirement seminar, I told Sondra, "I'm sure we haven't thought about everything we should plan and think about before retiring, but I feel that first Monday after my retirement date has been taken care of."

"What are you talking about, first Monday after you retire?"

My reply, "I'll explain it later."

The following is what we had planned and to some extent, completed. We (mostly Sondra) had made reservations to do a little traveling to those places we had never visited but wanted to when I retired.

Shortly after I retired in 1987, Sondra and I flew to Israel for a weeks' vacation that turned out to be the first of two trips we would make to the Holy Land. We returned some ten years later, in November of 1999 for a second visit. We were able to see many interesting sites and areas that we did not see on our first trip. During our post-retirement years, we flew to Hawaii. Then, we took our first cruise, on what is called the "inland cruise to Alaska." I told Sondra if the cruises I took in the Navy were as nice as the cruise to Alaska, I would have been a twenty-year Navy retiree. On our second trip to Israel, we were able to go to Egypt, where we saw the pyramids. While there, I rode my first camel (and my last). I was able to climb inside the largest of the famous three pyramids and view the inside chamber. Next, we took a cruise through the Panama Canal from Jacksonville, Florida to Los Angeles, California. We flew to England and visited many historical places there and also went to Scotland. After that trip, we started taking little weekend trips to places in Texas that we had never visited.

These were attractive when we recalled some of the times on our overseas trips we would get a little tired walking for long distances, and now on these short trips within Texas, we found we were also a little tired at the end of the day. If we thought about it, we didn't discuss it, but we were also several years older when we were making these "shorter" trips. I expect if you would have asked, "Do you think your age may have something to do with your getting tired?" Sondra and I both would have said, "Oh no, we aren't old enough for our age to cause us getting tired. It was probably something to do with the weather!" I expect what will prove to be our last overseas trip, was our flight and vacation when we traveled throughout Germany and Luxenberg. This trip proved to be one of the most interesting overseas trips we made.

As we age a little more each year and recall all the walking we did during those earlier trips; we thank the Lord for guiding us to take those types of vacations when walking was not an issue in determining where our next vacation would be. We still recall and laugh about some of the experiences we had, especially on our cruises. One that brought back some old memories was during our cruise on the *Grand Princess* ship of the *Princess Cruise* line. We took it in 2003 where we left from Jacksonville, Florida, and stopped at Cozumel, Costa Maya, and Belize City in the small nation of Belize. As we continued south, we stopped at the Isle of Roatan off the coast of Honduras where we swam with the dolphins (and have pictures to prove it).

Then continuing to Panama and going through the Panama Canal and its "locks," starting on the Atlantic side, seeing and feeling the "locks" close in front and behind us and the locks filling with water that caused our ship to rise. Once full, the gate would open slowly on the Pacific side, and we would continue our cruise. This experience was exciting for everyone if it was their first time going through the canal. I had encountered this, years before when the Navy ship I was on left the pier at Coco Solo, Panama, on the Pacific side and sailed to the Atlantic side of the Canal. Coco Solo was where I spent my last eighteen months in the Navy, on the USS *PC* 486, before being discharged. It located a couple of miles north of the city of Colon, Panama.

This cruise was a special event for me since it was 2003, and as we were going through the Canal, it dawned on me that fifty years before, in 1953, I reported onboard my first ship, the USS LST 1144. As we exited the last lock on the Pacific side and passed the pier that was my second ship's berth (USS *PC* 486); many memories flashed through my mind. One that brought a smile to my face was remembering the joke that the base personnel (and some crewmembers aboard our ship) used to joke with each other. Our ship had one five-inch .38 deck-mounted gun on its bow, twin 40-mm gun mounts, and the same number of 20-mm gun mounts were on both our port and starboard sides. We also had two racks of depth charges on our fantail (rear of our ship). Because of this amount of "firepower," we were referred to as the USS *Battleship* 486 that patrolled the Pacific side of the Panama Canal and kept all foreign intruders away from entering the canal zone if it was felt they posed a threat to the canal! At that time the Canal authority was the United States. The USA had not only the authority but also the responsibility under the contract with Panama, to protect, maintain, and govern the canal's operations. I heard that there had been some (probably enlisted personnel) suggest that a BB be painted on our bow, port and starboard sides in front of the numbers 486 to denote its honorary commission, as a battleship—that is, "BB 486." But all those antics were now just fifty-year-old memories. Seeing the pier that was our berth when we were in port was now empty because Panama was now responsible for the canal and its operation. There were no US Navy ships anywhere. The canal was no longer protected, at least by the US Navy.

We continued our cruise with stops in Costa Rica, where we were able to take a small boat trip up an inlet off the ocean and saw some of the prettiest wild birds in the world. We were told there are more beautiful colored wild birds in Costa Rica than in Canada and the United States combined. As we slowly drifted down the inlet, it was easy to believe the story was true. Each tree along the water's edge seem to have more than a dozen wild birds in their branches. All the birds seem to be competing to be the loudest and the prettiest "bird of the day."

We also stopped in Acapulco, Mexico, and saw the world-famous cliff divers make their dives. This was my second visit to Acapulco. As I indicated earlier, our PC 486 took a short R&R trip to Acapulco in the mid fifties. Now Sondra and I were enjoying our time in Acapulco, seeing the cliff divers "do their thing." I enjoyed it, even more, this time because I was with my wife. I remember thinking, as we were enjoying the beautiful sites, how much more enjoyable it was, seeing it with my wife than with a bunch of sailors! (With my wife I knew there were fewer chances of getting in trouble!) Eventually, we tied up in Los Angeles, California, where we caught a flight back to Dallas. In a week or two, after we had rested, we started thinking about taking a shorter cruise around the coastal ports and resort islands in the Gulf of Mexico a few years later. Today as we look at the pictures we took, we talk about the many exciting events we enjoyed, and they all remain fresh in our minds. All our vacations were at least a week long. To this day, we will often ask one another, "Do you remember when we were on vacation in…?" And sometimes our following conversations last for several hours, reliving the memories of yesterday.

When I retired from AT&T in 1987, I was fifty-five, and Sondra had just entered that decade. Today some thirty years later, we can still recall each of those vacations and agree we wouldn't have the stamina now to hold up, let along enjoy those places as we did at the time we took them. The best part about doing what we did was, we still have the pictures and better still, we still have the memories. Thanks to Thomas Jones and the psychologist's words, I can only give GOD the praise when He enabled Sondra and me to take the trips we took, at a time we enjoyed them to the fullest. It is sad to think there are probably many couples that never felt the fulfillment of their dreams when they retired like Mr. Jones felt when his wife died, and he realized the only thing he had was unfulfilled dreams. Sondra and I know the fun times they missed in not taking those vacations they had planned and talked about before he retired. We give GOD the praise in enabling us to enjoy our dreams and in a way, retaking them in our memories. Today we enjoy recalling and reflecting on those vacations we took advantage of at the time I retired, more than fifty years ago. And by the grace of GOD, we took steps before we retired, that enabled us to start fulfilling those dreams starting within weeks after we retired. We addressed the questions "Where did we want to go first?" "When did we want to go?" "What could we do at that time to minimize any problems that would hamper our going?" I give Sondra all the credit for calling, getting information on various cruises, costs, passports, etc. When the time came, she even packed my suitcase (not really). I remember thinking, "It just doesn't get any better than this!"

Following are "things" that helped us get started the right way, so we could enjoy the fun things in retirement, before or soon after the Monday following the date we retired. Maybe they will be of help to you:

1. If you have never taken a nice vacation…make reservations ASAP.
2. You might even take some mini vacations over the weekends and get used to being away from home.
3. Don't try to get all the "bucket list" items taken care of in the first month, leave a few for when you return from vacation!
4. Try sleeping late, have an extra cup of coffee at the breakfast table while still wearing your PJs. Doing this during the week will get you used to the free time you will have on vacation!
5. Get to know your neighbors ASAP. (Remember they can be free security "watchmen" on your home while you are on vacation!
6. Let your children know "Mom" probably won't be available for babysitting too much, until you get settled in, after returning from your vacation…maybe around the middle of NEXT year unless you are on another vacation!
7. Get your driver license address changed ASAP if it is not current. Then make sure you advise all your friends of your new address. Doing this will allow you to tell them about your vacation plans. It will also open the door for you to

call them after your vacation is over, to fill them in on how GREAT your vacation was.

8. Start lining up all your doctors and make appointments, starting with your "Family Doctor." They can be a help in your losing weight, start exercising programs, getting back in the routine of housework and yard work, etc. that are easy to forget about while you are on vacation!

   Notice how often the word *vacation* has been used? Remember, this vacation activity can be repeated every year, at least for the next few years after you retire.

If you have taken that very nice vacation, possibly a nice relaxing "follow-up," one like we took on the above cruise through the Panama Canal would be a good follow-up vacation. Don't check your 'to do' list off and say, "Well, we have taken care of the cruises, now let's take the lawn chairs out in the backyard and just take life easy." Big mistake, especially if both of you have relatively good health and 'down deep' you would like to take a nice cruise to someplace you have never been—start planning where, and when, you are going to take it, and do it now. Remember, any vacation is much more enjoyable if you can pay for it as soon as you make the reservations with the money you have saved over the previous year(s). If you planned, during your pre-retirement years for this capability, you will find you will enjoy each vacation more than having to think about paying off a loan when you return home—one thing you must keep in mind. You may also plan to visit your kids or relatives you haven't seen for several years. DO *not* view visiting friends and family as being the same as taking a vacation that you and your spouse have talked about for your fun and relaxation. They are both nice, but they are not the same!

"Grandma," or as I like to refer to Sondra, "that good-looking gal I met and married in Iowa, who was from Missouri, that I took back to Kansas. The woman I continued to move (with our children) all over Colorado, and from there, I took them to New Jersey to live in two different locations. Before I knew it, it was time for me to retire. Our two daughters had finished school and had married and started their own families and were living in Texas. Our son had finished high school and had the opportunity to play football at UTA, also in Texas. These situations resulted in all of our children living in Texas. Unfortunately, UTA discontinued their football program the following year after our son transferred from a college in Connecticut. Mom and I realized we had no family ties in New Jersey, at the time of my retirement. With all our kids living in Texas, and neither Sondra or I had any brothers or sisters, we decided to move to Texas. At least we would be closer to our kids. I should have known from my experience in AT&T; it is not a good idea to use as the only reason you retire to a different town is to be closer to one or more of your kids. If they are still working, they may transfer to another city by the time your moving van gets unloaded as you arrive in their hometown. But that is what we did. And that is what happened. We built a nice retirement home that we lived in for around twenty years.

All our kids are now grown, married, and have their own families. And guess what? Currently, our oldest daughter now lives in Oregon, and our son lives in Florida. However, our middle daughter still lives about ten miles from us in Waxahachie, Texas. Our oldest daughter in Oregon is a great-grandma now, and all her kids are in the State of Washington. They are retired and built a new home in Oregon and moved in during the last of 2018.

Our middle daughter and her husband built their Ranch home on their ten-acre farm West of Waxahachie about ten miles from us. Her three children all live in Waxahachie, married, and have jobs in that area. Her two girls both have two boys each. Her son married in 2016, and both he and his wife have jobs within the county. They are expecting their first child before the end of 2019.

Our son lives in Florida, where he and his wife have two boys and two girls. Their oldest son received a scholarship to college and has now graduated and is back in Florida working. The second son joined the Marines after graduating from high school. At this time, their two girls are living at home, and both are in high school. Our son also has a daughter (our granddaughter) who lives in Texas. She and her husband have a girl and a boy. Today it is difficult for children to remain close to their parents, geographically, especially when their jobs are in another state. We thank GOD that we have one of our children and her children, at this writing, who are all within a short drive from us.

I realize when you become grandparents, great-grandparents, and great-great-grandparents, you still like to keep in touch with all your family you can, *but* you can't expect them to have much time to visit with great-great-grandparents! That is the position Sondra, and I realize we are experiencing, in our family chain. I have to say our daughter who lives on a farm just West of town is good keeping in touch with Mom and Dad, as do all her children. They include us in our great-grandchildren's events—that is, birthday parties, school events, ball games, etc. Many don't realize it, but as people grow older, it makes them feel good when their family still invites them to their children's events, knowing sometimes they will not feel up to attending, but happy they were invited. If they can attend, they will be able to see how their great-grandchildren have grown, what they are doing, and how some of the younger ones are preparing to step out of the "nest" and become responsible citizens in our society.

I guess it was around the time Sondra and I realized our family titles of going from grandparents to great-grandparents and now to great-great-grandparents, we needed to start thinking about taking "one last cruise because it would probably be our last ocean cruise vacation." I didn't have any special place in mind, but I was ready to go. Little did I know that this cruise would be the most rememberable cruise we ever took. I can't take credit for planning and arranging all our retirement trips, but in case Grandma has something else for the future, I'll tell you the truth and admit if it were not for Grandma many of the trips we took and places we visited would not have happened. If it were not for Grandma, we wouldn't have all the memories we still enjoy today. That's another reason I thank GOD for Grandma!

I did not notice at the time, but my bride seemed to only talk about another cruise, one shorter than the Panama Canal cruise but just within the gulf area. The more we talked, the more she seemed convinced she had a good idea, and before I knew it, she had made it official. She has always handled getting the vacation plans taken care of, and seeing the details are complete. She mentioned to me one time how nice it was to take me along to carry the luggage and souvenirs she had bought. What a thoughtful woman!

We had talked about "one final cruise" and agreed if we were going to do it, we needed to do it now. Sondra checked the dates, costs, places we would be stopping. She handed me the check that was already filled out and said, "Here, sign it, and I'll mail it today." She has always known how to make me feel important, especially when it comes to paying for our vacations; she always lets me sign the checks. "What a gal!"

Sondra had scheduled us for a weeklong cruise around the Gulf of Mexico with stops at Costa Maya in Belize, the little island of Roatan Then back to Belize City in Belize, then up its coastline to Cozumel and then a nice relaxing cruise back to Galveston, Texas, where we left a week before.

One of the nice things about taking ocean cruises is they give excellent service. If you are hungry, you can get food twenty-four hours a day and snacks in between your meals. I don't recall if Sondra tried to get our cruise on a certain date or not, but the one she was able to book, left Galveston, Texas, on November 26, 2006, and returned to Galveston a week later. If you had asked me, I would have told you the time of our cruise didn't make any difference, "I was going for the ride."

The other nice thing that I have always enjoyed about ocean cruises is you are seated at a table with people you will be eating with each evening. By the time the cruise is over, you will have met and become friends with at least three other couples. This cruise was no exception. The other thing I looked forward to was at least one evening during the week is a "formal" evening. The men all wear their "tuxes," and the women come in their evening gowns. We never felt out of place since this was about our third or fourth cruise that had the "formal" evening meal. I was dressed in my tux that evening and waiting on "you know who" to get that one pleat in just the right place in her evening gown. We started toward the dining room and our table of friends. As we approached one of the passage-ways

Sondra said, "Let's turn here, I want to check something out that I saw this afternoon." Now, knowing Sondra and knowing we had been together all day and we had *not* been down that passage-way, I said, "Can't we check it out after dinner? We are going to be late."

"It will only take a couple of minutes."

"Okay, but you're going to have to make an excuse to the others as to why we are late."

As we started down the passage-way, I noticed a couple standing in the entrance to one of the cabins; both were all dressed up, tuxes, and gown like we were. I didn't think anything about it since this was "formal" evening. We had not reached the spot where the couple was standing before they entered the cabin, another couple came out, hugging and kissing each other. I did think that was a little strange, but they were young enough to be our grandchildren and could be on their honeymoon.

Sondra took my arm just as we were nearing the cabin and said, "This is the place I want to check out."

I asked, "What is it you want to check?" Just then I had a 'full view' inside the cabin, and there stood the couple we had seen in the passage-way, now standing face to face and the captain of the ship was reading their wedding vows to them. At first, I thought they might be someone Sondra knew from Missouri; maybe she had babysat one of them. Then I heard the captain say, "With the powers vested in me, I now pronounce you man and wife." As the captain turned to the groom, he said, "You may now kiss the bride."

With that, the couple kissed, turned toward the hatch (door), and walked out. Just as I was getting ready to ask Sondra, "Did you know either of them?"

The captain said, "Next," I turned around to see who he was talking to and saw Sondra and I were the only ones in the passage-way! The captain said, "Come on in, I can see the groom is a little nervous, but I assure you it is not going to hurt." I looked at Sondra, and she had that, "Got-yah" grin on her face and said, "Let's go." The captain assured us that, as the captain of the ship, while at sea, he has the authority to perform marriages that were official and binding." Then he proceeded to conduct the wedding ceremony with two witnesses I had never seen before or since. After he finished, he signed the certificate and handed it to Sondra, saying, "I always give this to the bride for safekeeping." With that, he wished us a long and happy life together and ended by saying, "Now that you have fifty years behind you, the odds are in your favor that it will work out.

The captain looked at me and, said, "I have found that couples who reach their fiftieth anniversary, the husband is usually more nervous than the wife is, getting married a second time. How do you feel?" I think I replied, "A little confused."

The captain replied by saying, "That's usually caused from old age more than the wedding ceremony." With that, we headed for the dining room and our friends, so Sondra could tell how she had trapped me. They all had a big laugh in hearing how she was able to pull it off. But for years, I would tell people, especially preachers, that "I am on my second marriage and the lady I'm married to now, I think I'm going to keep." That always gets some questionable looks from the preachers, that turns to laughter after I explain both marriages were to the same woman! I must say that cruise was not the longest, but it was the one I will always view as the most "rememberable" cruise we ever took.

Chapter 12

How to Retire with a Sense of Value

Are you living in a community whose cemetery
is the one in which you will be buried?

One of my younger great-grandsons asked me the other day if I knew how GOD and I were alike. Trying to sound as humble as I could, I replied, "No, I don't know, please tell me." I reached to catch my halo, sensing it starting to fall from my head as I heard his reply, "You're both old."

The question, "Are you living in the community whose cemetery is the one in which you will be laid to rest?" is not facetious. Think about this. If you are already retired, and you plan to move to that other community before you die, why are you waiting? Moving now will be easier, in all situations, than if you wait until your kids must handle all the arrangements and by that time you may be in a nursing home in a town where no one except your children knows you!

Moving now may enable you to join a local church and other organizations to develop friends who will remember you long after they attend your funeral. Hopefully, when you move, you will be moving near one or more of your children that you see or talk with at least one or two times a week.

This chapter is a summation of things GOD has shown me that are important and need to be "in place" as we near our final days here on earth. Remember neither you or I know when that will be, so I and my wife plan to follow my old Boy Scout motto, "Be prepared."

Are you at an age you feel you can say with certainty, "I know I am beyond the halfway point of my life."? At this writing, I was eighty-five on October 13, 2019, and my answer to that question was, "*Yes*, without any doubt, I am beyond the halfway point of my life, here on earth!"

One thing I have come to believe is what I call "My Final Retirement Years." My number 1 hope and prayer in life is that the wonderful lady GOD has given me as my wife will always be with me, in good health, right to the end. When it is time for one of us to join our heavenly Father, we have asked GOD, if it is His will, He takes both of us at the same time or takes the remaining one soon after He has called the first one home. Speaking for myself, I don't even like to think of being without my wife, Sondra, even one day.

Today we live close to our daughter Stephanie. She and Sondra talk with each other at least a couple of times a week. Just knowing we have one of our children close enough that if something major happens, she will be there to help if needed. It is not just for the comfort of knowing one of our children will always be just a phone call and a few minutes away, but the fact one of our children is near us, and today, all her children are within a few minutes from her home. This does give us the awareness of being physically close to some of our family.

Today we see national and international corporations require its employees to move throughout the United States (as we did) and even throughout the world. If there are no children close, geographically, it is very important that we talk with a lawyer or someone you have confidence in who will be able to take care of your wishes before and after your death. If there are no children, many times, you may have a close friend in the church that is in good health and would be agreeable to take care of your wishes. Remember, if you haven't taken care of this issue before you die, the government may end up with most, if not all your assets. It is very important that the above issues are identified and taken care of before you are no longer able to make the arrangements, or you are no longer alive. They need immediate attention very soon after you retire, if not before.

Also, if you have a living trust or, at a minimum, an up-to-date will, if you are not in the tax bracket with Bill Gates and Warren Buffet, you will still have the peace of mind, knowing that whatever you do have will go to the people or places that you want it to go.

The following is a big issue for many families today. There are times in our advanced years or when our health is not what it should be at our age; we need to say *no* when asked to help or do things that our doctors have advised us we could endanger our health and possibly that of another person if we did them. It may sound like a simple request from an organization we belong to or a community function that, in the past, we were actively involved. It can even be within our church. We must think about how we would feel if our involvement caused a friend to be physically hurt.

On the other hand, we don't want to start saying, *no* to every request we may be asked to help with, just because we are retired. Some people use the *no* response and any excuse they can think of to keep from doing what is needed and what they know they can do. If you tend to be a *no* type "responder" to requests for help you can give, think about this. Helping someone or some organization may help you as well. Being involved will give you the opportunity to get out of the house and be more involved in what is going on in the community you live in. (See Appendix A.)

If your health is good and the only thing you are doing today is reliving the blessings GOD gave you in the past but ignoring the blessings He wants to give you today, you are missing out on a lot of good blessings. Note, the key to these requests is, if you're in good health!

We often don't do things we know we can do because we know many people our age, can't do them? Do we realize what an irresponsible excuse that is? Are we going to be more satisfied when we reach that age that we can't do those things we used to do, and our excuse of yesterday is now valid?

We also need to be very careful when WE ask others to help, and some give us a reason why they won't be able to help, at least "at that time." We should be careful in doubting their words because the validity of their words is often known only by GOD, their doctor and the one being asked. We must remember when someone says they are unable to do what you are asking. Their words may be valid and pressuring them to do something that could endanger their health, even more, is something none of us wants to be viewed as guilty. At this point, if the one asking needs help, they might want to ask GOD?"

We all know that GOD shows us how great He is, every day. When we help someone in need, we have a feeling of satisfaction, especially when we respond in a loving and caring way. (See Appendix A.)

One other important point we sure don't want to be guilty of doing. If you ask someone to do different things and they tell you they won't be able to do them.

DO *not* Judge them as being lazy, not willing to help, or not wanting to get involved. Doing the above, you are trying to do GOD's job, and He has made it clear *you* and I don't have the authority to JUDGE others! But if people can't be found to take care of the need, your best action is to ask GOD!

Being an octogenarian, I know I am now a person who can no longer do many of the things that were asked of me ten or more years ago. I had a heart attack in 2001, resulting in triple by-pass surgery. In 2004 I had a pacemaker implant and a replacement in 2014. I have had a balance problem starting around 2010 and have passed out no less than four times in public places and once in my home, always for just a few seconds. At this writing, my balance seems to be worsening a little each year.

However, I praise GOD for how He has blessed my life. Before my heart attack in 2001, at the age of sixty-seven, I was jogging five miles without stopping, three times a week and working out in the gym on those same days. I was playing eighteen holes of golf two days a week, always walking versus using a cart. At eighty-four, I have given up golf and jogging, but my wife and I still work out at the "Y" five or six days a week doing a reduced program from our earlier years. I attempt to follow my doctors' recommendations on keeping in shape, at least for a man in his mideighties. I feel great, most of the time. Even when I must psych myself to go to the "Y," I know when

I finish, I will feel better. My point is, we can't let Satan convince us that we are too old to do what we know we can do and should do! (See Appendix A and D.)

Another truth in my life experiences is, "I know I'm not the man I used to be, but praise GOD I feel I'm more like the man GOD has made me be *today*." What I would call my number 1 excuse for not being able to do a lot of things I did in my sixties and seventies is plain and simple, it's "because now I'm in my eighties"!

"Many people would say I'm an old man by any standard, and I can't argue with their view. *But* I can still pray and ask GOD to take care of my family, my friends, my church, my SS class members, and Christians and Jews throughout the world and *yes* even the sinners' needs. I can still pray for my country, the United States of America, and all the men and women we have elected to ensure it remains the greatest nation in the world, and for our men and women who served in our military forces.

I give praise to GOD for reminding me of the times I forgot to thank Him for bringing me through the valleys of danger and despair and led me to the mountain tops on the other side. I thank Him for reminding me to refuse the requests I know I can't do and recognize those things I can't do safely and could even endanger the lives of others if I tried. I know, "With GOD, all things are possible." That does not mean I can do all things. I know that I can only do those things that He has enabled me and wants me to do today. Each Christian must answer that question for themselves, *not* for others. GOD is the only one that knows the answer for how you, me, and all humanity are doing. GOD's Word is very clear as to what His requirements are for having eternal life in heaven with Him, throughout all eternity!

Do you know if you are going to be there?

Today a reminder to myself—my belief and commitment to GOD and myself!

The following can be a good reminder to a new Christian as well as those who are not certain about their salvation, and all those in between.

On the *date* shown, I reviewed and updated the following questions to reflect my current feelings and beliefs.

As time passes, I commit to myself that I will review the following questions and make any changes necessary to show my true feelings and beliefs are as shown. I will do this to remind myself because GOD *already* knowns my real beliefs.

I know the clock of life is ticking and none of us know when it will stop. I believe when that time comes, it will be too late to change my answers, my beliefs and more importantly, too late to change my heart and mind. *Today* is the day to show GOD and myself my real feelings and *why* I feel the way I do.

*****

mm / day / year
The following are my answers as of this date: ____ / ____ / _______!

1. When was the last time I thanked GOD for the blessings He has given my family and me? _________
2. When was the last time I went out of my way to help someone in need to feel they have "value"? ___________
3. When was the last time I praised GOD for sending His only begotten Son, Jesus Christ, to die on the cross for my sins? __________
4. When was the last time I asked GOD forgiveness of my sins? __________
5. When was the last time I answered the above questions, and my answer was *not* "today"? __________
6. When was the last time I thought about the following statement? ___________

   Some say GOD, heaven, salvation, and the Bible are not real or valid. But Christians believe GOD's Word (Bible) says they are. Since no one can prove, either view is right or wrong with scientific proof; logic would suggest you wouldn't want to join the "doubters," knowing, *if* the Bible turns out to be right, the unsaved doubters will never see GOD, Jesus, or heaven!

7. If any of your answers to the first five questions were something other than *today* or its synonyms.
8. Ask yourself, "When am I going to look at them again?" __________
   a. If you didn't answer the questions, don't you think GOD is deserving of an answer from you? ____________
   b. If you feel you'll consider doing it sometime in the future, think about this, "GOD has not guaranteed any of us will see the sunrise tomorrow." What if you are not here tomorrow? What have you got to lose if you tell Him your beliefs today? ___________
9. You may have time today to change any or all your answers above if you feel they need to be updated. So why not do it *now* and check it later to see if you still agree with *today*'s answers, and if you don't, what caused your change of heart? _________
10. Signed: _______________________

To those who will remain unsaved:

Zechariah chapter 14 tells us the Lord will gather all nations to Jerusalem to fight against them. GOD, with all the holy ones, will fight against those nations and be victorious. As He stands on the Mount of Olives, it will split in two from east to west. At the end of the battle, we read in verse 9,

> The Lord will be king over the whole earth.
> On that day, there will be one Lord, and his name
> is the only name. (Jesus Christ)

I believe the King is coming. The answers to the above questions reflect my belief. If the Lord comes in *my* lifetime, do I believe I will be with Him through all eternity?

(See Appendix A: "Excuses—A Time to and a Time Not to Use Them.")

I have often thought when a need arises in our church, our community or one made known in the evening news; it is so easy to justify not doing anything because "I'm too old." After all, I'm in the eighth decade of my life. When I was younger, I was always ready and able to help mow the church lawn, paint the classrooms, haul off limbs, grass, and junk to the city dump in my pickup. I taught adult Sunday school class for over twenty plus years; I spent six-plus years with the "Bill Glass Prison Ministry," going to prison units throughout North Texas. My wife, Sondra, joined me during the last few years when we went to juvenile units. In my sixties, I went to Mexico on a mission trip with our church group. I even preached several times in one of the churches we attended when the pastor was not available. I did these things because I felt I could, and I felt I should.

When I start thinking about the things I was involved in, during my younger years, I catch myself feeling a little prideful. And that is when I seem to hear a voice inside me saying, "Remember who enabled you to do them." I know it was the Holy Spirit reminding me I should be thanking GOD for enabling me to do those things rather than suggest I did them because "That's the kind of guy I am." GOD does have a way to humble us when we start using those words, "I and me" versus "God and He."

If you have experienced this scenario in your life, I expect you may have also encountered the next step I found myself experiencing. Recently my doctor told me he didn't want me to stand on anything that had more than two steps on it and if I do and fall, he said, "Understand, don't come to me for treatment or pity!"

While I was still in the Navy and later: I passed out once when I jumped from our ship to the one tied up alongside us. I passed out for a few seconds, and I think the sudden jar to my body when I landed on the steel deck of the other ship may have been the cause of me passing out. However, some thirty-five years later, after I retired from AT&T, I passed out in public places three times and at home, once. Each time was only for a few seconds. The time I passed out at home, I hit the edge of a coffee table and caused a hairline fracture on my right collarbone. Before retiring, I continued doing the exercising activities I had been doing throughout my pre-retirement years with AT&T, without any problems. I wouldn't allow myself to believe I couldn't still do those same things years after I retired. I ignored the fact I was getting older. My point being, "We seem not to be able to accept the fact that many things GOD enabled us to do at the age of twenty-five to thirty, we *cannot* do at seventy-five to eighty." When I turned eighty-five in 2019, my beautiful (young) wife moved into that decade as she turned eighty. She is still vibrant and active, and she keeps me moving to keep up with her. There is no way I could carry on without her by my side, and I give GOD all the praise for her. "Thank You, Father!"

It seems to boil down to one simple issue—that is, if we do not know of any reason to not do what is asked of us, then we should evaluate why we should not do it. We need to realize that "man" is one, if not the most, predictable creature GOD ever created. Man is also one of the most unpredictable creatures GOD ever made. Even though He made man after His image, we are not GOD! Man is not all-knowing, all-powerful, and we sure aren't "sin-free." We must remember GOD never asks us to do anything He has not equipped us to do. GOD may have enabled us to do all kinds of things in our first six-plus decades, but that doesn't mean He wants us to continue doing them the rest of our life. GOD is indestructible; man makes the front page of the newspaper if he lives to be one hundred years old. If we feel GOD is asking us to do something today, and we know we can do it, we should probably "do it." If the answer is "*No*, I can no longer do it," we should then have a little talk with Jesus.

Not to belabor this point, but GOD has shown me the most valuable power He has given all of us to use, throughout our entire life, is the "power to *pray*." As believers, we all have the power to *pray*. We can do it anywhere, anyway and anytime. We can pray for our own needs, the needs of our family, friends and our country, even our enemies...any time and any place and GOD will hear us.

I don't know why it is so easy to listen to what I call, 'Satan suggestions,' when we want to do something that GOD's Word says we should not do. In my younger years, I did not fully recognize Satan's "trick of influence" that he can and does use on us.

An example of this is what we often encounter as we get older and don't care about doing much of anything when asked to do something in the church. Unknowingly, we grab one of "Satan's suggestions" as our justification for saying *no*. He makes us feel justified in saying *no* by causing us to think, "I've paid my dues, now I can sit back and take it easy and let the younger people take care of today's needs." Satan makes this seem so logical when He asks us, "Did GOD say you should do this?" It is important to know what GOD's Word does say and understand He does not expect only you or me to take care of all the worldly needs, especially if He has not equipped us with the talent to do them.

The following is a listing of "thought provokers" that the Holy Spirit brought to my attention during my adult years when I was asked to do something, and all I had to do was say, *yes* or *no* to opportunities *man* was asking me. The following have come to mind more than once during my adult years, before and after my retirement:

It seems so easy to think our abilities equate to our believing, if we are asked to do anything within the church, we should quickly answer, "Yes, I will do it." It is important to know what GOD's Word does say and understand He does not expect you or me to take care of all the worldly needs or even all the needs of the church we attend, especially those needs we know He has not equipped us to do. When we start thinking, "GOD feels I am so special that He wants me to take care of all the needs I am asked." We must remember, we are great in GOD's eyes, but none of us should feel we have been chosen to be the "elixir" for all things. Only GOD can fill that need.

Many today like to put time limits on GOD's words and when the Words of GOD are not what they like to hear or do, we tend to yield to Satan who reminds them, "GOD didn't say you have to do this or not do that, every day." Once we yield to his temptations, it can easily become our escape path to not serve GOD with the talent and abilities He has given us. However, we need to be careful that we don't use *no* when GOD's Word does say we need to do certain things all the time—that is, "Follow God's commandments."

I must admit I did not fully recognize the "trick of influence" that Satan uses on us when I first accepted Jesus as my Lord and Savior. The day I repented of my sins and gave my life to GOD and invited His Son, Jesus Christ, to be my Lord and Savior, GOD began to show me through His Holy Spirit what Satan will do to influence us against what GOD has equipped us to do.

(See Appendix B, July 19, 2009, "One Event out of the Spiritual Journey of Lloyd D. McJunkin.")

> What good is it for a man to gain the whole world, yet forfeit his soul? (Mark 8:36)

The following was part of an article I wrote in the "Thirty-Six Days Devotional Guide" at Farley St. Baptist Church in its UNITED IN THE JOURNEY campaign in 2009 in Waxahachie, Texas.

I came to know and accept Jesus Christ as my Lord and Savior at the age of eleven. Having attended SS for some five years prior, I had developed a (feeling) relationship with this wonderful man; my SS Teacher called Jesus. She told me how He was sent to earth by His Father in Heaven. She explained how He was born and grew up in a world of sinners and learned, by example, how GOD, His Father loved us so much that He let the sinners of the world, take the life of His only Son, as payment for all our sins.

At eleven years old, I knew it was time for me to ask Jesus to be my Lord and Savior." I didn't think I was a big sinner, but I believed GOD looked at all sin as not doing what He tells us to do. I knew I had done things that GOD did not want me to do, and I knew I needed to ask Him for the forgiveness of my sins and try not to repeat them.

Today I know the cost of accepting Jesus as my Savior is "faith." The feeling that came over me after professing my faith in Him as my Savior was unbelievable. As I look back, I see one thing did *not* take place. I was now in an older Sunday school class, and our new teacher seemed to feel we knew more about GOD and Jesus than most, if not all of us did. At eleven, many of us had questions, but we didn't know how to verbalize them. The result was *no* one actively helped me (at age eleven) to grow in the Word of GOD. I feel I grew very little Spiritually over the following fifteen years. I went to church, even while I was in the Navy, but many times I did not live the life of a "believer" the rest of the week. And I knew it and felt bad, AFTER I had sinned.

I recall those days of not following the ways I knew GOD wanted me to follow and I felt it was the Holy Spirit, within me that reminded me of the words of Jesus in Mathew 10:33 when He said, "But whoever disowns me before men, I will disown him before my Father in heaven."

And Paul in Romans 3:23 when he said,

> For all have sinned and come short of the glory of GOD.

Paul also tells us in Romans 8:26,

> In like manner, the Holy Spirit will help us in our times of need. When we do not know what to pray for, the Holy Spirit will intercede for us and utter groans that words cannot express.

I remember returning aboard ship more than once from an evening of sinful activities and laying in my bunk, asking GOD, not only for forgiveness but for His help in keeping me from repeating my sinful acts the next time I went ashore.

I remember times when I would do things without thinking if they were right or wrong. Later I would have this feeling in the pit of my stomach, and I realized I had sinned again, and many times, I felt I didn't have the right to ask for forgiveness. It would have been easy for me to blame my actions (sins) on others, but I knew that I had made the decision, not someone else. Without knowing what to do, I would carry the weight of my sins on my shoulders. I failed to remember the words of my SS Teacher who had told me that the blood of Jesus on the cross had washed my sins away. At that time, I had not heard what Jesus, himself said in John 14:14, "If you ask for anything in My name, I will do it." Once I became more aware of what GOD's Word says, I realized He would forgive us when we sin, even after we are saved. I found I would often think of this truth when Satan was trying to lead me to a sinful environment I had yielded to in the past, but now I knew I could say, "No way, I'm not falling for that line again."

Even after I married my wonderful Christian wife; for many years, I tended to play the role of, "Right or wrong, we are going to do things my way." My wife and later our children would sometimes question "why," but they knew there was a point that they needed to stop asking. Today I realize I was *not* always the ideal husband or father. Not to justify my actions at that time, but GOD reminded me more than once when I started putting myself down for some of the "wrong" things I did as a husband and father, He would point out that I was not the only a husband and father that was in that boat with me. I understood GOD was saying, "Regardless of what others are doing wrong, you need to strive to do as I say, and I'll take care of the others."

As time passed, it became easier for me to understand that GOD does have a plan for me. I could share with you many experiences during my younger years, where He brought me through situations that I could have been killed and left this world without ever really serving Him. Many times, I did not even thank Him for staying with me and forgiving my sins. I can't explain how He could love the person I was at that time, but I know He did, and His love continues to this day. Memories of what I have done and did not do after receiving GOD's gift of salvation reminds me of all the many blessings I missed. I know He has forgiven me, and I have forgiven myself, and I accept the fact that I will never be able to experience those missed blessings.

Today knowing I am coming nearer to the end of my journey here on planet earth, the joys of my life far outweigh the sorrows. Today I love to tell others about Jesus and all He did in my life. I pray this book will convey the power of GOD is felt by those in prisons and gyms and even in churches. A day does not go by that I do not smile and thank Him for His guidance and blessings. I thank Him even for the little blessings, because they remind me of the gentle touch of His hand on my life.

Today my life with my wife, Sondra, has proven to be much greater than I had hoped for in our marriage. I see in her the love of GOD. She has stood beside me, cared for me and sacrificed for me, and has made my life a living *joy*! Each evening during our devotions and prayer time together, we thank GOD for letting us be part of His family, for the many blessings He gives us each day, for our family, for our church, for the opportunities to serve Him. I know it took me longer than He wanted; to get on the pathway He wanted me on, and I thank Him for not giving up on me when I gave Him so many reasons to do so. I could add volumes to what surrounded each event mentioned above and many more events that I have not mentioned, but I leave that for another time.

I give GOD praise for guiding me to people and places that have helped me in my spiritual growth. I believe He has told me that my eternal life will be with HIM in that place where some call heaven, but where I like to call it HOME!

(See Appendix C, January 20, 2013, "Testimony of How Jesus Christ Became the Lord and Savior of Lloyd D. McJunkin.")

John 6:44 Jesus tells us,

> No one can come to Me unless the Father who sent me draws him, and I will raise him on the last day.

I, like many, accepted Jesus as my Lord and Savior at a young age and did not understand the full meaning in the above verse. Today I agree with a comment I once heard—that is, "The Holy Spirit opens man's eyes and hearts." The Holy Spirit is a very significant part in the Trinity because the Holy Spirit is within us and is our pathway to hear and talk with GOD, through Jesus, anytime or anyplace.

In Ephesians 2:8–9, Paul tells us,

> For it is by grace you have been saved, through faith and this is not from yourselves, it is the gift of GOD, not by works, so that no one can boast.

Then Paul gives us twelve simple words in the form of the question that believers need always to be mindful of when the world seems to be pulling us down—that is, Romans 8:31, Paul asks, "If GOD is on our side, who can ever be against us?"

Being an only child, I did not enjoy the opportunity of having an older brother or sister to use as a sounding board when I didn't understand what was going on in life. I felt I didn't have anyone I could ask as to why certain things happened to Me and how I should respond to these happenings.

I was not raised in what you would call a strong Christian home—that is, going to church with my parents on Sunday, asking a blessing over our food at home, or reading the Bible with my family. However, my grandparents (on my dad's side) lived only a few blocks from us, and my grandpa was what you might call a "black and white Christian," that is If the Bible says "You shall not take the Lord's name in vain." That is what it means, so don't waste time trying to get around the truth. He was a member of disciples of Christ church and delighted to 'discuss' the Bible with any or all who voiced some disagreement in what Grandpa might quote from the scriptures. He usually didn't have much trouble proving his point of view—that is, he did it, by showing the chapter and verse in the Bible.

I mention Grandpa McJunkin because he was the one that planted many seeds in my young mind that related to things like; the need and value of attending church, SS, and hearing GOD's Word. I admired Grandpa and loved him very much. I give him credit for generating interest in things relating to the church or as he used to say, "GOD's House."

Neither of my parents attended church, but that is another story. However, during my early school years, Mom would always make sure one of my older cousins would stop by on Sunday morning and walk with me to church. I think it was around the time I was in the second or third grade when I felt I didn't need an escort to go to church, and I told my mother, "I can do it myself." Unfortunately for a person, that became a motto I followed, often in the wrong way.

I sometimes think that GOD started working in my heart the Sunday our church called a new preacher (Bro. Carlson) to be our pastor. It was not his influence on my life as much as it was his wife's, Mrs. Carlson. *She became my new SS teacher.* She showed love for each of us kids in her SS class. I had not previously experienced the love she taught by "doing" in our SS class. It was a type of love never shown within my family, to the extent Mrs. Carson showed. Her love was different in that I seemed to feel it each time I was around her.

I had heard about Jesus before, but when Mrs. Carlson started telling us about *who* He was, *why* He came to earth, *how* He was loved, rejected and then crucified, *what* His life and death meant to all of us—young and old alike ... suddenly, things started to fall in place and have meaning. I feel Mrs. Carlson was sent by GOD into my young life to make a major impact on my being receptive several years later to the Holy Spirit's calling.

I realized I didn't know everything about Jesus Christ, and I sure didn't understand how anyone could do what the Bible said He did for someone like me. But as I kept hearing our pastor, Mrs. Carlson and others, talk about "faith," I began to understand I didn't have to know all the answers or understand the entire Bible to be saved. I was more than willing to accept the fact I could never do anything to earn my way into heaven. After all, at my age, I knew I couldn't do much that would earn me anything. It seemed that GOD was only asking me to acknowledge I was a sinner and try to stop doing sinful things. He wanted me to believe that Jesus Christ was His only begotten Son and ask Him to come into my heart (life) and be my Lord and Savior. That was what Mrs. Carlson had been teaching us in SS and I knew I wanted to be a part of His family. I knew then if I believed the things I had been told in SS and ask; GOD would give me Salvation and through His Son, Jesus Christ, be my Savior. If I did as He commanded, He would truly become my Lord and Savior. It was then that I knew there was nothing in this world that could stop me from doing what He wanted me to do.

I told my mother and father what I had decided to do. They both questioned me as to why I felt that I had to go forward the next Sunday and tell the congregation that I had invited Jesus Christ into my life as my Lord and Savior. I told them that I had already asked Jesus to forgive me of my sins and be my Lord and Savior and the Bible said I needed to share this with others and be baptized. That following Sunday (July

7, 1946) at eleven years old, I went forward and made my confession of faith before the church body and on (July 14, 1946) I was baptized.

If someone had asked me at that time what being with Jesus Christ throughout all eternity would be like, I probably would have said, "I don't know, but I know I'll be there with Him." I couldn't then nor, can I today comprehend the vastness of eternity or the fulfillment of being with Jesus, in person (Spirit), 24-7 but I know it will be greater and more wonderful than anything I have or ever will experience here on earth. I soon realized, however, that letting Jesus Christ be my Lord and Savior was up to me, and in many respects, that was not going to be easy. I recalled the significance of Paul's words in the book of Romans 14:12 when he points out, in the end, "Each of us then will have to give an account of himself to GOD."

I wish I could fill in the years between the time I accepted Jesus as my Lord and Savior and today with all kinds of wonderful things I did to glorify GOD's holy name, but I can't. There were times when I was in high school and in playing sports, I received recognition from my peers and spectators alike. I found this made it easy for me to feel prideful in ways I knew GOD didn't want me to feel. When I was in the Navy, I found I could do even more things that would often result in my shipmates viewing me as a "real sailor." Later, I realized it also brought sorrow to my Savior Jesus.

After returning to civilian life, I found I could fit in with the "in crowd" by doing things that were spelled out in the Bible as things I should not do. Although I didn't always yield to these temptations, there were times that I did. Today when I think of some of those sinful acts and know GOD has forgiven me, I still feel the pain of sorrow and ask myself, "*Why* did I do them?" I didn't know then, but now I truly believe the feeling of sorrow I experience was the touch of the Holy Spirit on me reminding me that the pleasure I thought life would offer was always short-lived, but the fulfillment of following His commands are lasting.

GOD brought a wonderful Christian woman into my life who not only married me but has put up with me for over sixty-four years, at this writing. She has given me three wonderful children who have given us nine grandchildren. Three of them have given us twelve great-grandchildren (as of this writing). There have been many times since that day, over seventy years ago, when I asked Jesus to be my Lord and Savior that I have asked Him, over and over, "Please forgive me, Father." I think how blessed I am that He still forgives my sins. Sometimes when I am thinking of this blessing, I seem to hear a soft and loving voice say, "I paid for your sins at Calvary because I loved you—even then. And I forgive you of your sins today because I still love you and have a plan for you." What a wonderful Savior we serve!

Since I've arranged my priorities of life more in proper order, I sometimes think of things in the church that I have been involved in doing. Things to help bring glory and honor to GOD's name. Like most Christians, I have received compliments, acknowledgments, and recognition for work within and outside the church. In my heart, however, the Holy Spirit reminds me of all the missed opportunities I passed along the way because I had taken my focus off the Lord. These were opportunities to serve my Savior at a time He was calling, but now they are lost forever. I also believe, without any doubt, that it was His Holy Spirit that deserves the credit in guiding me.

I have come to believe that, while it is nice when people acknowledge things we do in the service of GOD, we must always remember, all the nice words we might receive from humanity can never compare to those words we all look forward to hearing when we kneel before our Creator and hear Him say, "Well done, My good and faithful servant, welcome home!" I am so thankful that GOD has given me a passion for prayer, and a love to witness to those who have not found Jesus Christ as their Savior.

Prayer is the communication path to GOD by way of His Holy Spirit that lives within us and through His Son, Jesus Christ, who sits at His side. Witnessing is the opportunity we have that can help a lost soul find their Savior.

We must never forget the message the apostle Paul gives us in Philippians 2:9–11 when he wrote the following:

> Therefore GOD exalted Him (Christ) to the highest place and gave him the name that is above every name, that at the name of Jesus

> every knee should bow, in heaven and on earth and under the earth, and every tongue confess that Jesus Christ is Lord, to the glory of GOD the Father.

(See Appendix D: "'R' [Restaurant] Ministry Started: January 12, 2015.")

> Be careful not to do your "acts of righteousness" before men. If you do, you will have no reward from your Father in heaven. (Matthew 6:1)

When we do our "R" ministry, there are only three people involved—the waiter, Sondra, and me. If there is any doubt, we always inform the waiter that we are only the Lord's "instruments," it is GOD who is the "MESSAGE," He is the only one who can answer their prayer request and the only one deserving of their praise.

I feel led to explain how and why our "R" prayer ministry began. It started when our previous pastor in Granbury, Texas, retired, and an "interim" pastor was filling the pulpit until a new one could be called. One Sunday he mentioned, during his sermon, that he and his wife would sometimes stop on their way home from church and eat lunch at one of the restaurants. "Often, we will ask the waiter if they have something in their life that they would like us to pray for GOD to take care of."

On the way home that day, I mentioned to Sondra the comment our pastor made about asking a waiter if they could pray for a need the waiter had, anything in their life that he and his wife could lift to GOD. The more we discussed his comment, the more it caused us to ask ourselves, "Did GOD answer our prayer request that Sunday morning?" We had been praying that GOD would show us what He wanted us to do now that we could no longer do justice to the prison ministry, because of our physical limitations. We had been members of Bill Glass Prison Ministries for several years.

By the time we arrived home, we both felt this might be what GOD wanted us to do as a ministry to praise our Lord and Savior.

But how would we go about doing this seemed too simple—that is, "Just do it!" If it was not what GOD wanted, we knew we might be embarrassed and disappointed if we received negative responses like, "No, I don't have anything I want you or anyone to pray about." If we encountered that reaction, we felt we should discuss it again with GOD and make sure He did want us to go forward. The next week we were prepared for the worst response and "hoping and praying" for the best. We tried it out a couple of times with somewhat surprising and favorable results.

Then on January 12, 2015, I made a spreadsheet and recorded the first official response we received in our new "R" (restaurant) ministry.

As stated in chapter 10, when we asked GOD, if it was His will, to give us another ministry that would glorify Him. This request was made to Him. When I realized I had reached that point in life, I could no longer witness in the prisons the way it should be done. It was because of the physical impact it was having on me. To meet and witness with the prisoners requires a lot of standing and walking on the concrete floors and outside, in the exercise areas. The few times we could sit down, it was on a steel seat about twelve inches in diameter that was attached to a steel table. I can still remember trying to remain on my feet a little longer, knowing how hard those steel seats feel after setting on them for even a few minutes. It was getting to be a real challenge to witness the way I needed while trying to find a position that my legs were not in "pain," knowing that if I didn't, the pain would soon be felt in my back.

Near the end of my prison ministry, my wife, Sondra, joined the ministry and would go with me when we were visiting a "juvenile unit." At that time, she was in her late sixties, and I would always tell her that she was one of the older women that I had seen, who felt the calling to join the men when they were going to a "juvenile unit." As I recall, most of the ladies were probably around forty-five to fifty years old. Some of them had been doing this ministry for several years and seemed more accustomed to the concrete floors and steel seats.

There was, however, one "downside" in discontinuing our "prison ministry." It was more apparent to Sondra than to me. It centered on the reaction the young boys would show when they saw a woman that reminded them of their mother and quite often their grandmother. It was not uncommon that before Sondra could engage with one of them in a conversation, one of the young boys would come up to her and start talking. They would not be too far into their discussion before they would ask, "Would you like to see some pictures of my family?"

Sondra's answer would always be, "Yes." Then they would have out a box filled with many pictures of their family that always included their mother and grandmas. Their conversations would usually center around these two women they loved very much. They would tell Sondra how their mom or grandma had taken them to church and Sunday school when they were very young. Sometimes with tears in their eyes, they would say, "I know I did many things that "Mom" and "Grandma" always told me not to do. And I have told them, "I'm so sorry, and when I get out, I'm not going to do them again." Sondra told me she felt they were very sincere when they made those kinds of statements, and she would remind them they also needed to stay away from the people that influenced them to make the mistakes that caused them to be in prison at that time. They never seemed to disagree with her on that point.

Sondra was a retired nurse at the time she started visiting the youth units. Often, when we returned home and were discussing some of the more noteworthy events of the day; she would mention how she experienced like type situations in the hospitals when talking with young patients that were "hooked" on drugs. As a nurse, she found that you have to be careful and listen with an "empathetic" ear versus a "sympathetic" ear as these "young boys" poured out their sad stories.

She felt, "The reason many of the young boys we talked within the prison, was their families might have been too sympathetic with them at times they should have taken a firmer position."

She would always listen and without sounding like a drug counselor, point out to the young boys that they had to acknowledge to themselves that they knew when they were doing wrong things. Then she would tell them they had to stand firm against those who would try to convince them to do things that could and did send them to prison or the hospital.

My experiences with young boys were often much different. The examples I cited in chapter 10 were typical reactions I often incurred, except the young boy who indicated that after he was released from prison, he would kill his father if he continued to degrade him. Many of these young boys gave me the feeling they were thinking, "If you (meaning me) ever run into my father, tell him what I'll do if he treats me like he did before being sent to prison." You feel like putting your hand on their shoulder and say, "I understand," but I realized I didn't understand. Then I asked myself, "Why am I here?" I knew it was not to give them more "sympathy." I knew I was there to tell these young boys what GOD can do in their lives and what He has already done through His Son, Jesus Christ, to give them a new life.

I knew GOD was aware of our increasing problems caused by the long hours of standing on concrete and how sitting on steel seats were impacting my ability to effectively "witness." To answer our prayer requests and help us take care of our request, I feel GOD decided to bring to our attention, how we could continue "reaching out to those who need to hear about His love. The people we would be talking with would be in a different environment and be a different group of people than those we witnessed in our prison ministry. As important as "prison ministry" is, I knew GOD had others who would join that ministry that was younger and felt the calling to be a part of the effective way of helping those that were lost, to know GOD still loved them.

For Sondra and me, we were about to see that GOD had another group of people that needed to know GOD loves them and is ready to help take of their needs. He knew many in this group has to work on Sunday, many are single parents and have children to care for, and often they are very tired after spending their days standing and serving people all day long. He knows when they come home to their family; their needs await them. These are people who need Jesus Christ as their Lord and Savior as much, if not more, that the majority of the world because they are also His children. GOD was now going to show us He would view as our new ministry our showing these people that GOD knew of their pain and need and wanted His servants to remind them of His love for them. Little did we know the positive impact this would have on this new group of people. People who need the Lord, but often are not able to attend church on Sundays Many are single parents, raising small children, mostly women, who when they come home from work they are exhausted. They feel no one cares about them or understands their needs.

On January 12, 2015, Sondra and I felt GOD confirmed as a ministry for Him what we call our "R" (restaurant) ministry.

We feel GOD has affirmed His blessings on this ministry by sending to our table those who are not always able to attend church on Sunday. He has allowed us to talk with people who often don't know they can talk with Him, who is the only one that can take of their needs. I feel it also shows the "waiters," that our Lord cares for them, and He has sent two of His servants, to offer to lift their "prayer needs" with Him. We hoped when they heard two strangers telling them they always ask a blessing over their food and when they eat out they ask the one waiting on them, "Do you have something in your life that you would like us to ask GOD to help you with?" At first, we felt we might get all kinds of negative answers, for example, "No, I don't believe in that and don't want to discuss it." Bu, that did not happen until months later, and that was from only one person. To reassure us that GOD was in control, our first waiter responded with words that showed he needed help, and he knew it. (See Appendix D.) When given a "prayer request" we always told the waiter we would pray for them at that time and again during our "devotions" at the end of the day.

As time passed, we had some waiters tell us they felt GOD sent His servants that day, because they had just found out about a serious condition in their family and they didn't know what they could do, until we asked if they had something in their life they could pass on to GOD for His help. At that point, the words and how the waiters were responding suggested they were feeling a closeness to the Lord they had never felt before.

As shown below, GOD has sent "hundreds" of waiters to our table, and they have given us Hundreds of prayer requests of all kinds. In all these requests, Sondra and I felt so blessed as we lifted their needs to GOD, at that time and again during our devotions that evening. I might add a bit of humor as an afterthought—that is, we do this ministry not standing on concrete or setting on steel seats. It is done each time inside a restaurant, out of the hot or cold elements of the weather, sitting at a comfortable booth on soft padded seats, and lifting both our waiter's prayer request and our thanks for the food He has provided. We praise His name and thank Him for the meal we are about to enjoy. When GOD changed our ministry, He gave us one that enables us to do it "first class, in the comfort of soft seats and good food!" Sometimes I think I hear a soft voice repeating the words of Paul who said, in part, "God can do *all* things." Sondra and I believe that and give Him all the praise and glory for all He does for us and through us. For each prayer request we lift to GOD for a waiter, we feel so blessed for the waiter who honors us by sharing personal needs and hurtful experiences to themselves and friends and family.

The "prayer requests" given to us by the waiters have addressed every conceivable aspect of life. So many of them have been for other people that they know about and care about. Some of the requests seek GOD's help in finding a better job, their acceptance into college, the change of heart in their spouse, health issues for a friend or a family member, and then for themselves. They ask for blessings and guidance over our government leaders, especially our president. They ask for the healing of a pet that has been injured, is sick, or is suffering in its old age, for the money to buy or repair a car so they can use it to go to and from work. Some have said, "I have been blessed, and I would like to ask you to pray for peace and goodwill to once again be the "norm of the day" in America." When we think we have heard about every kind of request, someone will give us a brand new one. This new ministry has been such a blessing to Sondra and me! It humbles us so much when we realize how little man can do that is good and helpful to others when he tries to do it without GOD.

Again, without GOD, good things usually don't happen or don't last. With GOD, all good things are possible.

This ministry has been like an "elixir" for me on days that I didn't feel like going out to eat, but I did, I often didn't feel hungry, but I ordered. I didn't feel like asking the waiter if there were something in their life they would like for us to pray for GOD to take care of, but I did. I didn't expect them to have any out of the ordinary requests, but they did, and I didn't expect them to say anything more than a simple "Thank you," but they did.

My day was made complete when the waiter said something like, "You will never know how much you have made my day by showing your concern." But more than once, when that happened, I replied, "And you don't know how you have just made our day with your kind words."

When this would happen, I realized, my day started by my not feeling like doing anything. But the waiter's words of appreciation showed me what a "blessed day" the Lord had given us. I never thought I would feel so blessed when someone we had prayed to the Lord to take care of, then hearing how they thanked us made such a positive impact. Each day He shows us He is not just good, He is great, and it hurts when I think how I often disappoint Him in my thoughts, feelings, actions, and just plain stubbornness, and knowing that GOD is great all the time.

Almost all the waiters thank us again when they bring us our bill. There were a few that responded after we had finished eating, in a way that would kill any prideful feelings one might have (we hope and pray we have never felt prideful in the past and never will in the future while carrying out this ministry). But on bringing our bill, one waiter said again that she was so thankful for us wanting to pray for her needs. When we looked at the bill, it said, "PAID in full." We asked her if she had paid our bill and with a little smile, she said, "I think it was a couple who just left." Another time when we looked at the bill, we found it was only a note that read, "You will never know how much your kindness and your prayer has meant to me today. "Your bill has been paid in full! GOD bless you both." When we tried to find her, we didn't see her anywhere. One of the other waiters that we had asked if she knew where our waitress had looked around but came back and told us she had checked the kitchen and restrooms and our waitress could not be found, anywhere. Another time when our daughter and son-in-law, took us out to eat, he paid for our meals with his credit card. He noticed when she brought the receipt back; she had reduced it 50 percent. Our son-in-law told her, "You didn't have to do that." Her reply was, "I know, but you people didn't have to pray for me either, but you did." I couldn't help but think at that moment, "You can never outdo GOD."

It was back on January 12, 2015, that I made a spreadsheet and we recorded the first official response we received in our new "prayer ministry." We felt the quickness and sincerity in how the waiters have answered our question, made us both feel that GOD had definitely "blessed" our "R" ministry. We have experienced so many different requests that range from funny to heartbreaking, from personal to the needs of a friend. Just about every area you can think of, we have had a request for, and then He sends a new waiter to our table, and they have a "different need."

God is good—all the time!

The following are the results of what GOD has done and how He has led Sondra and me to serve as His instruments to reach out to those in need. "GOD is the Message. We are only His "messengers."

Between January 12, 2015 and January 12, 2019. In four years, we had 600 servers in 440 different locations give us 1,028 prayer requests. We also received an additional twenty-two praises to GOD for His help, love, and blessings in their lives.

During the time we've had our "R" minister, We have encountered only four waiters who did not have a prayer request. One did not give us a prayer request two different times. She shared with us some family issues that only GOD could take care of, but her response to our request remained, "No, everything is okay, I'll get by." We still prayed for her, both times.

As of July 31, 2019, we had 717 servers in 505 locations give us 1,147 prayer requests.

We also received an additional twenty-four praises to GOD for His help, love, and blessings.

(See Appendix E: "You Don't Need a Key to the Church to Be a Leader.")

The following is part of the SS lesson GOD led me to teach in our adult SS class in Granbury, Texas, on (December 29, 2014).

I want to tell you about a man GOD brought into Sondra and my lives some years ago when we were serving as leaders of our church's prayer ministry. I'll call him Fred, and he is with the Lord today. I remember pulling into the church parking lot to lead our Wednesday evening pray meeting and a smile would come on my face when I would see Fred in his car reading his Bible, waiting for us.

The first time Sondra and I met Fred was soon after he joined the church. He was in his eighties at that time. What made him different from most people was he seem to go out of his way not to be seen doing various things around the church. He was one of the humblest people I ever met.

He came to church on Sunday and sat in one of the pews near the back of the Sanctuary with his wife. He was friendly to those who spoke to him, but he was not one that would start a conversation. He and his wife attended a different SS class the one I taught so I don't know how vocal he was in class, but I soon became aware, he knew the Bible. As I came to know Fred better, I was reminded of the adage, "Never judge a book by its cover." Some of our members may have seen Fred was just a "quiet" member of our church.

I started to see who this quiet man was when he joined our Wednesday evening "prayer team." A year earlier, I attended a "prayer seminar" in Santa Fe, New Mexico, and heard the well-known Baptist preacher, W. T. Hunt speak. He said, "You will never have a successful and growing "prayer ministry" unless your congregation hears its importance from your senior pastor, on Sunday morning." Not too long after Fred joined our Wednesday evening prayer meeting, I noticed our small but faithful group seemed to take on a more uplifting attitude. We were a group where everyone prayed, however, often the prayers were general—that is, "Bless our church, our town, and our country, etc." Fred's prayers seemed to zero in on the needs of specific people within our church, town, and country. As time passed, I noticed our prayer warriors were doing the same, and the Spirit in their words seemed to be more sincere. I recalled those words of W. T. Hunt and thought, "Our 'prayer team' had grown by only one. However, Fred seemed to turn it into a body of prayer warriors who now prayed to Christ in a one-to-one attitude with 'to-the-point' prayers. Fred's impact on our prayer group was more than what one person would normally add. I thought GOD does work in strange ways sometimes."

From Fred's first Wednesday meeting with our "prayer team," I felt there was something about this Brother that we don't often see in others. He didn't seem to be the type of person who talked about what Christians should do or what he had done to please GOD. He just did it. Fred seemed to feel you accomplish nothing of value by telling others how great you are or relating all the great deeds you are doing or have done within the church IF you don't give GOD credit. I felt he was the type of person GOD sends to a church to inspire its members as to how great God is by what He does through His people.

I don't want to suggest it is wrong to tell others about things you have or are doing in the church, but we need to always give GOD the glory for enabling us to do what *he wants*. Many leaders share with others, activities and deeds they have done in the name of GOD, not to brag but to inform people what has been done and needs to be done, to have a growing church.

Fred was the type of person you had to catch doing something good to find out what he was doing to help make our church attractive to visitors and members. It made no difference to Fred if he found out you didn't like the things he was saying or doing. If he felt he was following GOD's Word, and the pastor was aware of his actions and didn't have a problem with them, he was going to continue.

Our intercessory prayer team consisted of six people, and with Fred joining I fondly referred to our group as "The Faithful Seven Prayer Warriors." I felt the name was well deserved because with few exceptions, every Wednesday evening, all seven would be in attendance.

I wondered if GOD might have sent Fred to help us understand the number of people present is not as important as the love and conviction in the hearts of those that are present. When I first heard Fred pray, I felt, "This man knows Jesus."

The original six "prayer warriors" lived in the town our church located. Fred, however, lived in another community. He drove twenty-two miles round trip each week to attend our prayer meeting. When you add another twenty-two miles he and his wife drove to church on Sunday morning, you might ask *why* would anyone drive that many miles each week when they have at least two Baptist churches in their hometown? I then asked myself more than once, "Could it be GOD had a plan for him at our church?"

Fred's faithful attendance to our prayer meetings seemed to have an impact on all our prayer warriors in many ways. Even though the attendance of the original six members was good, sometimes when the weather was threatening, one or two might not show up. I never felt they were looking for excuses not to attend, but since we were all over sixty, I knew they didn't care about driving in bad weather at night. However, Fred was there each week, rain or shine. I notice our original members attended more regularly when it became known Fred was an eighty-five-plus-year-old man who drove twenty-two miles to and from home to be in our prayer meeting every Wednesday evening.

I then noted Fred was not just at our Wednesday evening prayer meetings; he was almost always the FIRST one there. When I noticed he was usually waiting in the parking lot when Sondra and I arrived, I decided I should try to be there earlier and have the church open, so he did not have to wait in his car. Although it sounded like a good thing to do, even then, I still found it hard to arrive before Fred.

I started noticing during the week. If I had to go to the church to check on something in our SS classroom that GOD led me to teach one of our adult SS classes, I would often find Fred pulling weeds out of the flower beds. Some Saturdays I would find him sweeping the walk after the yard had been mowed that morning, knowing no one would be there to sweep them before church the next day. If the church was open, I often found him inside looking for things to tidy up that may have been overlooked by our cleaning crew, such as a bulletin that had fallen under a pew last Sunday. He might be straightening one of the chairs behind the pulpit that was out of place. The interesting thing about Fred doing these little things was, you had to catch him in the act because he would never mention to anyone what he had done. If Fred saw anything needing to be fixed, he would fix it if he could and never mentioned it to anyone.

What am I doing, in the eyes of GOD, that even comes close to Fred's service?"

During our prayer meetings, Fred seemed to talk to GOD as we might talk to a close friend. I felt if asked he would tell you, "That's who GOD is, the best friend anyone could have." Fred would lift-up those he knew were having problems (of any nature) because he knew they needed help and he believed GOD was the only one who could take care of their needs. Fred was a quiet man, but he was a serving-man. If you asked him to do something; he would if he could, and if he couldn't, he would help find someone who could.

I don't think of Fred as a man of many words, I think of him as a man of many deeds in serving GOD. He never mentioned what he had done, but over the years, his service to GOD became known by most members of our church family who caught him in the act of "serving."

The time that GOD showed Sondra and me Fred's real dedication and feelings toward GOD and the "importance of prayer" was on a cold winter Wednesday evening. All the TV stations where warning, "If you don't have to get out this evening, stay home because the bridges could freeze in some places, and we are expecting snow. If you break down on the road, the wind chill factor will be below zero." I told Sondra, "I can't believe Fred will get out in this weather, but if he does, he's already on his way, and we better go down and open the church, so he doesn't have to wait in his car." As we pulled in the parking lot of the church, there was Fred, sitting in his car reading his Bible. When we got out, he said, "It might be just the three of us tonight." It was as if he was thinking, "Since there are three of us, we are going to have a good time talking with GOD." That evening, I felt I had been in one of the most fulfilling prayer meetings I had ever attended, thanks to GOD for sending us, Fred. I told him how much we appreciated his taking that extra effort to take care of a need he saw. He was always quick to point out, "It is no big deal; any of our members would do it if they saw it first." I would laugh and said, "Okay, if you say so." Fred was a good and humble man in and outside of serving our Lord; in so many ways—and yet,

Fred, didn't have a key to open the doors of our church!

Fred was truly a "*humble*" man and a great Christian leader by example. I feel there are many "Fred's" living among us in the society we are a part of in the twenty-first century. Hopefully, GOD will send a Fred into your life and your church. Maybe they will show you, as "Fred" did me, that there is hope *if* our *faith* is in GOD.

> Keep on loving each other as brothers. Do not forget to entertain strangers, for by so doing, some people have entertained angels without knowing it. (Hebrews 13:1–2)

Fred seem to appear out of nowhere. After he died, some may have asked, "*Who was Fred?*"

(See Appendix F: "I Wish I Had Said That!")

The following are some thought-provoking comments I've come across over the years. I have no idea who first said them, but they probably have been repeated time after time. As I read each one, I thought,

"These are too good to read and not pass them on to others that may not have seen them." In reading the following statements, I thought several times, "I wish I had said that."

1. Dear God, I have a problem, and I think it's Me.
2. There is no key to happiness. The door is always open.
3. Silence is often misinterpreted but never misquoted.
4. Do the math, count your blessings.

5. As a child of GOD, prayer is kind of like calling home every day.
6. The most important things in your house are the people.
7. A grudge is a heavy thing to carry.
8. He who dies with the most toys is still dead.
9. Have a great day! The SON is shining, and He can certainly use you!
10. Be kind, for everyone you meet is fighting some type of problem in their life.
11. Live simply, love generously, care deeply, and speak kindly… God is watching.
12. Always remember some days you're the "big dog," and some days you're the "fire hydrant."
13. GOD loves you because of who GOD is, not because of anything you did or didn't do.
14. Everyone, including the church, talks about world problems are being caused by disunity between
15. Democrat and Republican "political" parties, and why these differences must be eliminated. Seems like removing disunity among all the Christian church denominations would be a good place to start.

(Appendix G: "GOD Can't Use a Person Like Me!"

If you think GOD can't use a person like you, read His Word and see what He used people like the following and think what Jesus told His disciples in Matthew 19:26,

> With man, this is impossible, but with GOD all things are possible.

1. Gideon was afraid. But GOD gave him the strength he needed.
2. Samson had long hair and was a womanizer. Some would feel today; he should still be criticized; but others would say, "He isn't doing anything that all young boys don't do." *But* look how GOD used Samson.

3. David had an affair and was a murderer. Of all people at that time, look at how GOD used him.
4. Moses had a speech impairment. But look at how GOD sent him back to Egypt to lead His people out of bondage and sent his brother Aaron with him to be his spokesman.
5. Daniel refused to yield to the law of the land that forbid the worship of anyone except to King Darius. When Daniel found himself in the lion's den for disobeying the law of man, he remained faithful to the law of GOD, look at how GOD saved Daniel.
6. Jonah ran from GOD. Look how he changed when GOD brought him back on dry land.
7. Naomi was a widow. But look at the faith she had.
8. Job went bankrupt. Look how he showed GOD's love when his possessions were returned.
9. Peter denied Christ. Look how GOD used him to become one of Jesus's greatest defenders and servants.
10. Peter denied Christ. Look how GOD used him to become one of Jesus's greatest defenders and servants.
11. The disciples fell asleep while praying. GOD knows all our weaknesses and we all have some.
12. Martha worried about everything. Don't a lot of us do the same.
13. The Samaritan woman was divorced, more than once. That was between her and GOD.
14. Zacchaeus was too small. Some of the real giants in the Bible were small in stature.
15. Lazarus was dead. Jesus showed how "GOD can do all things."

When you think GOD can't use you, think what He did with these people. Jesus showed the world what GOD could do.

The people shown on the previous page may have felt their weaknesses made them "unusable by GOD," and many people today would agree. But with GOD, all things are possible.

By ourselves, we would be right in saying GOD doesn't need man, none of us can do much to help GOD (He doesn't need help), but when GOD asks us and prepares us; we can do everything He wants us to do!

How can anyone doubt GOD is challenging people in the twenty-first century? Is the reason we doubt GOD is challenging people the same reason we are seeing people giving up on themselves? Could it be a lack of *faith*?

When we think GOD can't use us, aren't we saying GOD *is* limited as to what He can do? Don't we deny the truth in scripture like Matthew 19:26 when Jesus's disciples asked Him, "Who then can be saved?"

The Bible says, Jesus looked at them and said, "With man, this is impossible, but *with GOD all things are possible*."

Are we saying it's because we feel we can't do anything like Dr. Billy Graham, Dr. Martin L. King Jr., Mother Teresa, or like-type servants of GOD?

We need to realize the one thing each of these people did was what GOD asked them to do! Some took a little more encouragement than others, but their faith made the difference. That was also true in what Dr. Graham, Dr. King, and Mother Teresa did. Faith is all GOD asks of those who believe in His Son, Jesus Christ, as their Lord and Savior.

When we put ourselves down, we are judging ourselves and trying to do GOD's job. We are being influenced by Satan and in reacting this way, we not only miss out on serving our Lord and Savior, we also miss out on His many blessings He wants to give us.

If GOD is not using us, it's because we are not letting Him, and He will not force us. Our belief at that moment will be unchangeable. Never lose your *faith*! "There is no turning back in eternity!"

About the Author

In his mid-fifties, Lloyd was asked to teach an adult Sunday school (SS) class. After trying to convince God he was not qualified, he didn't know the scriptures, or didn't have time and there were many others in our SS class that were more qualified, God seemed to respond, "I agree with your third observation, but if you have faith in Me that you say you do, I'll take care of your other excuses, so what is your reason?"

Lloyd had no doubt what God could do, but he was not sure how much he could depend on himself. He accepted and began what developed into a period of more than twenty-five years of teaching adult SS classes in New Jersey to churches in Texas, and God kept His promise in more ways than one.

CPSIA information can be obtained
at www.ICGtesting.com
Printed in the USA
BVHW071014100521
606942BV00002B/88

9 781636 303505